THE REST IS HISTORY RETURNS

THE REST IS HISTORY RETURNS

AN A-Z OF HISTORICAL CURIOSITIES

GOALHANGER PODCASTS WITH

TOM HOLLAND & DOMINIC SANDBROOK

AND IAIN HOLLINGSHEAD

ILLUSTRATIONS BY ADAM DOUGHTY

BLOOMSBURY PUBLISHING
LONDON · OXFORD · NEW YORK · NEW DELHI · SYDNEY

BLOOMSBURY PUBLISHING
Bloomsbury Publishing Plc
50 Bedford Square, London, WC1B 3DP, UK
29 Earlsfort Terrace, Dublin 2, Ireland

BLOOMSBURY, BLOOMSBURY PUBLISHING and the Diana logo
are trademarks of Bloomsbury Publishing Plc

First published in Great Britain 2024

Copyright © Goalhanger Podcasts Ltd, 2024

Illustrations by Adam Doughty
Puzzles and quizzes by The Puzzle House

Goalhanger Podcasts have asserted their right under the Copyright,
Designs and Patents Act, 1988, to be identified as Author of this work

All rights reserved. No part of this publication may be reproduced or
transmitted in any form or by any means, electronic or mechanical,
including photocopying, recording, or any information storage or retrieval
system, without prior permission in writing from the publishers

A catalogue record for this book is available from the British Library

ISBN: HB: 978-1-5266-6864-6; TPB: 978-1-5266-6865-3;
eBook: 978-1-5266-6866-0; ePDF: 978-1-5266-6861-5;
Signed edition: 978-1-5266-8676-3

2 4 6 8 10 9 7 5 3 1

Typeset by Ed Pickford

Printed and bound in Great Britain by
CPI Group (UK) Ltd, Croydon CR0 4YY

To find out more about our authors and books visit
www.bloomsbury.com and sign up for our newsletters

*For Franz Ferdinand, Archduke of Austria-Este
and Sophie, Duchess of Hohenberg*

Contents

Introduction... 1

Anglo-American Rivalry: The Special(ish) Relationship: 200 Years Of Atlantic Antagonism..................... 3

Aztecs: The Final Confession of Hernán Cortés, Conqueror of the Aztecs................................ 9

Baghdad's Origin Story: The Arabian Heights........... 24

Bride of Christ: The Fourteenth-Century Italian Who Married the Messiah.................................. 36

Carthage: Roman Rumble in the Sicilian Jungle......... 44

Chaucer: In Conversation with the Man of the Fourteenth-century Moment.. 58

Colosseum Beyond Ridley and Russell: What the Amphitheatre Actually Meant to the Romans......... 68

Declaration of Interdependence: George III Responds to Jefferson and Chums............................... 76

Downton Abbey: A History of Domestic Service in Five Job Adverts.. 84

Exam: *The Rest is History*'s Exam... on the History of Exams... 91

Fashion Groovy Babies: What 1960s Fashion Tells Us About Post-War Britain.............................. 101

Freemasons: Six Ways Freemasons Have Shaped the Modern World... 111

Great British Quaker Off: The History of Chocolate in
   Six Recipes 120

The Hundred Years' War: Was Edward III the Biggest
   'Lad' in English History?....................... 129

Iron Mask: Who Was the Man in the Iron Mask?...... 142

Indiana Jones: The History Behind the *Raiders of the
   Lost Ark*....................................... 151

JFK: Top 10 Theories for the President's Assassination
   Analysed 159

Martin Luther King Jr.: The Biblical Book of Martin
   the Baptist..................................... 177

Library of Alexandria: Who Destroyed the Greatest
   Library in the World? 184

Historical Love Island: This Year's Winners........... 191

Love Island Personality Test........................ 198

Mitfords: The Family's Christmas Round-Robin
   Letters from the 1930s 200

Monkeys: Top Ten Monkeys in History................ 217

Napoleon: What sort of man was the young Napoleon?... 229

New York City: Welcome to The Jungle: a Tourist Board
   leaflet from 1978 242

Oppenheimer: The FBI's Oppenheimer Files 246

Paris in 1968: The Students are Revolting 257

Patagonia: Land of Their Fathers: The Welsh in Patagonia.. 267

Pregnant Pope: The Female Pope Who Was Stoned
   to Death.. 275

Quick-fire Quiz. 282

Romans and Sci-Fi: Why Have the Romans Inspired So Much American Science Fiction? 284

Saigon: Apocalypse Then: Our Man in Saigon in 1975. . . 291

Schools: 'Requires Improvement': Inspecting the First 500 Years of British Public Schools. 302

King Solomon's Mines: What Does a Bestselling Novel From 1885 Tell Us About the Victorians?. 319

The Tichborne Claimant: A Real Victorian Potboiler. . . . 328

Uprisings: Was the 'Peasants' Revolt' Actually a Peasants' Revolt?. 336

Vesuvius: #Pompeii: How the First-Century Natural Disaster Unfolded in Real Time 347

Wilde: The Importance of Being Oscar Wilde. 358

Witches: Why Were There Witch-Hunts in New England in the Seventeenth Century? 369

X-Rated Novelist: On the Psychiatrist's Couch with the Marquis de Sade. 377

Yuletide: Was Christmas Regifted by the Romans?. 385

Year Zero: Was 1974 the Worst Year in Post-war British History?. 392

The Great Puzzle Section 406

Acknowledgements 420

About the Authors 421

Index 422

Introduction

Sequels often end badly, whether the Second Crusade of 1147–1149; the brief second terms of Presidents Lincoln and McKinley, terminated in 1865 and 1901 respectively; or *Jaws: The Revenge*, released to near universal opprobrium in 1987. But we've had so much fun working on *The Rest is History Returns* that we're hoping to buck this trend. From Cortés to Chaucer, the Colosseum to chocolate, fashion to Freemasons, Hitler to Harry Potter, the Mitfords to monkeys, Pompeii to Patagonia, Saigon to de Sade, Wilde to witches – there is something in this A to Z to suit history enthusiasts of all shapes and sizes.

As Karl Marx almost said, history repeats itself, first as tragedy, second as farce, third as a podcast, fourth as a book of the podcast, fifth as a follow-up book to a book of the podcast.

This second instalment sees the return of some of our irreverent favourites, including another Historical Love Island (this year's winners are, if anything, even more surprising than last year's) and a smattering of Top Tens, including our analysis of the most popular conspiracy theories for the assassination of JFK and the monkeys who have made the biggest historical impact. Yes, we continue to ask the big questions that no one else has thought to ask – and to which everyone should want to know the answer.

The written word also gives us the space to delve more deeply into some thorny historical topics that continue to resonate today. What might the FBI files on J. Robert Oppenheimer have looked like? How could a more belligerent George III have replied to the American Declaration of Independence in 1776 (and how special actually was the 'special relationship' between Britain and the United States of America in the twentieth century)? How should Oscar Wilde's lawyer have wrapped up the closing speech for the defence? Did the young Napoleon display any signs of greatness? What might school inspectors have said about the first 500 years of British public schools? How would the destruction of Pompeii have unfolded if social media had existed in the first century AD?

And, perhaps most pertinently for 2024, a year of elections from Brazil to Bangladesh, India to Indiana, did the two dramatic unpopularity contests of 1974 help to make it the worst year (so far) in post-war British history?

We hope you enjoy reading it as much as we enjoyed producing it.

Tom and Dominic

Anglo-American Rivalry

THE SPECIAL(ISH) RELATIONSHIP: 200 YEARS OF ATLANTIC ANTAGONISM

The phrase 'the Special Relationship' was coined in 1930 by Ramsay MacDonald, the first Labour Prime Minister, popularised by Winston Churchill during the Second World War and widely used by almost every Prime Minister since to describe the (relatively) unique cultural, diplomatic, military and intelligence-sharing bonds between Britain and the United States of America.

However, as Hugh Grant's fictional Prime Minister points out in his rousing peroration in the 2003 film

Love Actually, it is a phrase that actually 'covers all manner of sins'.

For a peek behind the curtain, let's imagine how an unusually undiplomatic ambassador to Washington might have addressed some of these elephants in the room at a state dinner attended by Ronald Reagan and Margaret Thatcher in the mid-1980s.

⌇

Prime Minister, Mr President, Ladies and Gentlemen, what wonderful food we have been eating in the White House this evening! I have spent the final course thinking of how Rear Admiral George Cockburn sailed up the Potomac in August 1814, ate the banquet that President Madison had left behind in the hastily evacuated White House and then promptly burned down all the public buildings in Washington DC.*

Mr President, I'm so glad that you joined us for our dinner this evening. And I promise not to start any fires on my way home.

No, seriously, it's an honour to be asked to address you briefly on the theme of the Special Relationship between our two great nations, a relationship that has never been in better shape. And, I might add, it is a particular delight to be speaking as the final notes of 'The Star-Spangled Banner', a tune from a nineteenth-century London dining club repurposed

---

* Annoyed by Britain's naval impressment of British-born Americans during the Napoleonic Wars, and eager to attack British Canada while the mother country was preoccupied in Europe, the US Congress declared war on Britain in June 1812, the first time in the USA's short history. It didn't go well for the young country. Having quickly surrendered to the Canadians and aligned themselves with a French force whose fortunes were rapidly reversing, the USA found itself the target of a British blockade.

by the Americans to celebrate the British withdrawal from Fort McHenry in September 1814, ring around the room.*

Of course, that was all a long time ago – at least in your relatively short history as an independent nation. And our two countries have never fought each other again.

The war of words has sometimes been just as vicious, though.

I know everyone in this room has been charmed by President Reagan's many riveting anecdotes gleaned from his close reading of *Reader's Digest*. But not all British visitors have been so impressed by the repartee in the White House. In 1842, during his American tour, Charles Dickens found himself unbelievably bored by President John Tyler. He also grew tired of the constant autograph hunting and the balls attended by 3,000 people in his honour in New York. So he went to Virginia, where he encountered the three great evils of 'slavery, spittoons and senators'; to the Mississippi, which he described as the 'beastliest river in the world'; to Ohio, whose people he described as 'morose, sullen, clownish and repulsive'; and to the Midwest, which he thought marginally less impressive than Salisbury Plain.

No wonder he was eager to get back to Britain and write a journal and a novel depicting the Americans as crass, vulgar and obsessed with money.†

---

* Despite being brought to terms by the British burning of Washington DC, the Americans were able to turn the war of 1812 into a story of heroic, fledgling nation-building: partly through the retreat at Fort McHenry that inspired their national anthem; partly through a stinging defeat four months later in New Orleans, where Major General Andrew Jackson's forces killed 2,000 British soldiers in half an hour.

† Unsurprisingly, *Martin Chuzzlewit*, Dickens's least popular novel, went down incredibly badly in America, leading the writer Washington Irving to break off his long-standing friendship. There is an irony that one of Dickens's reasons for going to America – a country that had taken him to heart before he lambasted them for being obsessed with money – was to recoup lost royalties.

These days, of course, those stereotypes are grossly outdated. People on both sides of the Atlantic are now equally crass, vulgar and obsessed with money.

And to whom do we owe this unifying Anglo-American credo? Whence the long-term origins of a philosophy that greed is good, the market is king and individuals are more important than society? Which proto-neo-liberal can we thank as the inspiration for Thatcherism and Reaganomics?

Ladies and gentlemen, I give you Andrew Carnegie, a Scot who was born seven years before Dickens's visit to the USA, emigrated to Pittsburgh, Pennsylvania, smashed all his capitalist rivals and sold his steel company to JP Morgan for $303 million.

Did Mr Carnegie let militant trade unions stand in his way? Did he think his company might be better off in the dead hand of the government?

Did he hell!

And did the author of *The Gospel of Wealth*, a tract that argues that it is the duty of the rich to get rich in order to help others, feel guilty about being the wealthiest man in the world? Of course he didn't. As the Prime Minister might say, he was very much 'one of us'. He gave much of his fortune away, endowing parks, libraries, schools and museums* in both countries, a living embodiment of the Great Rapprochement of the late nineteenth century and the enduring notion that Britain and America should cooperate in the best interests of the world.

But I don't want to suggest that the traffic between our two nations has all been one way. In the twentieth century, we have been grateful for your (belated) military

---

* In 1905, Carnegie visited the Natural History Museum in London to unveil a cast of a dinosaur fossil whose discovery he had sponsored. 'Dippy' remained there until 2017.

support in both world wars; your helpful comments on India in the 1930s; your loan in 1946 (which we're looking forward to paying off by 2006); your gentle hand around our throat during the Suez Crisis in 1956; your insistence on storing US nuclear weapons in the Holy Loch near Glasgow in 1961; and your generous gift of a inferiority complex which none of us will ever quite manage to shake off.

And what have we given you in return in the last forty years?

Have we lived up to Harold Macmillan's intention to be the 'Greeks to their Romans', dispensing wise, world-wearied advice to a 'great big vulgar, bustling people, more vigorous than we are but also more idle, with more unspoiled virtues, but also more corrupt'?

Maybe not. But I like to think that we taught some of your three million GIs stationed in Britain in the Second World War that segregation was neither inevitable nor especially moral.*

We also cheered you up when JFK died by sending you James Bond and the Beatles, cheeky embodiments of ironic, post-imperial Britain that were no longer a threat to any of your interests.

And in the 1970s, when America was in the doldrums after Watergate and Vietnam, we made you feel better by being in an even worse state ourselves.

---

* According to George Orwell, 'the only American soldiers [in Britain in the Second World War] with decent manners are the Negroes'. Many of his countrymen agreed, rejecting demands to uphold the segregation of the US army and instead putting up signs in pubs saying, 'This place is for the exclusive use of Englishmen and American Negro soldiers'. This went down very badly with white US army officers, leading to serious disorder in Cornwall, Bristol and Lancashire. Dozens of black GIs were shot in the leg by US military policemen and sentenced to long periods of hard labour back in the United States.

So, Mr President, why not pay us a return visit and see how much has changed this decade? As the Prime Minister puts it, we have ceased to be a nation in retreat. And the Special Relationship has never been in ruder health.

We've left the 1970s behind, a period when Ted Heath said that the phrase 'was not part of his own vocabulary'.

We've forgiven Henry Kissinger for calling Britain a 'scrounger' in 1975, your travel writer Paul Theroux for comparing our hotels to prisons and the *New York Times* for uncovering a 'slowness at all levels and a mañana attitude that infuriates even Spaniards' in 1978 (as long as they never write anything disobliging about us again).

And now we're forging joint paths once more, committed to family values, low taxation, deregulation and a determination to bring down the evil Soviet Empire (although perhaps you could tell us next time you decide to invade a Commonwealth country, like Grenada).

So, ladies and gentlemen, please raise your glasses to many more years of the Special Relationship.

To never addressing our Prime Ministers disrespectfully when you think the microphone is off.

To being with you, whatever, wherever – regardless of British public opinion.

To not getting upset when a new American President calls someone else first or talks about their even longer relationship with France.

To always being at the front of the queue for trade talks.

Ladies and gentlemen, to this most special of Special Relationships.

Aztecs

THE FINAL CONFESSION OF HERNÁN CORTÉS, CONQUEROR OF THE AZTECS

Hernán Cortés, the Spanish conquistador who was born in 1485, became Governor of Mexico in 1521 and featured on Spanish bank notes as recently as 1992, has been variously depicted as a hero, a super-villain and a mediocrity who happened to be in the right (or indeed wrong) place at the right time. A mural by Diego Rivera in the Mexican National Palace, one of his more generous depictions, shows him as a green, knock-kneed, syphilitic monster.

Yet no one disputes the significance of Cortés's meeting, on 8 November 1519, with Montezuma, the Emperor of the Aztecs (also known as the Mexica),* who ruled over some six million people in a sophisticated kingdom spread over 80,000 square miles. A landmark date in world history, it led to a clash of civilisations that turbocharged European colonialism and spread Christianity into Mesoamerica.

What drove a man who was by turns godly and greedy, resourceful and rapacious? For a different insight, let's have a look at what Cortés's deathbed confession in 1547 might have looked like.

CORTÉS: Bless me, Father, for I have sinned.

PRIEST: We are all sinners, my child. But if we confess our sins, He is faithful and just and will cleanse us from all unrighteousness.

---

* The word 'Aztec' was coined in the eighteenth century, and popularised in the nineteenth, as a way of distinguishing the Mexica, the people who live in Tenochtitlan in the Valley of Mexico, from modern Mexicans. In Cortés's dialogue, we will refer to the Aztecs as the Mexica, as he would have done.

CORTÉS: I know, Father. But there has been an awful lot of unrighteousness.

PRIEST: Okay. Where do you want to start?

CORTÉS: At the beginning. My early life was pious, uneventful and obscure.

PRIEST: I'm glad to hear it. Our Saviour himself led a quiet childhood.

CORTÉS: I'm just getting going, Father. I was born in Medellín, Extremadura, a violent village near Spain's border with Portugal. After university in Salamanca, I decided to seek my fortune in the New World, leaning on a family connection who had just been made Governor of Hispaniola.* My departure from Spain was delayed until 1506 because I broke my leg while being chased by an angry husband.

PRIEST: You coveted your neighbour's wife?

CORTÉS: I did more than covet her, I'm afraid.

PRIEST: God forgives those who truly repent. You were a young man. And I'm sure you did not make this mistake again.

CORTÉS: Well…

PRIEST: Go on, my child.

CORTÉS: Life on Hispaniola was simultaneously very violent and very boring. The 300 or so Spanish were repressing the indigenous Taínos with ferocious ruthlessness, setting dogs on them and making them work

---

* Hispaniola is the island now divided between the nations of Haiti and the Dominican Republic.

in goldmines. Meanwhile, I found myself a job as a dull, pen-pushing notary in a dusty town in the south. I spent much of my time gambling, playing dice and womanising. You can still see the scar on my chin from a fight over a woman.

PRIEST: The Devil finds work for idle hands.

CORTÉS: He does indeed, Father. So I went further west, to Cuba, to keep out of mischief.

PRIEST: And did you, my child?

CORTÉS: No, Father. I was thrown into jail by Diego Velázquez, the Governor of Cuba, for refusing to marry a woman called Catalina Suárez with whom I had been flirting.

PRIEST: But you did marry Catalina? You made an honest woman out of her?

CORTÉS: Yes, Father. She was Velázquez's sister-in-law, so it made sense.

PRIEST: Hernán and Catalina, growing together in love and trust, united with one another in heart, body and mind, as Christ is united with his bride, the Church?

CORTÉS: Perhaps we could come back to that one, Father. You see, I was now working as Velázquez's secretary. In the early autumn of 1518, he was brought news that his nephew had met some friendly Totonacs on the Yucatan Peninsula. Sporting crystal plugs through their ears, noses and lips, these Totonacs told Velázquez's nephew that their streams ran with gold from the gold dust of the hills. He also met an envoy from the Mexica who showered him with gold necklaces and bracelets. When Velázquez heard this news, he sent me to the Yucatan Peninsula with a string of complicated instructions. I was to see where all the gold was coming from. I was to chart the coast to see if there was a shortcut to China and India. And I was to spread the gospel of Christianity.

PRIEST: So you were carrying out the Lord's work, my child – as well as the Governor's.

CORTÉS: Up to a point, Father. It wasn't long before I disobeyed Velázquez's orders. When he saw me strutting around Cuba in a black velvet cloak, a plumed hat and a gold medallion, he began to have second thoughts. He tried to cancel the trip, but I had already amassed eleven ships, stuffed with 500 Spaniards, as well as Taíno slaves, horses and dogs. I ignored Velázquez and set sail on 10 February 1519.

PRIEST: The spirit was strong in you, my child. You were burning with a zeal to spread the word of the Gospels.

CORTÉS: Thank you, Father. I suppose I was. When we landed on Cozumel, a tiny island within sight of the mainland, I ordered my men to replace the idols in the temple with an effigy of the Virgin Mary. We held Mass on the beach and turned upriver to the Mayan town of Potonchán.* Here we persuaded the Maya to embrace Christ and acknowledge the King of Spain as their overlord.

PRIEST: That's very impressive. How did their behaviour show that they had taken on board the teachings of our Lord and Saviour?

CORTÉS: They gave us twenty teenage girls whom we quickly baptised...

---

* The Mayan civilisation, which was spread across Guatemala, southern Mexico and northern Belize, dated back to 1,500 BC and reached its peak around AD 900 before falling into rapid decline.

PRIEST: How lovely.

CORTÉS: ...and used as cleaners, cooks and sex slaves.

PRIEST: I see. And you were still a married man?

CORTÉS: I was. It was a mortal sin. But La Malinche, a Nahua slave girl with an extraordinary facility for languages, became my right-hand woman, a vital go-between for all our interactions with the indigenous people. She blamed the Mexica for the horrors visited on her since childhood and she was desperate to get her own back on them.

PRIEST: So she used you.

CORTÉS: I'm sorry?

PRIEST: I'm not sure you need to be. Like Eve in the Garden of Eden, La Malinche manipulated you. It sounds to me as if she was a sex-crazed traitor who sold out her own people.

CORTÉS: But the Mexica weren't her people. And it was me who used her.

PRIEST: Maybe you both used each other.*

CORTÉS: Anyway, we met our first Mexica on Easter Sunday 1619. Dressed in fancy cloaks and feathered headdresses, they pitched up and gave us some gold. We gave them an armchair, which they didn't seem to like. Then we fired some cannons, organised a demonstration of

---

* The traditional Mexican interpretation of La Malinche is to view her as a traitor. More revisionist historiography has portrayed her as either a victim or as someone with agency. Intriguingly, Cortés never mentioned her in his letters, perhaps because he felt emasculated when the indigenous peoples started calling *him* Malinche instead of Cortés, giving some indication as to who they felt wore the trousers in the relationship.

Christianity and rode our horses around. The Mexica went white with fear.

PRIEST: 'Tremble, O earth, at the presence of the Lord, at the presence of the God of Jacob,' as the psalmist says.

CORTÉS: I think it was actually the horses and the cannons that made the Mexica tremble. I read out the Requirement,[*] in Spanish, and told them that we Spanish suffer from a sickness of the heart, which can be cured only by gold.[†] So they sent us more gold. And that was the moment when I decided to disobey my orders – again – and go inland to Tenochtitlan, at the heart of the Mexica kingdom.

PRIEST: 'For what shall it profit a man, if he shall gain the whole world, and lose his own soul?'

CORTÉS: There were times on that journey to Tenochtitlan, in the summer of 1519, when I did indeed lose my soul. I think of the night raids where men were tortured and women and children were mutilated. I think of the orgy of rape and pillage when we burned the city of Cholula.

PRIEST: 'The Lord shall cause thine enemies that rise up against thee to be smitten before thy face.'

---

[*] 'The Requirement' was a legal document that any Spanish captain arriving in the New World was obliged to read aloud when attempting to subjugate new people. Declaimed in Spanish, it contained a potted Christian history of the world, an assertion that the King of Spain was doing God's work, a declaration that the subjugated people were now Christian – and a warning that any breach of these obligations would result in death. Bartolomé de las Casas, a Spanish clergyman and fierce critic of the conquistadors, described it as 'unjust, impure, scandalous, irrational and absurd'.

[*] Cortés's heart disease, curable only by gold, is one of his most famous sayings – although the quote is so apt that many wonder if it was retrofitted to the facts.

CORTÉS: Well, yes, perhaps some of the smiting was justified. We saw a man with thirty wives and a town with human skulls lined up in their public squares. The Tlaxcalans were so impressed by our raping and pillaging that they decided to join forces against their sworn enemies, the Mexica.

PRIEST: So, again, you were being used by pagans.

CORTÉS: If you say so, Father. By November 1519 we and the Tlaxcalans were at the gates of the Mexica city of Tenochtitlan. It was the most extraordinary sight: a valley of some one and a half million people, a colossal patchwork of fields and farms. At its centre stood an island with causeways stretching like a spider's web in every direction to the shores of the lake. There were floating gardens, soaring pyramids, fairy-tale towers and thousands of canoes. It was all so wondrous that we could hardly believe it. Seville looked like a village in comparison.

PRIEST: 'The whole earth is filled with awe at your wonders; where morning dawns, where evening fades, you call forth songs of joy.'

CORTÉS: Yes, but we called forth a rather different song than the psalmist. On 8 November, we crossed the causeway towards the island, where we were met by Montezuma, the Mexica Emperor. Wearing a huge feathered headdress, he was borne aloft by the dignitaries of his powerful empire and surrounded by vast crowds of drummers and trumpeters. After we'd exchanged gifts, he led us into his palace and told us to make ourselves at home.

PRIEST: Maybe he had read the words of Hebrews 13:2: 'Do not forget to show hospitality to strangers, for by so doing some people have shown hospitality to angels without knowing it.'

CORTÉS: We were no angels, Father.

PRIEST: Maybe not. But this Montezuma did appear to be saying, 'Mi casa es su casa.'

CORTÉS: Well, yes, that's what La Malinche told us. But we decided to take it literally. I rather liked Montezuma's casa – and his gold. I coveted it, Father. And it suited my narrative to tell Charles V that Montezuma had immediately surrendered his lands to the King, thereby excusing my earlier decision to disobey Velázquez's orders to keep to the coast and my later one to 'recover' Montezuma's lands on behalf of the Spanish crown.

PRIEST: So, what really happened? You were taken prisoner by Montezuma?

CORTÉS: Actually, yes, I think we were. It wasn't very clear, to be honest.* Montezuma and I kept on going hawking and hunting together, but we Spanish were under constant guard. After a couple of months, we started wondering whether Montezuma had a specific fate in mind for us. Perhaps he intended us to be his bodyguards? Or worse? The palace where we stayed was right next to his zoo, which included dwarves, hunchbacks and amputees. Were we going to be the latest exhibit? Others were worried that we'd be ritually slaughtered at the feast of Toxcatl to mark the Spring Equinox. We'd seen their shrine to the Mexica

---

* Historians have struggled to explain this dynamic: Cortés's claim to have imprisoned Montezuma, while the rest of the Mexica went peaceably about their business for the next few months, seems highly implausible. The historian Matthew Restall suggests that this may have been a massive exercise in projection – and that the tables were turned.

god Huitzilopochtli in the temple. We'd gazed on the writhing stone serpents of their idols. We'd peered inside their stinking braziers and seen blackened lumps of human flesh.

PRIEST: What does it say in the Book of Exodus: 'You shall have no other gods before me'? You're talking about infidels, my child, brutal in their pagan ignorance.

CORTÉS: I am. But our brutality ended up being more than a match for theirs. We managed to take Montezuma hostage. Meanwhile, news reached us in Tenochtitlan that the gold I'd already sent back to Charles V had been spotted by a furious Diego Velázquez, the Governor of Cuba and my old boss. He sent a gigantic, red-bearded Castillan called Pánfilo de Narváez and a thousand men to teach me a lesson. I set off with eighty to surprise him in the dead of night. After one of my pikemen had gouged out Narváez's eye, the rest of his men joined me and travelled back to Tenochtitlan. We now had a sizeable army, equipped with gunners, crossbowmen and a European immunity to smallpox which soon killed around a third of the indigenous population.

PRIEST: God was on your side against these idolaters. Does it not say in Exodus 9: 'I will send the full force of my plagues, so you may know that there is no one like me in all the earth'?

CORTÉS: But it wasn't the smallpox that killed Montezuma. And it wasn't the stones, bricks and arrows thrown by his own people when we took him out on the roof to reason with the crowd. No. We manacled the King of the Mexica and stabbed him up the – well, use your imagination.*

---

* No one knows exactly how Montezuma died. Matthew Restall gives five theories: killed accidentally by Aztec projectiles; killed on

PRIEST: Why?

CORTÉS: I think he'd been talking to Narváez behind my back.

PRIEST: Then they would both have had you killed. You did nothing wrong, my child. You took an eye for an eye.

CORTÉS: If you say so, Father. Montezuma had certainly outlived his usefulness as a hostage. I'd returned to Tenochtitlan to find my men starving and trapped by thousands of angry Mexica. Having killed our precious hostage, we had no choice but to escape. On the night of 30 June 1520, we muffled the horses' hooves with cloths, packed up as much treasure as we could and tried to sneak out across the causeway. But Mexica suddenly piled in from all sides. The wooden bridge collapsed. Around 600 Spaniards died. We call it La Noche Triste.

PRIEST: It's an apt name. It sounds like an absolute tragedy.

CORTÉS: It was. We lost all our gold in the lake.

PRIEST: I meant all those lost souls.

CORTÉS: Oh, those. Well, the rest of us were in a terrible condition, trudging back into the mountains, constantly harried by Mexica guerrillas until we ended up back among our old Tlaxcalan allies. They took us in and bandaged our wounds. And after some debate about whether

---

purpose by Aztec projectiles; killed by a rival; suicide; and murdered by the Spanish. The least likely theory is the one advanced by Bernal Diaz, a conquistador and chronicler of the expeditions, who claimed that Cortés and his officers bandaged Montezuma's wounds and wept over the Emperor's death. A sixteenth-century history, based on indigenous sources, supports the notion that he was murdered by the Spanish. Inevitably, we've gone for the most salacious method of death, contained in a Jesuit source.

they should join forces with the Mexica to finish us off, or join forces with us to finish off the Mexica, they opted for the latter. Doña Luisa, a Tlaxcalan princess who had married one of my right-hand men, said that we Spanish were like grasshoppers. Kill some of us, she said, and more plagues would arrive.

PRIEST: She was right. Our God – the one, true God – is slow to anger and quick to love. But He can also smite His enemies with frogs, lice, flies, locusts, darkness and dead firstborn children.

CORTÉS: If only it had been just the firstborn children.

PRIEST: What do you mean?

CORTÉS: The only way we and the Tlaxcalans could secure victory was by being viewed as the most lethal, most terrifying fighting force on the continent. So our first target was a hill town called Tepeaca that commanded the vital trade route from Tenochtitlan to the coast. We rounded up all the women and children, branded their cheeks with the red-hot letter G for Guerra and sold them as slaves. The surviving men were dragged back to be sacrificed.

PRIEST: You sacrificed them?

CORTÉS: No, we allowed our Tlaxcalan allies to tear them apart with dogs.

PRIEST: But...

CORTÉS: It gets worse, Father. By December 1520 we were ready for phase two. On New Year's Eve, we hit the town of Texcoco, the crucial breadbasket for the Mexica, looting and burning their priceless maps. We sacked the beautiful mansions and gardens of Iztapalapa. And by the following June we were in a position to avenge La Noche Triste and attack Tenochtitlan itself. As well as 700 infantrymen, equipped with light steel swords for which the Mexica clubs were no match, we had hundreds of gunners and crossbowmen and twelve newly built ships. It was Goliath versus David, a modern force attacking a Bronze Age city. Some of our men were captured and ritually sacrificed, their beating hearts ripped from their chests and offered to the Mexica god Huitzilopochtli. But still we pushed on, flattening the town as we went, penning the Mexica in the north of the city. They unleashed their sacred Quetzal Owl, a man dressed from head to toe in green and gold feathers, who was meant to make us quail in terror. We shot him. In August, as the civilian bodies piled up on the streets, we gave the Mexica one last chance to accept our terms. They refused them. And so on 13 August 1521, we launched our final attack and captured their new Emperor.

PRIEST: None of this shocks me, my child. As the Lord says, 'It is mine to avenge. I will repay.'

CORTÉS: But we took our vengeance too far, Father. Cuauhtémoc, the new Emperor, who was a cousin of Montezuma's, refused to tell us where the gold was. So we tied him to a pole, poured oil on his feet and set him on fire. He merely smiled, as if he were taking a steam bath. We searched everyone, everywhere, for gold – in their mouths, their ears... We pillaged lakeside towns. We set dogs on their dignitaries. We tortured their priests.

PRIEST: But this gold belonged to Charles V, did it not? You were only trying to render unto Caesar the things which were Caesar's.

CORTÉS: If you say so, Father.

PRIEST: And you won Mesoamerica for Christianity, did you not? Charles V made you Governor. You helped to transform Spain's place in the world economy.

CORTÉS: Yes, but it was all in vain. Conquering Tenochtitlan was the high point of my career. I have spent the rest of my life fighting accusations of corruption from Velázquez and others. The last six years of my life have been spent in total obscurity in Seville. And now you see me on my deathbed a broken, forgotten man.

PRIEST: But a repentant one, too?

CORTÉS: Yes, Father.

PRIEST: And no doubt still succoured by the love of your dear wife, Catalina?

CORTÉS: Well, Father...

PRIEST: Go on, my child.

CORTÉS: I'm afraid to say she had an unfortunate accident. After hearing about our victory in Tenochtitlan, she decided to leave Cuba and join us there. Not long after Catalina's arrival, La Malinche gave birth to a boy whom she christened Martin Cortés—

PRIEST: The same name as your father?

CORTÉS: I know – an extraordinary coincidence. On the evening of 1 November 1522, I held a party in my mansion on the lake. We had a row. Catalina went to bed before me. I followed soon afterwards. And then in the middle of the night, I woke the household and told everyone that Catalina had had a fit and died. It was such a shame because the last words we'd spoken were such cross ones.

I was so grief-stricken that I ensured she was buried in great haste before anyone could see the body. Then I married someone else.

PRIEST: You murdered Catalina?

CORTÉS: Yes, I think I did, Father.[*]

PRIEST: Are you sorry for your mortal sin?

CORTÉS: Not really. She was cramping my style.

PRIEST: Do you want to go to hell?

CORTÉS: Okay, fine. I'm sorry about killing my wife. And I'm really sorry about everything else.

PRIEST: The smiting and the pillaging? Don't worry about it. I absolve you from your sins in the name of the Father, and of the Son and of the Holy Spirit.

CORTÉS: Amen.

---

[*] Cortés denied killing Catalina – but then he would say that, wouldn't he?

Baghdad's Origin Story
THE ARABIAN HEIGHTS

Once upon a time, a powerful podcaster called Dominic Sandbrook ruled his digital fiefdom with kindness and compassion. He had recently hosted episodes on British fashion in the 1960s, British fascism in the 1930s and British boarding schools in the nineteenth century. He had even sneaked in a few cheeky plugs for his books, including The Great British Dream Factory: The Strange History of Our National Imagination, available from all good booksellers.

He was one of the happiest men alive.

Or so he thought...

BAGHDAD'S ORIGIN STORY

One day, he returned to his computer screen from a horse ride in the shire to find his heart broken. The Rest is History *was not, as he had believed, going to do four episodes on Aladdin, Sinbad and Ali Baba and the Forty Thieves. They were not going to talk at length about the angry, cuckolded Sultan charmed by Sheherazade's wonderful storytelling in* Arabian Nights. *Instead, someone was trying to smuggle in a series of podcasts about Islamic theology and the rise of the city of Baghdad.*

Dominic was furious. And what he did next was so terrible that it has gone down in history. Every afternoon he hired a different producer, only to put him or her to death the following morning. Oxfordshire trembled under his terrible reign. Parents hid their children away in law schools so that they wouldn't go into the media. No one knew when this terrible diktat would end.

But then one morning, a handsome, young(ish) man named Tom Holland said to his family, 'I'm going to volunteer to speak to Dominic about this.'

Their eyes filled with tears. 'Why would you do that?' they said. 'You are too handsome and young(ish) to throw your life away. He will kill you, too.'

'Trust me,' said Tom.

Dominic eventually agreed to speak to Tom one evening, on condition that he didn't inter—

'The night is long,' interrupted Tom, 'and I'm not sure I can sleep, knowing that I too might die tomorrow. So may I tell you a story to pass the time?'

'Okay,' said Dominic. 'But if you say the word "sacral", I will have you killed before sunrise.'

And so, when Dominic was settled in his chair, Tom began...

The Slave and the Saddle

This is the story of Baghdad, a city that lives in the imagination, as well as in the history books. Not only was it a great imperial city, like Rome or London, it was also the centre of gravity in the Islamic world at the end of the eighth century.

Yet only a few decades earlier, Baghdad had been a tiny, anonymous Christian village on the banks of the River Tigris. And to understand this remarkable transformation, we need to go back another century.

After the death of the Prophet Muhammad in 632, the Arab armies wiped the floor with their Roman and Persian rivals. By the early eighth century, their empire stretched over five million square miles, from the Atlantic to the walls of China. The Umayyad dynasty ruled this vast area, which included Spain, Egypt, Syria and the entirety of the Persian Empire, from their base in Damascus.

In an era when nothing happened without the approval of God, the Umayyads could point to the sweep of their conquests and say that they were favoured by Allah. At first, they wanted to keep this favour to themselves, preserving their distinctive Islamic identity by making it very difficult for non-believers to convert to Islam. Their empire was multicultural and still predominantly Christian, not just in the former Roman provinces but also in Mesopotamia.

This balance shifted over time. Following the example of Muhammad himself, who had both owned and freed many slaves, the Umayyads imported thousands more from across the empire. A tithe of slaves was often part of the deal when a city surrendered to the Arabs. The people of Zaranj, a fortress that commanded the approaches to the Hindu Kush, agreed to send the Umayyad court 1,000 of their most beautiful boys, each holding a golden cup, as part of the terms of their surrender. Abd al-Malik, the fifth Caliph, who suffered from such terrible halitosis that he was able to kill a fly with a single blast of his breath, liked to categorise his slave girls: the Berbers were best for pleasure, the Romans for housework and the Persians for childbearing.

Many of these slaves eventually became Muslims. Meanwhile, other non-believers grew tired of the sumptuary laws saying that non-Muslims could not dress like an Arab, wear a sword like an Arab or even sit straight in a saddle like an Arab. And although Jews and Christians, the 'people of the book', were well treated, they resented paying the *jizya*, the tax on non-Muslims. And so some of them converted, too.

And yet these conquered peoples did not simply absorb the teachings of Islam; they also shaped it. This was a golden age for Jewish scholarship, a period when the *yeshivas*, the rabbinical schools in Mesopotamia, were developing the Talmud, the spoken law, alongside the Torah, the written law. It is probably no coincidence that this period saw the development in the same region of the *hadiths*, the sayings attributed to great figures from the Muslim past, and especially the prophet Muhammad, which complemented the Qur'an, the written word of God.

Early Islam was also influenced by Zoroastrianism, the religion of the defeated Persians. Neither the practice of praying five times a day nor the belief that apostates should be put to death are to be found in the Qur'an – both are clearly derived from Zoroastrian practice.

This legal and theological melting pot was dangerous for the Umayyads, an autocratic dynasty keen on drinking, partying and frolicking with slave girls and boys. Perhaps, thought some of the new Muslim converts, the Umayyads weren't the defenders of the faithful. Maybe they were actually a sinister apostate regime who had carelessly – or even deliberately – neglected the teachings of Muhammad.

And maybe – as the Umayyads faced military challenges on the frontiers, sectarian splits closer to home and the rise of a rival Arab dynasty – God didn't favour them after all.

*

Tom fell silent.

'I hope you're not going to leave the story on that cliff-hanger,' said Dominic.

Tom smiled. 'I will tell you the next part tomorrow,' he said. 'As long as you let me live.'

'Very well,' said Dominic.

'Although, if you're a member of the Rest is History Club, you can listen right away,' said Tom.

'Don't push your luck,' said Dominic.

The next evening, when Dominic was settled in his chair, Tom began...

The Blood-Shedder and the Bloody Skull

In the early eighth century, the Umayyads suffered a series of military defeats: in the land of the Franks, in the far west of their empire; in Northern Transoxiana (southern Kazakhstan today), in the far east of their kingdom; and in Constantinople, where they repeatedly tried and failed to defeat the surviving rump of the Roman Empire.

Watching these defeats carefully were two powerful sects with strongholds in the modern Middle East: the Kharijites and the Shia. They didn't have much love for each other: Ali, Muhammad's cousin and his rightful successor, according to the Shia, was assassinated by the fundamentalist Kharijites in 661 after he'd expelled them from his army. The Kharijites' tendency to slice open the bellies of those they condemned as infidels did not win them many friends among other Muslims either. But the two sects had common cause in hating the decadent and heretical Umayyads. In 745, after a string of sectarian uprisings, the Kharijites took a chunk of Iraq and proclaimed their own caliph – and the Umayyad dynasty descended into civil war.

Meanwhile, the Abbasids, who claimed direct descent from Abbas, Muhammad's uncle, were establishing themselves as a serious rival to the Umayyads. Their first move came via intermediaries in Khorasan, a vast region that includes modern Turkmenistan, Afghanistan and eastern Iran. On 9 June 747, Abu Muslim, a Persian agent of the Abbasids, unfurled their black flag of war near Merv, where the last Sasanian king had died fleeing the Arabs. Tapping into those buried loyalties – and a Zoroastrian tradition that their deposed kings had also considered themselves appointed by God, just like the Abbasids – Abu Muslim conquered much of modern Iran and Iraq within the next sixteen months. On 28 November 749, al-Saffah, the great-grandson of Muhammad's uncle, was proclaimed the first caliph of the Abbasid Caliphate.

Al-Saffah's first task was to defeat the last caliph of the Umayyad Caliphate. When Marwan, a grizzled, curly-haired veteran of many campaigns, lost the Battle of the Zab, on 25 January 750, he fled to Egypt, where his Abbasid pursuers chopped off his head, removed his tongue and fed it to a cat. Al-Saffah, which means 'the blood-shedder', rounded up the final living Umayyads, butchered them and draped their bodies with carpets while his friends picnicked to the sounds of their dying groans.

He also ordered the tombs of the Umayyad caliphs to be dug up, their corpses scourged with whips and their skulls used for target practice before being smashed into hundreds of tiny pieces.

*

'This is fantastic stuff,' said Dominic. 'Absolute scenes. But you've barely mentioned Baghdad. Let alone Aladdin.'

'Be patient,' said Tom. 'All will be revealed if you let me live another day.'

'All right then,' said Dominic.

The next evening, when Dominic was settled in his chair, Tom began…

Daddy Small Change and the Demons

Al-Saffah, the blood-shedder, lived another three years, shedding as much blood as he could before he died of smallpox. In 754, his elder brother took the throne name of al-Mansur, the victorious one – a better title than his other nickname, Abu Duwaneek, which translates as

BAGHDAD'S ORIGIN STORY

'Daddy Small Change', a reference to his effective marshalling of the economy.*

Al-Mansur considered a few options before settling on what would become Baghdad as his capital. He rejected the Umayyads' Damascus, despite its fame and its beauty, on the grounds that the Abbasid power base lay in the east. They needed to look to the rising of the sun, not to its setting, as the Caesar-like Umayyads had done. He also rejected Kufa, a key city in Iraq, on the basis that it was rife with heretical Shi'ites and Kharijites. On one visit, his Persian guards had proclaimed him a god. Al-Mansur objected, whereupon his guards tried to kill him and he had them all put to death.

Al-Mansur therefore decided to build a new capital from scratch in Mesopotamia, the richest possession in the entire caliphate. He laid Baghdad's first foundation stone himself in the summer of 762, and the city quickly fulfilled his boast that it would be the crossroads of the universe, the meeting place for east and west, the past and the future.

Matching Rome in its imperial heyday, Baghdad's peak population of a million souls made it the largest city in the world. You could buy almost anything in the vast market in Karkh in the south of the city, whether spices from as far afield as Indonesia, brought up the Tigris by enterprising merchants, or rich, delicious cakes made with sugar cane from Mesopotamia itself. A huge single market operated all the way from Fez to the gateway of China.†

---

* To al-Mansur is attributed the gloriously Mafiosi maxim: 'He who has no money, has no men, and he who has no men, watches as his foes wax great.'
† Wealthy Muslim traders exported many goods in this era as well, most famously orange trees to Spain.

Scholars also flocked to the city, putting it on a level with Classical Athens or Renaissance Florence in terms of influencing the way in which the world thinks. Baghdad was key to the development of *fiqh*, the science of jurisprudence, which resulted in four rival schools of Islamic thought which still hold sway across North Africa and the Middle East today. Al-Mansur also embarked upon an ambitious intellectual project, known as the House of Wisdom, which commissioned translations of almost all writings from Ancient Greece.

Populated with international scholars, Christian doctors and Zoroastrian astrologers, Baghdad was an extraordinarily cosmopolitan melting pot. This multiculturalism was reflected in magnificent architecture that included numerous nods to the city's great predecessors. Al-Mansur's round city walls, forming a perfect circle, reflected a Sasanian fondness for similar designs.* The gates were said to have been crafted originally by demons for King Solomon. The park for wild beasts was a tradition that stretched back to the Assyrian kings. And the 120-foot green dome atop the 360,000-square-foot Palace of the Golden Gate emulated Umayyad palaces, albeit on a vastly bigger scale.

*

Dominic stifled a yawn.

'Am I boring you?' asked Tom, anxiously.

'Not at all,' said Dominic. *'I will spare your life one more day. But I want more blood and gore in tomorrow's story. I want Aladdin, I want Ali Baba, I want—'*

---

* The city's circle was so perfect, said al-Jahiz, a famous essayist who ended up crushed to death under a pile of books, that it looked as if it had been poured into a mould and cast.

'Okay,' said Tom.

The next evening, when Dominic was settled in his chair, Tom began...

One Thousand and One Translations

Much like Baghdad itself, the stories in *Arabian Nights* are a cocktail of different cultural traditions, which include the pre-Islamic Sasanian Empire and fifteenth-century Cairo, as well as ninth-century Baghdad.

Working from a fourteenth-century Egyptian manuscript, they were translated into French at the beginning of the eighteenth century by an orientalist called Antoine Galland under the title *Les mille et une Nuits* (*One Thousand and One Nights*). As well as adding the story of Sindbad from a manuscript found in Constantinople in the 1690s, Galland also included the stories of Aladdin and Ali Baba, which he had been told by a Syrian monk. Later translators of a work more commonly called *Arabian Nights* include Sir Richard Burton, the British explorer who infamously disguised himself as a Muslim in order to enter Mecca.

Many of the other stories can be dated to Abbasid-era Baghdad. They feature characters such as blacksmiths, butchers, conjurors, policemen, tanners, dung collectors, masseurs – and, of course, criminals – who rarely feature in other literature of the time. They also include a range of historical characters, albeit rendered with about as much accuracy as the British royal family in *The Crown*. For example, Harun al-Rashid, the fifth Caliph, is portrayed as a kind of Bruce Wayne, cleaning up the mean streets in disguise, whereas in reality he was rather pious and austere.

However, the storytellers had no shortage of real-life drama to draw upon. Viziers, Caliphal prime ministers who feature in many of the stories, were tremendously powerful – until they weren't. The Barmakids, an originally Buddhist family from Afghanistan who had converted to Islam, served the first five Caliphs loyally until Harun had them all wiped out, probably because Ja'far, his vizier and closest friend, had been having an illicit affair with his sister.

It is also said that Harun only succeeded to the throne because his mother, a beautiful former slave from Yemen called al-Khayzuran, poisoned his older brother (like Nero, he was also trying to kill her) and instructed a large-buttocked slave girl to finish him off by sitting on his face.

Harun's equally beautiful wife, Zubaidah, who features in *Arabian Nights*, asked everyone who saw her to kiss the hand of her monkey. One general was so furious at this indignity that he drew his sword and chopped the monkey in two.

*

'Tom, this is absolutely splendid stuff,' said Dominic. 'A tour de force. You could go on for a thousand and one podcasts.'

'Thank you,' said Tom, relieved. 'But sadly the Abbasid Dynasty didn't. By the time the Mongols destroyed Baghdad in the thirteenth century, the city's golden age had already long vanished. After Harun's death, there was another spectacular succession crisis in a caliphate without primogeniture. Two brothers fought each other, leading to endless conspiracies and revolts by the Shias and Kharijites. By 865, there were two caliphs, one in Baghdad, one in Samarra, eighty miles to the north. In 869, the African Zanj slaves who had been working on the sugar cane fields launched a terrible uprising. Basra was

BAGHDAD'S ORIGIN STORY

sacked. Armies rampaged across Iraq. Tens of thousands of people died. And Baghdad never recovered the security, the supremacy or the geopolitical centrality that it had enjoyed under Harun.'

Dominic looked at Tom tenderly.

'That is a shame,' he said. 'But do you know, I think I have finally recovered my own equilibrium, thanks to your marvellous storytelling.'

Dominic took a deep breath.

'Could someone as good and clever as you like me back after all the terrible things I have done?' he asked.

'Of course,' said Tom.

And from that moment on, Tom and Dominic were the happiest pair that ever lived, their stories retold over and over again, all across the world (albeit less often in France).

Bride of Christ

THE FOURTEENTH-CENTURY ITALIAN WHO MARRIED THE MESSIAH

In the fourteenth century, a young Italian woman living in Siena claimed that she had married Jesus Christ in her bedroom, sealing their vows with a ring made from his circumcised foreskin. Facing only sporadic scepticism from her contemporaries, she became the most celebrated woman of the age, healing the sick, performing miracles and influencing Papal politics.

Canonised within a century of her death at the age of thirty-three, she continues to hold up a fascinating *mirror to the relationship between God, men and women.*

This is the extraordinary story of St Catherine of Siena.

A plague on fair Siena

The twenty-fourth of twenty-five children, Catherine was born to a dyer and a very full-time mother on 25 March 1347.*

Siena was in a state of turmoil during Catherine's early childhood. Although sufficiently rich and sophisticated to rival neighbouring Florence in its golden age, it was hit hard by the Black Death from May 1348 onwards. Shops closed. The wool industry went into a deep freeze. Plague pits were dug across the city. Perhaps inevitably, Catherine lost several of her siblings, having already lost her twin sister, Giovanna, who had been sent out to a wet nurse while her mother concentrated on Catherine.

Siena's problems were compounded by the Hundred Years' War raging on the other side of the Alps. When King Edward III of England defaulted on his Italian bank loan in 1345, the resulting financial crash hit Siena badly.

The Church was also in crisis, thanks to Pope Clement V moving the Papal capital from Rome to Avignon in 1309. A period referred to as the 'Babylonian Captivity of the Papacy', it saw popes live in great luxury in France, feasting in banqueting halls, and living a life of grandeur in exquisite gardens and opulent private steam rooms. Meanwhile,

---

* Raymond of Capua, Catherine of Siena's biographer, describes her mother as 'filling the house with children like a fruitful bee'.

public displays of religiosity were rising rapidly in the face of widespread death, famine and destruction.

Merry Magdalene

Despite being born into all this chaos, Catherine was a happy, normal child who was given the nickname 'merry' as a young child.

She was especially close to Bonaventura, one of her older sisters, who had once shamed her rakish husband into behaving better by going on a hunger strike. Bonaventura introduced Catherine to fashion when her little sister was fourteen, a move that Catherine's rather partisan biographer, Raymond of Capua, blamed for Bonaventura's death in childbirth shortly afterwards.

'Almighty God,' wrote Raymond, 'unable to bear the sight of His chosen bride being drawn even the slightest bit further away from Him, Himself removed the obstacle that was preventing her from uniting herself with him. For Bonaventura, having led her sister into the way of vanity, shortly afterwards found herself about to give birth and, young as she was, died in doing so.'

Catherine's parents quickly produced another obstacle to any divine union, insisting that she marry Bonaventura's widower. She refused to comply with their demands, committing herself to virginity,* suppressing her emerging

---

* According to Raymond of Capua, Catherine's pledge to remain celibate was a response to the Devil tempting her by 'bringing her vile pictures of men and women behaving loosely before her mind, and foul figures before her eyes, and obscene words to her ears, shameless crowds dancing around her, howling and sniggering, and inviting her to join them'.

femininity by cutting her hair short, trying to make herself look ugly and refusing food. When her anxious mother took her to a spa with hot springs, Catherine deliberately scalded herself.

But Catherine did not feel alone in her teenage rebellion. Having had her first visions of Christ when she was only five years old, she was desperate to see her Saviour again. Her prayers were answered when a tortured, bleeding Christ appeared in her bedroom for a chat. They married soon afterwards: the Virgin Mary gave her away; St Paul was a witness; David, the psalmist, played the harp; and Christ placed his bloody foreskin on her finger, which no one else could see, as a sign of their eternal union.

The Messiah's mission

There doesn't appear to have been any erotic element to Catherine's marriage. Instead, she was instructed by her new husband to bear witness to the people of Siena. Having joined the Dominicans as a lay sister, she dedicated herself to the service of the poor, sometimes by stealing from her parents. On one occasion, when she had given her father's expensive wine to some beggars, she appeased his fury by miraculously producing more wine.

More miracles followed. Bread was made from rotten wheat. Plague victims were healed. Her own mother was brought back from the dead. Other mothers had milk restored to their dry breasts.

Bodily fluids featured heavily in the public appearances of a woman who had married a bleeding saviour. Having drunk the pus from the diseased breast of a lay sister, a taste she described as 'radiant with the sweetness of heaven', she was rewarded by Christ offering her the wound from his side. On another occasion, she comforted a condemned man in prison, accompanied him to the scaffold, picked up his decapitated head and drenched herself in his blood. She started to display stigmata, the marks of the wounds that Christ had suffered on the cross.

Catherine also gained huge attention from her fasting, her displays of asceticism and self-abnegation becoming more extreme in her twenties. Sometimes surviving for long periods on only water and the Eucharist wafer, she was told by Christ to return to her parents' table and eat. Yet she often ended up sticking twigs down her throat to induce vomiting.

Riots, Rome and last rites

In her mid-twenties, Catherine's activities began to take on a more political nature. In 1371 she deliberately walked through riots in Siena, bringing peace back to the streets. In 1375, she persuaded the people of Pisa and Lucca to abandon a league against the Pope and sign up to his authority.

Having miraculously been made literate by Christ, she wrote and dictated hundreds of letters, including one to Pope Gregory XI, exhorting him to return to Rome. Despite remarking upon her 'intolerably dictatorial tone, a little sweetened with expressions of her perfect Christian deference', Gregory XI was impressed when she visited Avignon as Florence's ambassador in 1376. Not only was it remarkable for Siena's great rival to choose Catherine as an ambassador, she was also widely credited with persuading the Pope to return to Rome in January 1377.

This miracle, however, did not endure. When Gregory XI died fourteen months later, the Cardinals ended up electing two popes: one Italian and one murderous aristocrat from Geneva. Catherine backed the former, Urban VI, who drew heavily on her support, summoning his cardinals to hear her speak in November 1378.* Indeed, it is possible that without her backing, the Great Papal Schism, which lasted until the restoration of Rome's authority in 1417, would never have taken place.

Catherine died less than two years after her visit to Rome, having undergone a final act of asceticism by attempting to survive a month without drinking any water. Her body was buried in Rome; her head was preserved in Siena; and she was canonised in 1461 by Pope Pius II.

Saints, syndromes and secularism

Catholics take Catherine's story on faith, pointing to her miracles, her saintly suffering and her influential writings which saw her declared a 'Doctor of the Church' by Pope Paul VI in 1970. In 2010 Benedict XVI said that she 'still today speaks to us and impels us to walk

---

* Pope Urban VI wrote of Catherine: 'The weak woman puts us all to shame. I call her a weak woman not to make little of her, but I want to emphasise that she is a woman and belongs to what is by nature the weaker sex. By nature, it is she who should show fear, even in situations where we would feel no danger. But on the contrary, it is we who play the coward while she stands undaunted, and by her rousing words, imparts to us her own courageous spirit.'

courageously toward holiness to be ever more fully disciples of the Lord'.

Those of a more sceptical mind, influenced perhaps by modern psychology, might well wonder whether this troubled teenager, plagued by survivor's guilt about her twin, distraught at her older sister's death and fearful of sex with a widowed brother-in-law she didn't want to marry, turned food into a weapon against her parents – while the anxious people of Siena and beyond projected their spiritual desires onto someone who today might have been diagnosed with anorexia.

Is there a way of reconciling these two extremes: the saintly and the secular; the fourteenth century, in which everything is spiritualised, and the twenty-first century, in which everything is rationalised (and often medicalised)?

There is certainly an argument to say that describing Catherine simply as anorexic is both reductive and anachronistic. The Middle Ages did have a fledgling understanding of eating disorders – and no one ascribed these labels to Catherine. A more interesting insight provided by her story is into the role of religion, women and food in this period.*

In a time of failing harvests, there was a sense that the deadliest of the deadly sins was gluttony. To decline food, therefore, was the ultimate renunciation, especially for women, who were charged with the provision, preparation and serving of meals. And to do so while refusing mortal marriage and attempting to live off the Eucharist – the literal body and bloody of Christ, according to Catholics – elevated Catherine above the normal rank of women.

---

* This relationship is explored in Caroline Walker Bynum's wonderful book, *Holy Feast and Holy Fast: The Religious Significance of Food to Medieval Women*.

Catherine's rebellion against her allotted gender role and her elevated understanding of Christ reveals the paradox at the heart of Christianity: to be inferior relative to those who have status is, in itself, a source of power.

It is a message that still resonates in any age, pious or pagan.

Carthage

ROMAN RUMBLE IN THE SICILIAN JUNGLE

CARTHAGE

It was the heavyweight clash of the millennium. Between 264 and 146 BC, Rome fought three titanic wars with Carthage, then a great imperial city on the most northern tip of Africa, now a residential suburb of Tunis. By the end of their existential struggle, known to history as the Punic Wars, one side had been wiped off the map; the other had risen to become the dominant power in the western Mediterranean, well on its way to establishing one of history's great empires.

How did this feud begin? What was the story of the First Punic War? The first time Rome and Carthage faced off was a showdown that lasted twenty-three years, fought largely on the island of Sicily that stood between their two power bases. The two cities resembled a pair of boxers in their prime, each in search of a knockout punch. Watching the confrontation closely from their ringside seats were the Greeks, their numerous city-states overshadowed by a new generation of superpowers.

So given that every classic fight needs a top-quality commentary team, let's imagine that our eyes and ears for this boxing bout are two of the most famous Greeks of the era: Pyrrhus* the adventurer-prince who fought both Rome and Carthage, and Polybius the historian.†

---

* Pyrrhus, Prince of Epirus (c. 319–272 BC) was a second cousin of Alexander the Great who, like his uncle, was happy to invade anywhere if he thought it would make for a good story. After fighting the Romans in Italy and the Carthaginians in Sicily, he seized the throne of Macedonia, invaded the Peloponnese, and was killed in a street battle in Argos by a tile dropped on his head by an Argive mother. *Technically*, this makes him dead by the start of the Punic Wars, but never mind.

† Polybius (c.200–118 BC) was one of a number of Greek aristocrats taken to Rome as hostages in 167 BC, as part of Rome's takeover of the mainland Greek city-states. Although he wasn't allowed to leave,

Preliminaries

POLYBIUS: Good evening, ladies and gentlemen, and welcome to our coverage, live from Sicily. It's 264 BC, and have we got a corker of a fight coming up! Joining me in the commentary box this evening is a prizefighter that many have called one of the modern greats. It gives me great pleasure to introduce Pyrrhus, King of Epirus!

PYRRHUS: Evening, everyone. It's nice to be up here in the audience for once, rather than going into that ring. And thank you for that flattering welcome, Polybius. But let's get one thing straight: I had a good career, but I'm not in the same league as the two we're going to see tonight. I've gone toe-to-toe with both of them, and Rome and Carthage are the best fighters this sport has ever seen. Period.

POLYBIUS: That's a big claim, Pyrrhus.

PYRRHUS: I'm telling you, Polybius, this is going to be a historic evening. If you're tuning in at home, don't go anywhere – you're going to want to tell your grandchildren that you watched this.

Polybius mixed in high society and seems to have made the best of his unfortunate circumstances. The surviving sections of his history of Rome's rise to greatness are some of our most important texts from the period.

Carthage: Profile of a champion

POLYBIUS: So, Pyrrhus, Carthage – where do we even begin? Carthage is a legend of the sport, the undisputed heavyweight champion in the region.

PYRRHUS: Phenomenal reserves of character. Superb technique. Carthage has the whole package.

POLYBIUS: You can see Carthage's vital stats coming up on your screens at home now. Lebanese descent – from the city of Tyre, to be precise – but based in Tunisia since moving there for commercial reasons in 814 BC.

PYRRHUS: Yes, she's been in this region for over 550 years, but she's still very proud of her Lebanese heritage. As many of our viewers will know, she oversees the western part of a huge trading network based in Tyre, the oldest continually inhabited city in the world. We Greeks call her people the Phoenicians – or 'the purple people'.* And no one in the Western Mediterranean comes close to matching Carthage, whether in the ring or in raw financial muscle.

POLYBIUS: What I find interesting about Carthage is that she has never copied the current trend for throwing her weight around outside the ring and building a property portfolio overseas. Her fights are for money, not land: as long as Carthage is making a profit in merchandise and defending her corner, she's not interested in expanding beyond her Tunisian base.†

---

* The Greeks gave them this name because of the 'purple people's' most famous export, a fabulously valuable purple dye made from Levantine molluscs. The Latin for 'Phoenician' was *Punica* – which is where the Romans got the name of the Punic Wars from.

† Another power that prioritised profit over territorial expansion was the early British Empire – until they came to realise that they could do both.

PYRRHUS: Right. So she's used her wealth instead to buy the best equipment, the best support team, the best mercenaries. There's nobody wealthier in the whole division. And then there's Carthage's famous fighting style, which we call 'Naval Warfare'.

POLYBIUS: Yes, thanks to 'Naval Warfare', it's very hard to go toe-to-toe with Carthage over a long period of time.[*] Opponents get worn down. No one can withstand their onslaught across the full twelve rounds.

PYRRHUS: Although I must say: the one thing Carthage has always lacked is the knockout punch. Again and again, Carthage wins on points – and then carries on trading with its defeated enemies. The Greeks that have gone up against them tend to walk out of the ring with their heads held high: defeated, but not humiliated.

POLYBIUS: Absolutely right, Pyrrhus. And that's why the situation here on Sicily is so complicated, isn't it? Carthage is the heavyweight champion, but they've never gone to the effort of stamping out every challenger from the east end of the island, where our fellow Greeks have founded many colonies.

PYRRHUS: Carthage is in phenomenal shape. None of the locals have the calibre to take that Sicilian heavyweight belt from them.

POLYBIUS: None of the Greeks, no. But what about the Romans? Shall we turn to tonight's challenger?

---

[*] Carthage's navy boasted 350 ships at the start of the Punic Wars. Their well-trained crews were widely feared for their oarsmanship, their speed and their ability to ram the enemy.

CARTHAGE

Rome: Profile of a challenger

POLYBIUS: So, Rome. Definitely the underdog in this fight, but she's a rising star and it's certainly too early to write her off.

PYRRHUS: I agree, Polybius. This is a fascinating encounter, because Carthage and Rome are such dissimilar fighters. Rome is younger and hungrier, and having worked her way through the Italian middleweight division, she has now run out of challengers.

POLYBIUS: Give our viewers a quick overview of Rome's origin story here, will you, Pyrrhus?

PYRRHUS: Sure. So, Rome was born in 753 BC, answering at first to a dynasty of kings, notably Romulus, who had been raised by a wolf along with his twin Remus. I'll let our viewers decide whether or not they believe that. We do know for sure that by 509 BC, Rome had a falling-out with her final king and became a republic. But if I had to pick *the* defining moment in Rome's early career, I'd go for her defeat by a Gaulish boxer in 390 BC.* At that point Rome was still on the local boxing circuit of Latium, just one of dozens of lower-league fighters trying to make a name for themselves. The loss stung – Rome was humiliated. Rome took a long hard look in the mirror and said,

---

* We don't know exactly what happened – it's shrouded in later legend – but we're sure that a tribe of Gauls conquered Rome at around this date. The later Romans liked to believe that an army of reinforcements rescued the captured city in the nick of time, which sounds suspiciously convenient.

'This isn't good enough. If I'm going to compete seriously, I need to change my whole mindset.'

POLYBIUS: And what did that change look like? A better diet? More time in the gym? Rewatching *Rocky III*?

PYRRHUS: Every normal fighter throws in the towel occasionally. Not Rome – Rome will endure any amount of pain rather than give up. And if Rome's opponent throws in the towel, Rome will simply wait a bit, challenge them again, and knock the stuffing out of them all over again. Rome hungers after that knockout punch. It's unique. And, frankly, it's terrifying.

POLYBIUS: It sounds intense.

PYRRHUS: It's unbelievable. After that night of anguish in 390 BC, Rome has spent the past 120 years picking fights with every boxer in mainland Italy and hammering them to kingdom come. Take the Samnites, for example – they lived in the wild mountainous region of southern Italy and were considered pretty tough – but Rome absolutely clobbered them between 343 and 290 BC.

POLYBIUS: And of course, you've fought both of our boxers tonight. Tell us, Pyrrhus: how do they compare?

PYRRHUS: The first time I met Rome in the ring, in 280 BC, I won on points, but it knocked the stuffing out of me.* When I fought her again five years later, she won outright.

---

* Invited by the Greek city of Tarentum to help them in their fight, Pyrrhus defeated Rome in two battles, but he took heavy losses on both occasions, and Rome rejected his reasonable terms of surrender. After the second battle, Pyrrhus is reported to have said, 'Another victory like this and it will be the ruin of me' – which is where the phrase 'pyrrhic victory' comes from.

CARTHAGE

You can knock her down, but she just keeps coming back at you. I've never seen anything like it.

POLYBIUS: And how does that compare with your experience with Carthage?

PYRRHUS: After losing those two fights with Rome, I came here to Sicily and found myself in the ring with Carthage. We had no particular beef – I just wanted another opportunity to make a name for myself. It was all very gentlemanly, and after I lost, we hugged it out.* But with Rome, there's an intensity, an absolute refusal to accept anything other than the opponent's annihilation. And that's scary. You can't help asking yourself: 'Am I sparring with someone who's actually a psychopath?' That mental advantage has seen her win knockout after knockout in the middleweights.

POLYBIUS: And now she's bulked up and gone up a weight class for her first heavyweight fight. It's a big challenge, isn't it? At this level, even tiny weaknesses get exposed.

PYRRHUS: They do. But let's see what happens. Rome has come to Sicily full of bravado, looking for fresh challenges and muscling in on Carthage's traditional territory. This fight – between the upstart and the reigning Sicilian champion – has been inevitable for months.

POLYBIUS: It's a mouthwatering prospect.

---

* Before leaving Sicily in 275 BC, Pyrrhus (who evidently had a knack for saying memorable things – which is why it's a shame he missed his true calling as a boxing commentator) is supposed to have said, 'What a killing field we are leaving here for the Romans and Carthaginians' – a prediction that proved horribly accurate.

The opening round

POLYBIUS: Okay, the seconds are out of the ring, the crowd is going wild, and it's time for the main event on this warm night in Sicily in 264 BC. Will Rome, the plucky young challenger, live up to the hype? Here we go...

PYRRHUS: Oof, look at that. Carthage is showing some real pedigree here, and Rome just isn't sure what to do.

POLYBIUS: Those jabs are coming thick and fast. Carthage's 'Naval Warfare' tactic is giving her a huge advantage.

PYRRHUS: Rome has got to figure out how to adapt fast.

POLYBIUS: Hang on, Pyrrhus. What's going on here? This is some audacious stuff. Rome, whose entire career has been built on getting up close and walloping opponents, seems to be copying Carthage's totally different approach. I don't believe it. She's trying out the 'Naval Warfare' manoeuvre herself.*

PYRRHUS: Absolutely extraordinary. Rome is reinventing its entire M.O. right in front of us, learning on the fly when the fight is already under way.

---

* Having never had a navy before, Rome initially struggled to fight such a strong sea power, especially as the war revolved around control of the island of Sicily. When a solitary Carthaginian warship fell into Rome's hands, Roman carpenters studied it and built a hundred copies in double-quick time, sending them into battle against the Carthaginian fleet – albeit with mixed results at first, since Rome didn't yet have the well-trained crews and experienced naval commanders to go with their fancy new ships.

CARTHAGE

POLYBIUS: This is nuts.

PYRRHUS: Only Rome would dare to do something like this.

POLYBIUS: It can't possibly work – ohhh. There, I told you: Rome's stumbled at a crucial moment and has been knocked right down onto the canvas. These things take years of practice, and unfortunately that's probably the end of—

PYRRHUS: No, look! Rome's got right back up and is still going for it with the same 'Naval Warfare'—

POLYBIUS: Ouch! Another huge blow to the temple from Carthage and Rome has gone sprawling. This might not be a long fight.

PYRRHUS: But no, Rome's just got back up – *again* – and is carrying on as though nothing's happened. Just look at Carthage, who is starting to realise that Rome's a bit mad. This is no ordinary fight.

POLYBIUS: What's Rome doing now? I've never seen anything quite like it. Rome has got Carthage in a headlock. This is totally unorthodox.

PYRRHUS: Elegance is out the window, training is out the window. Carthage clearly doesn't know how to handle this.

POLYBIUS: She can't get away from Rome's grip – and Rome has landed a shattering punch on Carthage's jaw. And another. Does that move even have a name? I'm going to call it the *corvus*! What is Rome doing? They're locked together and punching the living daylights out of one another.*

---

* In 260 BC, Rome's sheer bloody-mindedness led to its first great naval success, thanks to the *corvus* (Latin for 'crow'), a boarding ramp with a sharp 'beak' at one end. When this mad invention was dropped onto the enemy deck, it punched through the planks and locked the two

POLYBIUS: And there's the first bell. Phew! Everyone breathe. The first four years of this fight seem to have flown by in the blink of an eye. I'm exhausted just watching this.

The exhausting middle rounds

PYRRHUS: And here we go: round seven, the entire decade of the 250s has flown by, and I just can't imagine how they're still on their feet. What a slugfest we're seeing.

POLYBIUS: They both deserve to be champions – but only one can win. Sicily has never seen a fight like this one, and Sicily will be the prize for the winner.

POLYBIUS: This feels personal now, doesn't it? When we started this evening, seventeen years ago, there was no bad blood, but now you can tell that these two absolutely loathe each other.

PYRRHUS: Rome are definitely winning on points. She's giving Carthage an absolute pummelling in her own backyard.

POLYBIUS: Rome has got the run of the ring.*

PYRRHUS: Sensational stuff. What we're seeing here is nothing less than a total realignment of this weight category. Is it all over?

---

ships together, rendering ineffective the Carthaginians' defter handling of their ships. Once the *corvus* was deployed, Roman legionaries swarmed onto the enemy ship and engaged in their beloved hand-to-hand fighting.
* By 247 BC, the Carthaginian territory in Sicily was reduced to just two besieged port cities.

CARTHAGE

POLYBIUS: Carthage's only hope in the final rounds is to go defensive, tire Rome out, and hope to squeak a victory on points in the final round. Look – she's focusing on staying out of the reach of Rome's deadly gloves. Carthage is just running down the clock now. What's the plan – is Carthage hoping something will turn up?

Winner takes all

POLYBIUS: It's 241 BC – and we're into the final round now.

PYRRHUS: We all thought Rome had nothing left in the tank, but her friends and family are cheering them on like wild things.

POLYBIUS: It seems to be giving Rome an extra burst of strength.*

PYRRHUS: Twenty-three years after the fight began, Rome is now outfighting Carthage with orthodox 'Naval Warfare' tactics.

POLYBIUS: Absolutely wild. Think back to where these two were in the first round. Rome has been on the most brutal learning curve imaginable.

PYRRHUS: Rome stuck at it, and it's paying off.

POLYBIUS: Carthage is taking a huge pummelling.

PYRRHUS: There's only one way this is going to go now.

---

* To be precise, a financially exhausted Rome asked its citizens to pay for one last fleet, which in 241 BC managed to break the stalemate and secure Carthage's surrender.

POLYBIUS: Carthage is tottering against the ropes... And there it is! Carthage's corner has thrown in the towel.

PYRRHUS: Rome wins! Rome is the champion! Raising both boxing gloves to the sky, Rome starts to celebrate as the enormity of the moment sinks in.

POLYBIUS: Absolute scenes. She gave it everything, but it's official now – Carthage has been dethroned. That final round was one too many for Carthage.

PYRRHUS: Carthage's corner is not happy. They're exchanging angry words.

POLYBIUS: I'm not surprised. Carthage stands to lose out financially in a huge way from this upset. Think of all those lost sponsorship deals. She's gone from filthy rich to broke, overnight. And notoriously, Carthage owes a lot of money to her support team.

PYRRHUS: Rome's never had this problem, because Rome's team is all composed of their own relatives. But Carthage's support team is heavily reliant on mercenaries from North Africa, Greece and Sardinia, among others. They haven't been doing their job through any particular love of Carthage. And now Carthage can't pay...

POLYBIUS: Oh dear. It's turning really ugly just next to the ring. There seems to be an actual fight. Carthage is being attacked – by Carthage's own support staff. These are really, really unpleasant scenes. I can only apologise to the viewers. Nobody wants to see that.

PYRRHUS: This was already a bad-tempered evening, but this is just making it worse.

CARTHAGE

POLYBIUS: Meanwhile Rome is still in the ring, lapping up the moment. Rome is a heavyweight champion for the first time, the complete master of Italy and Sicily. They'll be talking about this across the entire Mediterranean circuit. You know what, Pyrrhus? I don't think this is the end.

PYRRHUS: I reckon you're right. This is a night of humiliation for Carthage, and she will be desperate for a rematch.

*

Rome's peace terms were predictably punitive. Their impact on Carthage was made all the worse by the resultant trauma of the Mercenary War. It took the city two decades to recover. Eventually, in 218 BC, Carthage's resentment against Rome inspired a young general called Hannibal to march over the Alps and invade Italy from the north, launching the Second Punic War – which Rome also won, although they came close to catastrophe in the early stages. With Carthage thoroughly beaten and reduced to a minor power, the Third Punic War (149–146 BC) was a one-sided affair which saw Rome raze Carthage to the ground and slaughter its inhabitants.

Chaucer

In Conversation with the Man of the Fourteenth-century Moment

Geoffrey Chaucer is widely viewed as the venerable grandfather of English literature, a writer whose challenging Middle English has sent generations of undergraduates scurrying for their CliffsNotes study guides.

In reality, he is an unusually accessible, worldly and fascinating author. Poet, courtier and well-connected diplomat, Chaucer lived a colourful life at the heart of fourteenth-century English society. His cutting-edge poetry, written in English, rather than Latin or French, challenged both literary and social conventions. And The Canterbury Tales, *his last and most famous work, provides historians with a fascinating window into fourteenth-century England.*

If a contemporary newspaper had sent its arts correspondent to interview him in the last year of his life, this is how it might have gone.

Canterbury Courier
18 April 1400

'We Creatives Have Got to Take Risks'

In conversation with Geoffrey Chaucer

eoffrey Chaucer is all smiles as he welcomes us into his desirable super-prime London home, glamorously located in the garden of Westminster Abbey. But while the interior is as chic as one would expect from a refined friend of royalty, Mr Chaucer himself is surprisingly down-to-earth for someone who's achieved true literary stardom.

'Don't mind the clutter,' he says with a light laugh. 'I only moved here in December.'

Waving us into a chair, he adds, 'Make yourselves at home. Since the wife died and the children left home, it's just been me and the servants, and now that I'm nearly sixty, I can't bring myself to waste time tidying up.'

Reclining in an ornate chair and stroking his neat white beard, he seems relaxed as he chats exclusively to the *Canterbury Courier* about life, poetry and his hotly anticipated forthcoming book.

What a stunning location!

Isn't it?! I've always liked a view. In the 1370s, when I was Controller of the Wool Customs for the Port of London, I was given a grace-and-favour flat right above the Aldgate where the road from Essex comes through the city walls. It was a wonderful spot for a people-watcher like me. Unfortunately, it was also the gate that the rebels came through during the Peasants' Revolt in 1381. That was a very frightening day, hiding with my family as the peasants poured into London right under our feet.

Hold that thought – we'll come back to the Peasants' Revolt. First, can you tell us a bit about your early life? Did you always want to be a writer?

I'm sure your readers would like a story about the artist's difficult relationship with his parents, but I'm afraid I'll have to disappoint them. I spent a very happy childhood in the 1340s[*] in the parish of St Martin Vintry, a cosmopolitan London ward full of Italian and Flemish merchants. My only real trauma was the same as everyone else's – the arrival of the Black Death in 1348. I was very lucky. My father was the key player in the London wine import business, so Edward III appointed him the royal wine-importer and sent him to Southampton, which was much less affected than London. We survived, but all our London relatives were wiped out. My parents inherited a great deal of their property, which is perhaps rather vulgar and tasteless to admit. Then again, lots of my old-fashioned readers think I'm vulgar and tasteless anyway.

---

[*] It is thought that Chaucer was born around 1342, but no one is entirely sure.

So you were set up for a high-flying career?

Yes – I became a page in the household of Lionel, Duke of Clarence, the second surviving son of King Edward. He's been dead for thirty years now, of course, but he gave me my start in life. Those were the golden years of the court of Edward III, and there I was, still a young lad, seeing all the jousting tournaments and dressing in the latest styles. You should have seen me in my buttock-exposing mini-tunic! I was such a fashionista! Best of all, though, we got to fight the French.* In 1359, we went on a raid and made it all the way to the walls of Paris. The following year, I was captured and Edward personally sent £15 to ransom me, which was the sort of decent thing he used to do. It was all very hairy, looking back on it, but for a hot-blooded young man like me, this was terrific stuff.

You didn't want to remain a soldier?

That spell in a French dungeon persuaded me that I wasn't cut out for a military career, so I became a diplomat instead.

And did you enjoy that?

I loved the travel. I loved meeting people. I loved reading the Italian greats: Dante and Boccaccio and Petrarch. And in 1374, as I mentioned, I was appointed Controller of the Wool Custom, which meant I was responsible for organising the entire wool trade from London to the Continent.

You're a man of many talents. How on earth do you find time for your writing?

Well, I don't do literary festivals. And I don't do podcasts. So I've had plenty of time to write throughout my life, alongside my civil service career.

---

* The Hundred Years' War (see page 129), a dynastic struggle between the French and English kings, lasted from 1337 to 1453.

Your first literary success was *The Book of the Duchess*, written in 1370 when you were in your late twenties. Can you tell us a bit more about that?

It's a eulogy for my friend's wife who died of plague.

Your 'friend's wife'? You're being very modest. You're talking about John of Gaunt, aren't you – King Edward's son?*

Well, yes. My wife's sister Katherine married John after he was widowed. Imagine! Me, the great-grandson of a pub landlord related to the King! I'm an example of how the old social categories are getting blurred, and that's something that's fed into a lot of my writing. John of Gaunt was always very good to me.

Although your association with him almost got you killed, didn't it?

Yes, but I don't blame him. The monopolies of the English wool merchants were bad for business, and we wanted to revitalise the trade by involving the Europeans. But the English traders didn't like the idea of competition, and they hated the state meddling, as they saw it, on the side of foreigners. So they fought us at every turn.

When the Peasants' Revolt reached London in 1381, the poor Flemish merchants became a target. The rebels hated John of Gaunt for hawking off wool licences to foreigners, and so they sacked his palace. Fortunately, he was away at the time, but my colleague, Sir Richard Lyons – he ran the wine trade while

---

* John of Gaunt was the third surviving son of Edward III, which made him the younger brother of Edward, the Black Prince (Richard II's father) and Lionel (the one who'd employed Chaucer as a page). He was also the father of Henry Bolingbroke, who was exiled by Richard II. When John of Gaunt died in 1399, Richard tried to block Bolingbroke from inheriting his property, so Bolingbroke invaded, deposed Richard and became Henry IV. This is also the plot of Shakespeare's *Richard II*, so if you haven't seen it yet we've just spoiled it for you (although it did come out a while ago).

I ran the wool trade – had his head chopped off by the mob in Cheapside. That's why it was so terrifying when I was trapped in the Aldgate flat above the rebels – if they'd known I was there, that would have been the end of me.

That sounds like a close shave.

It certainly was. And it's not the only time I've almost lost my life for doing my job. It also got a bit touch-and-go in the mid-eighties, when there was a power struggle between the royal family and a group of barons calling themselves the Lords Appellant. The Lords Appellant got the upper hand for a while: lots of us lost our jobs; some of my friends were executed for treason. But when the royal faction finally saw off the Lords Appellant, Richard II gave his surviving supporters their jobs back. I was appointed clerk of the king's works, responsible for maintaining royal buildings like the Tower of London and the Palace of Westminster.

You've certainly lived life to the full, haven't you?

I like to think so. But I'm more or less retired now. When Henry IV took the throne from Richard last September, he granted me a very generous pension, as he'd known me as a family friend for years.

To what extent do you think your life has influenced your writing?

Oh, it's been a huge influence. England has changed enormously since I was young. There's more money changing hands, for one thing. It's now possible for someone like me to improve their place in society over the course of a single lifetime, which would have been unthinkable before the Black Death. I think that sense of new possibilities – of lives in a state of flux – has been at the front of my mind while I've written my poems. Earlier, I mentioned discovering Dante, Boccaccio and Petrarch during my diplomatic career. In *Divine Comedy*, *The Decameron* and *Scattered Rhymes*, those Tuscan writers were doing radically fresh things with literature which I wanted to bring to England.

What sort of things?

They wrote in their mother tongue, instead of in Latin or even French. People used to assume that the vernacular wasn't suitable for proper literature. But English can be just as worthy a language for great poetry. Even the King of England speaks English now.*

But you've encountered some opposition along the way, haven't you?

I'm delighted that up-and-coming writers see me as a trailblazer. But yes, you're right, back in the sixties when I was starting out, the literary establishment saw me as a bit of a rebel, ripping up the rulebook. I had some scathing reviews in the *London Review of Illuminated Manuscripts*. It was only in the eighties, when I had successes with some of my poems about love, especially the *Parlement of Foules* and *Troilus and Criseyde*, that I finally began to feel people were taking me seriously. But we creatives have to take risks, and we can't pay too much attention to the critics. It always takes them at least a generation to get used to newfangleness.

'Newfangleness' – that's one of the words you've invented, isn't it?

Well spotted. Yes, I'm always trying to keep up with the zeitgeist, in my poetry and in my life.† We should celebrate the

---

* Henry IV, crowned in 1399, was the first King of England to speak English as his first language since the Norman Conquest of 1066.
† A good example of Chaucer leaning into social and economic change is the time he exploited a legal loophole and accidentally tainted his reputation for 150 years. In 1873, a legal document was discovered in which it was stated that a woman called Cecily Chaumpaigne agreed not to sue Chaucer for her 'raptus'. *Raptus* is a Latin word that can mean rape, seizure or abduction. Subsequent Chaucer scholars worried that

joyous variety of existence. And that, more than anything else, is what my current project is all about.

Ah, yes, as I'm sure you're aware, there's been a lot of chatter about this new book, but you've been keeping the details firmly under wraps. Can you tell us anything about *The Canterbury Tales*?

Well, that's just its working title. But I like to think it will have something for everyone. It's certainly the most ambitious thing I've ever written. My concept is that thirty pilgrims are travelling from Southwark to Canterbury, to pray at the famous shrine of St Thomas Becket, and along the way they have a competition about who can tell the best story. I've put myself in as one of the characters, and my friend Harry Bailly – the well-known Southwark landlord – features as the innkeeper in charge of the competition.

Who doesn't love a literary in-joke?

Indeed.

I'm fascinated by your premise. Why a pilgrimage?

They bring together people from all walks of life, so it gives me a chance to tell a wide variety of stories, while presenting a vivid cast of characters. I've set it in April because this is when plague season is over and spring begins. It's a celebration of modern life in all its forms.

---

he might have raped Cecily – until 2022, when another document was found in the British National Archives, clarifying the situation. It turns out that Cecily was a maidservant, and Chaucer had poached her from her old boss with the promise of a higher salary. The Statute of Labourers, introduced in 1351 to regulate wages during the manpower shortage after the Black Death, meant she couldn't voluntarily swap employers. So the 'raptus', it seems, was a legal fiction that Chaucer had kidnapped her, a situation that wasn't covered by the Statute. Unfortunately, this nifty legal dodge made Chaucer look like a potential sex offender for 150 years.

Can you give us any more juicy details?

Well, the first story, 'The Knight's Tale', is a traditional chivalric romance set in ancient Greece at the court of King Theseus.* It's exactly the sort of romance that one might expect in a book like this. But really I'm just setting up the reader's expectations in order to subvert them, because after the first tale, things get anarchic pretty quickly. A drunk pilgrim – a miller – refuses to wait his turn and tells a bawdy story about an adulterous carpenter's wife. I don't want to give too much away, but it's absolutely filthy. And the whole thing just gallops on from there.

I can't wait. Do you have a publication date yet?

Not yet. We'll see how I get on.†

And you give an interesting place to women in your stories, don't you?

Yes – I'm trying to reflect modern society in all its variety and turbulence. I know it will ruffle lots of feathers, but that's half the fun of it. There's one woman in particular that I'm working on, called the Wife of Bath, who's been married five times and been on lots of pilgrimages – she's what I like to call a Strong Female Character. I've decided she's from Bath because of the booming wool industry there, which has caused all sorts of

---

* Film buffs will notice that this is not the setting of the Heath Ledger film *A Knight's Tale*, which features Paul Bettany as Chaucer. Although *A Knight's Tale* was inspired by all things Chaucerian, the story isn't based on any of the *Canterbury Tales* – it's more of an enjoyable hodgepodge, which would have surely met with Chaucer's approval.

† Unfortunately Chaucer did not get on for much longer. He died in October 1400, leaving the *Canterbury Tales* unfinished – though it was an instant hit all the same. Chaucer's descendants also did pretty well for themselves. His granddaughter, Alice Chaucer, married the Duke of Suffolk and became one of the richest people in England. Alice's son married the sister of Richard III, and her grandson became Richard's heir to the throne. If Richard III hadn't given battle in vain, Chaucer's great-great-grandson might have become the King of England.

social change and turned the old-fashioned status quo on its head. She has strong opinions about sex, and she thinks the writings of the Church Fathers always favour men because they were written by men.

This sounds like racy stuff.

It is! I felt quite naughty putting that on the page. But there's a serious point here. Here in the year 1400, there are women who have amassed property and enjoy increasing levels of agency in society. English women have more rights than their predecessors, as well as their counterparts in Europe. This is all very new, and I find the kaleidoscope of modernity a tremendously exciting topic for a writer. Nobody's ever given the common people a voice in literature before – certainly not in English – and that's my aim with the *Canterbury Tales*. Who knows? Maybe it'll catch on.

Colosseum Beyond Ridley and Russell

WHAT THE AMPHITHEATRE ACTUALLY MEANT TO THE ROMANS

In 2024, almost a quarter of a century after Gladiator made a star of Russell Crowe, Ridley Scott is releasing a sequel to his Oscar-winning film. Although the original took considerable liberties with the characters of Marcus Aurelius, Commodus and Maximus Decimus Meridius, Commander of the Armies of the North (who didn't, sadly, exist), its depiction of the Colosseum as the awe-inspiring, terrifying symbol of Rome was remarkably faithful.

It's a symbol, however, that many have misunderstood over the years. The Colosseum wasn't inaugurated until AD 80, over a hundred years after the end of the Roman Republic. There are no records of Christians being fed to lions. And perhaps most surprisingly, the Romans didn't even call their main amphitheatre the Colosseum, a misattribution for which Lord Byron was partially responsible in the nineteenth century. In his narrative poem 'Childe Harold's Pilgrimage', Byron mistranslated – and probably misattributed, to the Venerable Bede – an eighth-century prophecy which referred to the Colossus, the statue built by Nero, not the Colosseum, which the Romans called 'Caesar's Amphitheatre'.

Byron's words, however, still capture the symbolism of the building across the millennia: 'While stands the Coliseum, Rome shall stand; When falls the Coliseum, Rome shall fall. And when Rome falls – the world.'

And he was right to insinuate that gladiatorial contests in Caesar's Amphitheatre and its many predecessors were always more than simple entertainment. Here is what they meant to the Romans.

The rites to Rome

The first gladiatorial contests, which stretch back to the third century BC, began as funerary rites, offering the gods a tribute of armed violence to propitiate the souls of the dead. These funerals, slaughtering slaves bought cheaply for the purpose, were often staged in Rome's Forum, the central open space between the Palatine and Capitoline Hills.

Originally named *munera*, from which we derive the English word *munificence*, the funeral obligations slowly morphed into *spectacula*, a show that deserved to be watched more widely. Fans clamoured to watch the most talented fighters and the most dangerous spectacles in the same way as modern crowds thrill to boxing matches, Formula One crashes or fast bowling in cricket.*

But even as the primary purpose of appeasing the souls of the dead began to fade, gladiatorial contests still remained more than simple spectacles.

Standing room only

In the middle of the second century BC, the Roman Senate brought in legislation to stipulate that spectators had to stand while watching gladiatorial contests, thereby affirming their virile, masculine character. This was in response to paranoid Roman moralists fearing a lapse in standards if citizens sat down comfortably to watch the bloodshed. *Seditio*, the Latin word for seating, is the origin of the English word *sedition*, the act of inciting people to rebel against authority.

Interestingly, English football has witnessed similar panics in recent decades about losing its virile working-class spirit in a namby-pamby era of all-seater stadiums,

---

* Dominic writes: Tom made us write that.

corporate sponsorship and the seditious prawn cocktail sandwich brigade.

Civis Romanus sum

In the latter centuries of the Republic, as Rome grew into a great power, gladiatorial combat became a means of maintaining social cohesion. To watch the gladiators fight was a key perk of citizenship, a common experience fostering a shared sense of civic Roman identity.

As warfare moved far beyond the limits of an expanding Rome, gladiatorial contests also reminded its citizens of the militarism underpinning Roman greatness. The oath taken by gladiators before a fight – 'I will endure to be burned, to be bound, to be beaten, and to be killed by the sword' – was modelled on the oath sworn by a Roman legionary.

Toys for boys

In the final years of the Republic, gladiators became a way for ambitious politicians to project their power and image, a prelude to the twenty-first-century trend of petro-dollar plutocrats buying up English football teams (or indeed Silvio Berlusconi buying AC Milan).

Unsurprisingly, it was a young Julius Caesar who blazed this trail, using his father's death in 85 BC as an excuse to dress up 320 pairs of gladiators in silver armour for a *munera* for his father's soul. Alarmed by the largest gladiatorial display to date, the Senate introduced legislation to rein in further extravagance.

However, the cat (and the bears, the tigers, the elephants and the snakes) were already firmly out of the bag as far as extravagant gladiatorial contests were concerned. When Augustus became the first Emperor in 27 BC, he staged a show featuring 10,000 gladiators.* A novel by Petronius, written during the reign of Nero, the fifth Emperor, describes 'strange, ravening creatures borne by our fleets... the padding tiger is wheeled in a gilded palace to drink human blood while the crowd applauds and cheers'.

As well as becoming more lavish, gladiatorial contests also grew more regimented, a way for the early emperors to woo and control the masses. Having revived the notion of the Roman census (the reason Joseph and Mary supposedly had to travel to Bethlehem for Jesus's birth), Augustus saw gladiatorial games as a stone-and-flesh reflection of society, the newly segregated amphitheatres giving Senators the best seats.

There were also potential pitfalls for emperors identifying themselves so closely with these displays. Claudius, the fourth Emperor, was a sickly, scholarly man with little interest in martial matters. Having once royally messed up a naval display in a temporary lake by implying that the gladiators didn't have to fight, he had to hobble out of his seat and harangue them in person.

---

* This suspiciously round number was quoted by Suetonius, a Roman historian who had access to Augustus's records. It is possible that 10,000 was simply Latin for 'bigly', as Donald Trump might have put it.

Fighting after Rome burns

Despite all these extravagant displays, it took more than a century – and ten emperors – for Rome to build a permanent amphitheatre.

The Colosseum was the brainchild of Vespasian, a rugged, no-nonsense, turnip-munching soldier who took power in AD 69, the fourth Emperor that year. Still coping with the chaos following the death of Nero, the new Flavian dynasty needed to stamp their authority on the urban fabric of the city. Nero had inadvertently given them an opportunity to do so by building an enormous pleasure palace and garden in the wake of the Great Fire of Rome in AD 64. Aware that it was viewed by the senatorial elite as a display of imperial self-indulgence, Vespasian knocked it down and filled the lake with concrete, thereby creating a vast, valuable brownfield site in the centre of the city.

Building an enormous amphitheatre – the Colosseum – on this prime slice of real estate would kill multiple birds with one stone.

While evoking the long Roman tradition of gladiatorial contests, it would also serve as a visual reminder of the Flavians' great military triumph, defeating the Judeans and capturing Jerusalem in AD 70. Vespasian and Titus, his son and successor, were *imperatores* – generals – in the strictest sense of the word, not lyre-playing, mother-killing weirdos like Nero, who had never led an army.

They used Judean slaves and treasure (although most of the money came from taxes on the eastern half of the Empire) to build Caesar's Amphitheatre, a building comparable to the great wonders of the world, according to the Roman poet Martial. Adorned with huge statues and beautiful awnings, it dominated the Roman cityscape in much the way that cathedrals would later loom over medieval towns.

Titus Anomalous

Vespasian didn't live to see the inauguration of the Colosseum in the summer of AD 80, the second year of Titus's reign. It was a challenging time for the new Emperor: Rome was ravaged by plague; fire had destroyed the Temple of Jupiter twice in a decade; and Pompeii and Herculaneum had just been entombed by the eruption of Vesuvius, leaving thousands of souls denied the usual funerary rites. As well as providing the usual entertainments on the grandest ever scale, the Colosseum therefore offered the chance to appease these restless spirits, an echo of the earliest gladiatorial contests.

Titus also seized the opportunity for a spot of reputational sport-washing. As head of the Praetorian guard, the imperial bodyguard, he had been known as a bloodthirsty libertine. Turning over a new leaf, he declared himself motivated only by the desire to avoid polluting his hands with blood. This desire manifested itself, somewhat ironically, in dragging all the informers he had previously employed into the Colosseum during its inauguration – and having them lashed with whips and smashed with cudgels.

The poet Martial, whose first book in AD 80 celebrated the shows held in the Colosseum, wrote approvingly of the punishments and executions carried out in the amphitheatre. A fusion of Cirque du Soleil and snuff movies, stagecraft and ritual, justice and myth, these public tortures included a bear eating the intestines of a chained man (an echo of the punishment of Prometheus) and a woman mounted by a bull (an echo of the story of Pasiphae).

The confessions of posterity

The last reference to gladiatorial fights came around AD 435, half a century after Christianity had become the state religion of the Roman Empire. A violent, sacral ritual originally designed to appease the lost souls of the dead didn't sit easily with the message of the Gospels.

However, some Christians proved themselves unable to resist temptation. *The Confessions of St Augustine* describes Alypius, the theologian's equally religious friend, reluctantly attending a gladiatorial contest in the late fourth century.

'As soon as he saw the blood, he drank it in with a savage temperament,' writes St Augustine. 'He did not turn away, but fixed his eyes on the bloody pastime, drinking in the madness, delighted with the wicked contest, drunk with bloodlust. He was now no longer the same man who came in, but was one of the mob he came into, a true companion of those who had brought him there.'

After the fall of the western Roman Empire, the Colosseum became variously a chapel, a cemetery, a castle and a workhouse for repentant prostitutes under Renaissance popes. Its design has continued to inspire sports stadiums in the twentieth and twenty-first centuries. But its enduring fascination for tourists – and Hollywood – probably owes more to the equally enduring interest in the bloodiest aspects of human nature than we might care to admit.

Declaration of Interdependence

GEORGE III RESPONDS TO JEFFERSON AND CHUMS

Few countries have a better origin myth than the United States of America: a tyrannical British king determined to curtail the liberties of his loyal subjects; a beautifully worded Declaration of Independence that spoke to the hearts of all freedom-loving Americans; a plucky guerrilla force led by George Washington, which overcame extreme odds in Boston, Delaware and Valley Forge to defeat the mighty British army; and a fledgling republic, underpinned by a near-sacral constitution, which continues to inspire reverential devotion almost 250 years later.

No wonder Lin-Manuel Miranda made such a good musical out of this promising material – and Mel Gibson such a dreadful film.*

---

* A review in the *Guardian* dismissed *The Patriot*, released in 2000, as 'flag-waving rot'.

DECLARATION OF INTERDEPENDENCE

Amid all the hagiography, however, the British perspective has been somewhat sidelined, not least because (spoiler alert) the American Revolutionary War turned out badly for the away team, who surrendered to Washington at Yorktown in 1781 and signed the Treaty of Paris recognising American independence two years later. In Miranda's musical Hamilton, *George III, the only British character, is – somewhat unfairly – played for camp laughs, whereas he was actually a highly cultured monarch (at least until his madness set in decades later).*

Here is how the King might have responded to the Declaration of Independence on 4 July 1776 if he had been advised by a couple of robust eighteenth-century podcasters.

The Unanimous Declaration of George III

Buckingham Palace, 6 July 1776

Dear Jefferson *et al.*

Thank you for your press release, the contents of which have been noted.

In response, I would say that we hold <u>these</u> truths to be self-evident, <u>that some men are created more equal than others</u>, that they are endowed by their Creator with certain <u>debatable</u> Rights, that among these are Life, Liberty, <u>Property</u> and the pursuit of Happiness <u>within the context of a tax-paying society</u>. That to uphold these rights, Governments are instituted among Men <u>and Monarchs</u>, deriving their just powers from the consent of the governed, that whenever any People becomes destructive of these ends<u>, it is the Right of the Government to respond as it sees fit, especially when falsely accused of a long train of abuses and usurpations amounting to absolute Despotism</u>.

Such has been the patient sufferance of this government; and such is now the necessity which constrains it to respond. The history of the present King of Great Britain is a history of repeated injuries and usurpations by a vocal minority of his American subjects, all having in direct object the establishment of an absolute Anarchy over these States.

To prove this, let Facts be submitted to a candid world.

DECLARATION OF INTERDEPENDENCE

Thirteen years ago, at the end of the Seven Years' War, my American colonies were wealthy, healthy and prosperous. The average American was two inches taller than the average Englishman. Not only could more of you read and write (a fact we have learned to regret recently),* your franchise was also much wider than ours (you like to bang on about 'No taxation without representation', but Manchester doesn't have an MP either). And in an era like ours, when it is easier to get from Boston to London than from Boston to Charleston – and where your George Washington has never even visited New England – there seemed little chance of a sense of a united 'American' identity emerging.

With your help, we secured your borders and guaranteed your liberties by expelling the Catholic French from North America in 1763. And yet the problems of peace proved more taxing (if you'll forgive the pun) than the exigencies of war. Our national debt had almost doubled, to £137 million. The interest alone on that debt was £5 million a year, more than 60 per cent of our annual budget. The French wanted revenge. So was it not fair to ask you to pay your way for your own defence, especially when the average American paid only six pence a year in taxes, fifty times less than the average British taxpayer, the most taxed citizen in Europe?

The Sugar Act, about which you made such an unseemly fuss in 1764, actually cut the duty on imported molasses. You were only up in arms about it because it also clamped down on smuggling, which was rife in New England. Yes, we threatened to send your merchants to be tried in a Vice Admiralty Court in Nova Scotia, but we have always dealt with customs violations in similar ways in Britain. Long experience has taught us that local juries who have benefited from smuggling tend to reach sympathetic verdicts.

The following year, you made even more of a kerfuffle about the introduction of a tax that had been levied in England since

---

* In a highly literate society, pamphlets condemning the King and his ministers reached a wide audience. *Common Sense*, written by Thomas Paine, a British exile who travelled with Washington during the American Revolutionary War (and later ended up imprisoned in revolutionary France), was the most popular of these.

1694. The rate of this Stamp Act, as Lord Grenville, my Prime Minister, pointed out, was a tenth of what is paid in England. And while we're on the subject of prime ministers, might I remind you that I have precious little power over Parliament. If you knew your John Locke as well as you pretend to do (I enjoyed your thinly disguised bit of copy and paste in the Declaration of Independence), you'd be aware that he published his *Two Treatises of Government* in the immediate aftermath of the Glorious Revolution of 1688 that established the principle of parliamentary sovereignty. So I suggest you stop haranguing me as if I had any influence over my ministers. I am not Charles I, and you should be jolly careful that your Washington doesn't turn out to be an Oliver Cromwell.

Your response to the introduction of the Stamp Act was simultaneously violent and childish. I was especially amused to hear that Richard Henry Lee, a Virginian who signed your Declaration of Independence, was so outraged by the perceived infringement on his liberty that he forced his slaves to re-enact the protests against the legislation – before applying for the job of stamp distributor himself.

Regardless, we repealed the Stamp Act in 1766 (which, in retrospect, might have been a mistake). The Townshend Acts, which we passed the following year, introduced limited duties on external trade, provoking another furious cycle of pamphleteering, boycotts and violence. My Redcoats were sent to Boston to keep the peace. On 5 March 1770, a huge mob carrying cudgels and bricks (no, not snowballs – I've seen that Paul Revere engraving and it's more than a little misleading) cornered a small number of troops who fired in self-defence. Five Bostonians tragically lost their lives. But did we try to sweep this under the carpet? No. Your very own John Adams, another signatory to your Declaration of Independence, defended the soldiers in court, saying they were 'facing a motley rabble of saucy boys, negros, and molattoes, Irish teagues and outlandish jack tars' (and yes, I had to look up some of those words in Mr Johnson's nice new dictionary). Two of the soldiers were convicted of manslaughter, and had their thumbs branded.

DECLARATION OF INTERDEPENDENCE

In 1770, we repealed the Townshend Acts (which might have been a mistake), with the exception of the duty on tea (which might have been a mistake too). Nevertheless, your reaction to the Tea Act of 1773 was even more hysterical. Now I know you don't care much about the fortunes of the East India Company, but this legislation wasn't just about rescuing its falling revenues following a famine in Bengal. Neither did it impose a monopoly, as you tried to claim. It simply allowed the Company to offload cheap, surplus tea, benefiting everyone in the colonies except the smugglers. So forgive me if I don't feel too sympathetic towards the sixty Bostonians who 'blacked up' as Mohawks and threw 342 chests of tea worth £10,000 into the sea, causing serious ecological damage into the bargain.

You described our subsequent legislation, which included the closure of the port of Boston until the ruined tea was paid for, as the 'Intolerable Acts'. But they weren't half as intolerable as the wanton destruction that even Benjamin Franklin, another signatory to your Declaration of Independence, described as an act of violent injustice. I thought your response to the Quebec Act in 1774, which you also considered 'intolerable', particularly egregious. We were not attempting to harness the twin evils of Catholicism and authoritarianism as Paul Revere seemed to think. Nor were we seeking to rain down Canadians – and other 'savages' – upon the thirteen colonies. We were simply attempting to solve the legacy problem of French inhabitants in North America by introducing a successful piece of legislation that caused no backlash in Canada itself.

Incidentally, you made a similar hullabaloo when we tried to protect the Indians from further western encroachment with the Proclamation Line in 1763. Do you spot a pattern here?

What was most revealing, I thought, was the fact that the legislation which got you most worked up was the Dunmore Proclamation of November 1775 exhorting slaves to rise up against their owners. Now I know this was a little cheeky.* But

---

* Lord Dunmore was no Abraham Lincoln. He later became Governor of Barbados, where he failed to free a single slave.

there is a paradox, is there not, in declaring all men equal when many of the men who put their names to that declaration hold other men as enslaved property?* Perhaps you have read *Taxation no Tyranny* by Samuel Johnson, the great lexicographer, in which he wonders: 'How is it that we hear the loudest yelps for liberty among the drivers of negroes?'

Despite all this, I was still willing to forgive and to forget. But by 1774, you already appeared hell bent on confrontation. After electing your first 'Continental Congress', attended by twelve of the thirteen colonies, you started stockpiling weapons and contacting ammunition traders in Holland and Spain. On 19 April 1775, when a hundred of my Redcoats attempted to find these weapons in Lexington and Concord, shots were fired, over a hundred British and American men lay dead and we were at war with one another.

Now, if I were truly a tyrant, my troops could easily win this war. Like the Romans – perhaps you have read the first volume of Edward Gibbon's *The History of the Decline and Fall of the Roman Empire*, which was published this year – they would annihilate the rebel strongholds, torturing, pillaging and enslaving as they went. The Royal Navy would blockade and bombard Boston until you begged for surrender.

But how can we win hearts and minds as well as battles? How can our generals plan campaigns when your guerrillas insist on hiding behind trees and running away to the back country? And how can we resupply our troops when it takes two months to cross the Atlantic?

No, the best we can hope for is to keep the Spanish away from Gibraltar; to stop the French joining the war (or at least hope that any intervention proves so ruinously costly that they

---

* This thorny question goes to the heart of the current debate in America about the nation's history. In 2019, the *New York Times* published the '1619 Project', an attempt to reframe the story of the country's origins by focusing on the year in which enslaved black people first arrived in Virginia, a deliberate counterbalance to the story of an American Revolution that has often glossed over the issue of slavery.

DECLARATION OF INTERDEPENDENCE

revolt against their king within a decade); and to hold on to our other – more important – thirteen colonies in the region.*

After all, it's difficult to imagine the thirteen American colonies on the eastern seaboard amounting to much over the next 300 years.

Yours ever (but probably not),

George R.

---

* Tobacco, the main crop in Northern America, made around £750,000 per year, whereas the sugar cane, molasses and rum from the West Indies fetched almost £4 million.

Downton Abbey

A HISTORY OF DOMESTIC SERVICE IN FIVE JOB ADVERTS

'A steaming silver tureen of snobbery servicing the instincts of cultural necrophilia' was the historian Simon Schama's damning verdict on Downton Abbey, Julian Fellowes's 2010 ITV drama set in a fictional Yorkshire stately home. Almost ten million viewers disagreed, propelling the show through six seasons, eight weddings, seventeen deaths (including *two of Lord Grantham's beloved Labradors), 69 Emmy nominations and a Wikipedia checklist of every major global event between 1912 and 1926 ('No, Carson, I don't think this Herr Hitler chap will amount to much, despite what I have just read about his so-called putsch in a Munich beer hall in this newspaper you have just given me.')*

The show's success confirmed a near-insatiable interest in an upstairs–downstairs dynamic that reached its height in Edwardian Britain – before falling into rapid decline.

Here we take a different angle on a century of social history by looking at how a series of employers and employees might have advertised in a newspaper's Situations Vacant column.

Wanted: Housemaid with common sense (1874)

Large townhouse in London W1 seeks young housemaid eager to swap her father's humble cottage for cleaning, starching, polishing and scrubbing. Lady of the house is the anonymous author of *Common Sense for Housemaids* (Thomas Hatchard, 1853) and although the successful candidate is not expected to be intimately familiar with all 542 words of the section entitled 'Sweeping, ways of', she will be rigorously tutored to adhere to these principles.

As such, she will learn to be 'light of foot and gentle in her movements' and never to 'flaunt about in vulgar finery' or 'mimic her mistress in manners'. After her own family and the family of her mistress, 'tables and chairs should be objects of deep interest, claiming the next place in her affections'.

This is an aristocratic dwelling, not one of those burgeoning middle-class homes eager to ape the mores and manners of the upper classes by returning to a meagrely staffed Victorian villa after a pen-pushing day in the office. Housemaids will be treated fairly, but they will also be reminded of the sign in the servants' hall: 'Know your place'.

Normal hours are 6 a.m. until 10 p.m., sometimes longer, overtime always unpaid.*

---

* One of the reasons factory work ended up becoming more popular than service was because, although the work was still gruelling, at least the hours were fixed.

Wanted: Butler to supervise household (1910)

Large estate in Derbyshire owned by former Viceroy of India* seeks experienced, educated butler to serve at luncheon and dinner, open the front door in a supercilious manner and run a household of over 100 domestic staff, including footmen, valets, gardeners and grooms. There currently being no housekeeper, thanks to Mr Lloyd George's vindictive 'People's Budget',† the successful applicant will also have ultimate responsibility for the large number of female servants, who outnumber the men twenty to one.

This is not one of those 'modern' dwellings, so popular in America or continental Europe, which believe that so-called labour-saving devices are an adequate substitute for young women's hands bloodied and blistered by polish, turpentine and carbolic soap.

Please only apply if you are 5'10" or taller. You may bring your own servant.‡

---

* Any servant to Lord Curzon (Viceroy of India, 1899–1905, Chancellor of Oxford University, 1907–1925 and Foreign Secretary, 1919–1924), would have had their work cut out. On visiting friends in the country, he found himself unsure how to open a bedroom window one evening. When he discovered that all the servants had gone to bed, Curzon simply picked up a log and smashed the glass to let in the air.

† Put forward by the Chancellor of the Exchequer David Lloyd George and his then-Liberal protégé, Winston Churchill, the Budget of 1909 paid for pensions and a burgeoning welfare bill by introducing a new rate of income tax for the wealthiest, as well as taxing landed estates. This novel redistributive approach was fiercely opposed in the Lords, including by the log-throwing Curzon.

‡ In their 1910 report, the Rowntree Foundation declared that not having a servant was a marker of absolute poverty. At a time when 1.5 million of the 4 million women in the British workforce were servants, even servants had their own servants.

Wanted: Middle-class lady help (1928)

Did you spend the Great War in a munitions factory or working as a bus conductress? Are you widowed or single and relying financially on your brother or father or male cousin? Are you reluctant to consider a life of polishing the front door now that you can finally vote in general elections?*

If so, why not apply to Gertie Maclean's Universal Aunts agency? Set up seven years ago with the motto 'Anything for Anyone at Any Time', we have found positions for hundreds of 'lady helps', who will do anything from delivering a pair of Purdey shotguns to Verona to advising on how to lay the table for a dinner party.†

And best of all, you don't need to live with your employer, so there's no chance you'll end up being looked down on by Virginia Woolf or George V.‡

---

* 'My butler votes, why can't I?' was one of the Suffragettes' memorable slogans.
† Gertie Maclean kept notes on her prospective 'aunts'. Among the many gems was this intriguing profile: '32-year-old Pansy Trubshaw. She understands cricket and foreign stamps, but not much else.'
‡ 'My brains are becoming soft by constant contact with the lower classes,' wrote Virginia Woolf to her sister. 'I am sick of the timid, spiteful servant mind.' Her fellow modernist, Katherine Mansfield, agreed. Having fired her cook, 'a dishonest, hateful old creature', she moaned that it was 'dreadful enough to be without servants, but to be with them is far more dreadful'. George V, meanwhile, used to take photographs of the rooms in his various palaces, enabling him to give his servants a rocket if anything was put back in the wrong place.

Position sought: Manservant (1937)

Jewish refugee from Vienna seeks work in respectable British household. Applicant holds domestic servant visa and some knowledge of catering sector having worked for thirty years in stockbroking and stayed in many of the grand hotels of central Europe.*

---

* This was the genuine experience of one well-educated refugee turned manservant. As well as having to deal with the significant drop in status, many of the affluent refugees in the 1930s found themselves shocked by the levels of discomfort endured by their English employers living in unheated Victorian villas, using toasting forks instead of electric toasters and eating herrings for lunch.

> **Wanted: Wife for modern man (1971)**
>
> Widowed civil servant seeks kindred spirit for companionship – and maybe more. Much-loved first wife outlived by brand-new 'Liberator' washing machine, a Christmas present from yours truly, reducing her daily hours of domestic servitude from twelve to only eight. The household also retains two vacuum cleaners, named Polly and Daisy, like my parents' maids, and a dishwasher, like the Duke of Bedford.*
>
> Household contains no children – and no copies of Germaine Greer. Hobbies include stamp collecting, the film soundtrack of *Sound of Music* (and definitely *not* the Beatles) and watching *Upstairs, Downstairs* on the television while bemoaning the fact that no one in this country wants to be a servant any more.†

---

* The Duke of Bedford was pictured at the Ideal Home exhibition in 1959, manfully (and unconvincingly) unloading a dishwasher. His Grace's less enlightened grandfather had resisted electricity until 1930 as he didn't want the workmen looking him in the eye.

† The precursor to *Downton Abbey*, *Upstairs Downstairs* ran for five series in the 1970s and won multiple awards. Lucy Lethbridge, our guest for the episode on this subject and author of *Servants: A Downstairs View of Twentieth Century Britain*, recalls reading, in an unpublished PhD thesis, that the actors who played the cook and the butler were given the smallest dressing rooms, despite being the biggest stars, whereas those playing the aristocratic Bellamys could reapply their make-up in voluminous luxury.

Exam

THE REST IS HISTORY'S EXAM...
ON THE HISTORY OF EXAMS

Pens out. Notes away. You have twenty minutes (twenty-five minutes for those with extra time) to answer the following questions on the history of public examinations. Calculators, smartphones and blogs by Daisy Christodoulou* must not be used.

Your time starts... now. Good luck.

---

* We are grateful to Daisy Christodoulou, author, educationalist and Director of Education at No More Marking, for the crash revision course (and PTSD) she gave us as our guest for this episode.

Question 1:

Where, in the seventh century AD, did the first exams originate?

A) Rome: the popes needed professional help with all the paperwork

B) China: the Tang Dynasty was establishing one of China's greatest empires and wanted to improve the recruitment system for its high-flying civil servants, or 'mandarins'

C) Byzantium: the Constantinople-based emperors compensated for their shrinking empire by increasing their number of palace bureaucrats

D) The Anglo-Saxon Heptarchy: a single exam system was thought the best way of consolidating a sense of national pride

Question 2:

What was the Chinese 'eight-legged essay?'

A) An 11+ exam for the best grammar schools, sat over eight hours
B) A school-leaving exam written in groups of four students
C) A compulsory creative writing exercise for primary school students about a dog who makes friends with a cat
D) A torturous exam essay on Confucian classic texts which involved jumping through pedantic hoops to satisfy the mark scheme

Question 3:

Why was the exam system accused of toppling the Chinese Empire in the nineteenth and early twentieth centuries?

A) The grade boundaries were too high, leading to a revolt by disgruntled working-class students unable to break into the ranks of the civil service

B) The exams were too easy, leading to a revolt by disgruntled middle-class parents who had wasted their savings on unnecessary tutoring

C) The population grew but the number of civil service places did not, leading to a revolt by disgruntled graduates who had done well in the exams but not quite well enough to get a job (a process named 'elite overproduction' by social historians)

D) Students were fed up with being examined on Confucian classics which no one could understand

Question 4:

At the start of the seventeenth century, an Italian Jesuit called Matteo Ricci played an important role in the story of exams. What was it?

A) As one of the first Westerners to travel to China, he spread the word about their impressive exam-based system for recruiting civil servants

B) He managed to persuade the Pope to reverse an earlier ban on exams as heretical

C) He made exams much cheaper and easier to scale by writing on paper rather than animal parchments

D) He pioneered anonymity in public exams by inventing the candidate number

Question 5:

In 1788, Prussia introduced the Abitur, Europe's first modern, standardised exam system.* This replaced an older, medieval system, common throughout Europe, which was difficult to scale to cope with millions of candidates. What was this medieval system?

A) A scholar took on an apprentice, or *padawan*, who would mark younger pupils' work for him, until the scholar was satisfied that the *padawan* was a fully fledged academic

B) Candidates were subjected to the *disputatio*, a theological debate with monks – a system which evolved into the modern PhD viva

C) Female candidates would line up for a newspaper photographer and jump as high as possible in the air. The higher the jump, the higher the grade

D) 'Exam by Water', whereby a student was tied up and thrown into a pond. If they floated, they were deemed to have revised insufficiently hard

---

* The Abitur is still in use in Germany today – old Abits die hard.

EXAM

Question 6:

Hong Xiuquan was a student in nineteenth-century China whose reaction to failing his exams was the most extreme in history. Why?

A) Having repeatedly failed China's state exams, he led an uprising, set up his own state with its own exam system, declared himself the younger brother of Jesus Christ, and began a holy war that killed between 30 and 50 million people

B) In an attempt to improve his grade, he slept with his teacher: their child was Chairman Mao

C) He shot the Imperial Invigilator, triggering a civil war between pro-exam and anti-exam factions

D) He lobbied the government until it invented extra time and resits

Question 7:

Which European country was particularly slow, idiosyncratic, ad hoc and confused when it came to implementing exams?

A) France: every time the government tried to impose exams, the horse-and-cart drivers blockaded the roads and set fire to their wheels

B) Prussia: the army repeatedly clashed with the left-wing teaching unions over their refusal to allow military uniforms in the examination room

C) Poland: the country was invaded by a neighbour every Easter, disrupting everyone's revision timetable

D) Britain: different religious denominations were used to running their own schools, their own way, and didn't want a uniform system. This explains why there are still so many different exam boards today

Question 8:

The nineteenth-century British philosopher John Stuart Mill was broadly in favour of exams. But what were his concerns?

A) He worried that teaching to the test would fail to equip pupils with real-world knowledge

B) He wanted to abolish coursework, as he thought it put too much pressure on parents

C) He worried exams would suck all the best and brightest into a civil service that he thought largely pointless

D) He thought Philosophy the only subject worth examining

Question 9:

Apart from schools, which nineteenth-century British institution had a long, messy culture war about whether or not to adopt exams?

A) The army: the modernisers wanted greater professionalism, but the traditionalists were offended by the idea that you could no longer buy your way to a high rank

B) The brand-new Football Association, which wanted all its players to have a certificate in Latin and Greek

C) The municipality of Birmingham, which wanted to impose exams on anyone trying to move to the city

D) The House of Commons, where politicians voted heavily against a bill requiring them to meet baseline intellectual requirements

Question 10:

In 1858, the University of Cambridge administered the first proper exams in England.* Which of the following subjects was NOT in the exams?

A) English Composition

B) English History

C) Geography

---

* Cambridge University's first set of exams were not for existing or prospective undergraduates (the university wasn't ready to give up on nepotism just yet) – but for local school-leavers who wanted to get a certificate of education.

D) Virgil

E) Anything connected to science or maths

Question 11:

Which of the following was NOT one of the questions in the 1858 English Composition exam?

A) Give an account of the late Indian Mutiny

B) Contrast the life of a soldier with that of a sailor, both in peace and war

C) Write a letter to a friend in Australia announcing your intention to emigrate, and ask him for information

D) Write a speech from the perspective of an eighteen-year-old woman, arguing why you should be given the vote

E) Discuss the change produced in the habits of the people by railways

Question 12:

Which of the following was NOT a real question in the 1858 Geography exam?

A) Draw an outline map showing the coastline of Europe from the mouth of the Danube to the mouth of the Rhine. Mark the chief rivers and the chief ranges of mountains

B) Draw – and colour in neatly – an oxbow lake

C) Describe accurately the situation of the following places: Genoa, Londonderry, Mecca, Rio de Janeiro, Singapore

D) Describe in words the course of one of the following rivers, mentioning the chief towns upon its banks: the Thames, the Severn, the Rhone, the Danube

Question 13:

Moving into the twentieth century, which is the fake question in this 1950 Scottish Leaving Certificate History exam?

A) What changes did Henry VIII make in regard to the Church, and for what reasons?

B) Trace the chief steps in the development of South Africa from the Great Trek to the Union Act of 1909

C) What were the reasons for the collapse of Napoleon's empire?

D) Is it more helpful to think of King James (r. 1685–88) as James II of England, or James VII of Scotland?

E) Describe the domestic problems that faced the British government from 1905 to 1914 and explain the measures they took to solve them

Question 14:

A maths paper that was awarded a grade E in 1968 would have got which grade in 1996?

A) A
B) B
C) C
D) D
E) E
F) U

―――

Please sit in uncomfortable silence until an invigilator has lost all the papers.

Answers: 1b, 2d, 3c, 4a, 5b, 6a, 7d, 8c, 9a, 10e, 11d, 12b, 13d, 14b

Fashion Groovy Babies
WHAT 1960s FASHION TELLS US ABOUT POST-WAR BRITAIN

For a few glorious years in the mid-1960s, London was the undisputed fashion capital of the world, a swinging metropolis unrecognisable from the smoggy, rationed, bombed-out city of 1945. And regardless of

whether you know your Bazaars from your Bibas, your Jean Shrimptons from your John Stephens, your King's Roads from your Carnaby Streets, the story of post-war British fashion provides a wonderful clothes horse on which to hang a wider analysis of other social changes in the period.

Make do and spend

The boom in the post-war fashion industry was a conscious reaction to the boxy, utilitarian austerity of the Second World War. Clothing rationing was introduced by the Board of Trade in 1941 and tightened the following year, forbidding turn-ups, double cuffs and double-breasted suits for men and puffed sleeves on blouses for women. Men's socks were limited to nine inches. The only items of clothing allowed elastic were women's knickers. And no garment could boast more than three buttons.

In 1943, the government released the slogan 'Make Do and Mend', which quickly permeated the public consciousness.

While preparing for her wedding in 1947, Princess Elizabeth was inundated with extra ration coupons from well-wishers, which she had to return as it was illegal to share them. When clothing rationing was finally ended in 1949 (five years before food rationing) and the economy began to boom in the 1950s, people were eager to dust off their wallets and put their grey wartime memories back in the wardrobe.

Gay dog clothes

Although most of this story is about the growing purchasing power of young women, the first example of a fashion subculture in the 1950s was the Teddy Boys. Like the New Look, Christian Dior's famous February 1947 collection that rejected the austere androgyny of the 1920s and 1930s in favour of narrow, feminine waists and lush, sweeping skirts, Teddy Boys also looked back to the more romantic Edwardian era. Suddenly flush with extra cash, young men could now spend it on a fancier collar, a nicer waistcoat, tapered trousers and lashings of Brylcreem.

Not for the last time in the history of twentieth-century fashion, the press didn't approve. Inundated with letters from older readers complaining about young people wasting their money on clothes, they described Teddy Boys' apparel as 'gay dog clothes'.

Rocking around the Mods

By the mid-1950s, the Teddy Boys had been replaced by the Mods, who wore tight black trousers and jackets, ordered Italian coffee in 'Espresso Bars' while listening to jazz and drove Vespa or Lambretta scooters (which probably looked cooler in Naples or Rome than in the morning drizzle on the Elephant and Castle roundabout in south London).

In an increasingly globalised world, the Mods' great rivals, the Rockers, attired in jeans and white T-shirts while listening to American rock 'n' roll, were influenced by the likes of James Dean or Marlon Brando.

In May 1964, these two tribes fought each other – and the police – for more than two days in the seaside towns of Brighton, Margate and Clacton, leading to a widespread moral panic about youth violence.

The cult of youth

By 1960, there were five million 'teenagers' in Britain, a term first coined in America in the 1930s and not widely used in Britain until the 1950s. These teenagers were spending £830 million every year, a 50 per cent increase from the 1930s. Although accounting for only 5 per cent of total consumer spending, they spent 20 per cent of their money on clothes.

No surprise, therefore, that an editorial in *Vogue* magazine in 1959 noted that 'young' was the adjective of choice for all fashions, hairstyles and ways of life.

Mary Quant, the daughter of Welsh school teachers who studied fashion at Goldsmiths in the early 1950s, took this obsession with youth to another level when she opened a shop called Bazaar on the King's Road in west London in 1955. Taking inspiration from children's clothes, it sold bright, jolly, thigh-skimming pinafores, often adorned with polka dots and stripes and made out of tartan or gingham.

Now that fewer people were working in factories or houses heated by smoky coal fires, there was more of a market for delicate, brightly coloured clothes. Nevertheless, Quant's claim that her shop saw duchesses jostling with typists to buy the same dress was somewhat misleading. Her pinafore dress featured in *Vogue* in 1960 cost seventeen guineas, the equivalent of three weeks' wages for a young woman working in an office.* However, her designs did become genuinely mass market, especially after she signed a deal in 1962 with JC Penney, one of the largest clothing chains in the United States, which sold her clothes in 1,700 branches across the country.

Mainstream media influencers

By 1960, there were ten million television sets in Britain, a 32 per cent increase in three years, piping music programmes such as *Ready Steady Go* directly into the nation's homes. And even if you managed to avoid being influenced by the fashionably dressed pop groups on the TV, you probably bought one of the myriad new magazines, such as *Romeo*, *Boyfriend* or *Honey*, all of them bombarding teenage girls with the message that if you wore the right clothes and make-up, you'd get the right boyfriend (and maybe even the right job).

The proliferation of these magazines, as well as the launch of advertisement-funded ITV in 1955, led to the launch, in February 1962, of newspaper colour supplements. The first, in the *Sunday Times*, featured the model Jean Shrimpton. The *Observer* and *Sunday Telegraph* soon followed suit.

---

* Clothes were definitely becoming cheaper, however. Back in 1939, a standard man's overcoat would have cost the equivalent of £1,000 in today's money. No wonder people made them last thirty years.

The cult of celebrity

The glossy magazines made celebrities out of the photographers as well as the models. Some, like Antony Armstrong-Jones, who went to Eton and married Princess Margaret, came from traditional stock. Others, most famously David Bailey, who left school in east London at fifteen, were a new breed of working-class hero. Fashion, said Bailey, allowed him to 'pursue his three main interests: photography, women and money' (he dated the model Jean Shrimpton, among many others).

Lesley Hornby, aka Twiggy, one of the most famous fashion models in the 1960s, also came from a humble background. The daughter of a suburban carpenter, she was discovered by the fashion editor of the *Daily Express* in her local hairdresser in 1966.* 'The Cockney kid with the face to launch a thousand shapes', ran the newspaper's headline on 23 February.

Universal British exports

Jean Shrimpton, one of Twiggy's great heroes, is credited with taking the mini-skirt to a global audience in 1965 – although the fashion correspondent for the *Sunday Times* had already dubbed 1963 'the year of the leg'.

On 30 October 1965, Shrimpton attended Melbourne racecourse dressed in a short white shift dress made from

---

* Twiggy's boyfriend at the time called himself Justin de Villeneuve, although his real name was the more prosaic Nigel Davies.

synthetic orlon fabric which she had been paid £2,000 (the equivalent of a year's wages for an average Australian) to advertise. Local newspapers were outraged that the hemline ended a few inches above her knee, not to mention the fact that she was wearing no hat, no gloves and no stockings. The rest of the world, however, was delighted.

By the mid-1960s, Britain had swapped its old political empire for a new global cultural hegemony, symbolised not only by a fashion industry that was briefly the centre of the world, but also by the success of other exports, from Beatlemania to James Bond. Provincial American teenagers even aped British slang, wandering into stores called 'The Carnaby Store' or 'The Soho Emporium' in suburban Iowa and declaring the clothes 'groovy' or 'fab' or 'gear'.

Kings of the Swingers

Not only was London exporting its clothes and its culture overseas, the world was also coming to London, a city whose declining ports and manufacturing industries had left plenty of cheap office and housing space for the kind of young, trendy people mocked in the Kinks' song 'Dedicated Follower of Fashion'. The capital hosted three million tourists in 1965, twice as many as in 1960.

In a cover story in April 1966, *Time* magazine famously dubbed London the 'swinging city'. Some were doubtlessly swinging more than others. Another American journalist wrote that 'English girls took to sex as if it's candy and it's delicious'. Others thought all this hype a convenient myth for randy men and greedy brands. In August 1966, the fashion editor at *The Times* wrote an article about travelling on the Tube. She counted twelve cardigans, thirteen pairs of sandals and not a single mini-skirt.

The white heat of PVC

'We are living in the jet age,' said Harold Wilson, the Labour party leader, during the 1964 general election campaign, 'but we are governed by an Edwardian establishment mentality.' Promising the voters the 'white heat' of technological revolution, the victorious Wilson vowed to sweep away thirteen years of complacent Conservative rule (Sir Alec Douglas-Home, the incumbent PM, was the third Old Etonian in a row in Number 10) with a ruthless focus on scientific change.

This political enthusiasm for all things modern was reflected in the world of fashion, notably in the blocky op-art movement pioneered by Bridget Riley and André Courrèges. Why wait for the future, they reasoned, to wear PVC mini-skirts and travel around by jet pack when you could do at least one of those things right now in 1966?

Beetling back to the future

Few trends last long amid the white heat of social revolution, as one year's 'groovy' young thing becomes the next year's 'square' has-been. After a few years fetishising the future, the flower-power hippy movement that took hold from around 1967 was a distinct backlash against industrial modernity, turbo-charged by fierce opposition to the Vietnam War.

Just as the Teddy Boys had taken inspiration from the Edwardians, some in Britain now looked further into the past, to the Victorians, semi-rehabilitated and open to irony once the Empire was safely in the past. The Beatles, who were always two years ahead of everyone else in terms of fashion, led the way with *Sgt. Pepper's Lonely Hearts Club Band*, released in May 1967 and inspired by late Victorian music hall. The album's cover depicts them wearing moustaches and uniforms, driving a craze for both.

The following year the Beatles went on a pilgrimage to India, dressed in Indian clothes and did what they were told by the Maharishi, inverting over a century of British cultural imperialism during the Raj.

The end of the party

'The people who are in control and in power, and the class system and the whole bullshit bourgeoisie is exactly the same, except there is a lot of fag middle-class kids with long, long hair walking around London in trendy clothes,' said John Lennon in an interview in *Rolling Stone* magazine in 1971. 'Apart from that, nothing happened. We all dressed up, the same bastards are in control, the same people are runnin' everything. It is exactly the same... The dream is over. It's just the same, only I'm thirty, and a lot of people have got long hair.'

Lennon moved to America with Yoko Ono in August 1971, following the zeitgeist. The fashion party, such as it was, was largely over for now for London. As far back as 1968, America had regained its cultural ascendancy, mainly thanks to California's grip on slang, fashion and music.

In a modern world dominated by trainers (sorry, *sneakers*), hoodies, jeans, T-shirts, Elon Musk and the Kardashians, one might say that they have never looked back.

Freemasons

SIX WAYS FREEMASONS HAVE SHAPED THE MODERN WORLD

What do Oscar Wilde, Winston Churchill, the Duke of Wellington, Cecil Rhodes, Rudyard Kipling, Wolfgang Mozart, Joseph Haydn, Robert Burns, Arthur Conan Doyle, Peter Sellers, Nat King Cole, Oliver Hardy, Henry Ford, Buzz Aldrin,* Walt Disney, the Duke of

---

* Buzz Aldrin, the second person to step on the moon, asked permission from the Grand Lodge of Texas to set up Tranquility Lodge. The paperwork that Aldrin took on his lunar expedition is now held in Waco, Texas, which hosts an annual (earthly) meeting of the Tranquility Lodge.

Edinburgh, Sir Alf Ramsey, Arnold Palmer, Shaquille O'Neal, fourteen presidents of the United States and five kings of England have in common? The answer, of course, is that they are or were all Freemasons.

But what exactly is a Freemason, given that the likes of Edward VII, George VI and President Truman are not famous for their ability to shape stone with their bare hands? And how have they influenced the history of the last 300 years?

---

1. Freemasons fuelled – and reflected – the Enlightenment

Although Freemasons are fond of using symbols such as King Solomon's Temple and the Eye of Providence to suggest an ancient pedigree, the Grand Lodge of England – and the movement in an organised form – wasn't established until a meeting in 1717 chaired by Sir Christopher Wren, at the Goose and Gridiron pub near St Paul's Cathedral.

These early Freemasons drew upon several centuries of less well-defined stonemason lore that was vigorously encouraged by the Master of Works in James I's government, a Scot called William Schaw (1550–1602). Eager to flatter the senior stonemasons he needed to work on buildings such as Stirling Castle and the Palace of Holyrood in Edinburgh, Schaw introduced them to Classical and Renaissance philosophy, while helping them to organise themselves into a fledgling trade body.

The first Masonic Lodge of this kind appeared in

Edinburgh, in 1599. During the next century, these lodges spread all over Scotland and England, attracting not just callus-handed stonemasons, but fashionable gentlemen eager to explore the intellectual concerns of the age. The stonemasons' elaborate initiation rituals began to take on a more philosophical bent, the Masonic Lodges using columns, chessboard floors and other symbols as mnemonics to guide people through them.

By the eighteenth century, the main surviving link between Freemasonry and stonework was the symbolic accoutrements of gloves, aprons, set squares and lead weights used in the rituals. Freemasonry had become firmly associated with the principles of liberty and freedom, reinforced by the *Constitution of the Freemasons* which committed its members from 1723 to the unusually progressive values of civility, scientific and artistic education, religious tolerance and meritocracy. The gloves worn by Freemasons ensured that you didn't know if you were shaking hands with a duke or a dustman.

These Enlightenment associations were further fuelled by the secretive oaths sworn during initiation ceremonies.* Amid a great deal of theatrical flummery involving blindfolds, swords, zipped body bags, feigned deaths and restorative man-hugs, prospective Freemasons made three promises: to be a nice chap; to find out a bit more about the world; and to consider death a serious business.

The fierce secrecy surrounding these unexpectedly banal pledges proved a clever recruitment tool, while also

---

* In a less secretive age, you can find these oaths on the internet, albeit not on the website of the United Grand Lodge of England which instead details the £51.1m donated to charity in 2020; the four important values of integrity, friendship, respect and service; and how to join the 175,000 Freemasons from all backgrounds belonging to more than 7,000 Lodges in England and Wales.

creating a quasi-religious sense of belonging that transcended contemporaneous debates about Catholicism, Protestantism and High and Low Church.

Amid the emerging scene of London private members' clubs, it also helped that Freemasons' unusual rituals were accompanied by the more relatable rites of networking, feasting and getting smashed.

2. The USA is the Land of the Free(masons)

The Freemasons' watered-down deism was especially popular with the American Founding Fathers, notably George Washington, who led the colonists to victory against Britain in the American War of Independence.

Aware that the fledgling republic had neither God nor history on its side, President Washington needed to imbue the capital that bore his name with a sense of secular sacredness without offending anyone. As a Freemason himself, he used a Masonic ceremony, including chanting, drums and consecration with wine (there were no blindfolds or man-hugs, sadly), when he laid the first cornerstone of the Capitol building in September 1793. The ceremony proved so popular that it sparked a fashion for Freemasonry across the new American republic – and a backlash thirty-five years later.

In 1828, the year before Andrew Jackson became the seventh US President – and the third Mason to hold that office – a group of politicians convinced that Freemasons were secretly running the government created the Anti-Masonic Party. Although short-lived, it included Presidents John Quincy Adams and Millard Fillmore among its members.

3. Masonic civil rights campaigners marched on Masonic Washington

Just as the Founding Fathers' understanding of all men being created equal did not extend to America's enslaved population, Freemasonry's Enlightenment credo of social, religious and racial tolerance somehow precluded membership for African Americans.

Undeterred, a black Bostonian called Prince Hall founded Prince Hall Freemasonry in September 1784. Its members have included many of the black soldiers in the American Civil War in the 1860s; Thurgood Marshall, the lawyer who argued the landmark *Brown v. Board of Education* case in 1954 and later became the first African American Supreme Court Justice; the civil rights leader Jesse Jackson; and Rosa Parks, who was a member of a rare female Masonic organisation.

The National Association for the Advancement of Colored People (NAACP), which played a pivotal role in the Civil Rights movement, was largely funded by Masonic donations.

4. The Empire on which Freemasonry never set

Although Britain lost her thirteen colonies in 1776 to Brother George, the British Empire's subsequent 'swing to the east' made the most of Freemasonry to further her imperial gains in Asia. Not only did Freemasonry act as a kind of overseas welfare, social and networking system for lonely British soldiers, sailors and merchants, it was also instrumental in giving native elites a degree of conditioned access to their British rulers.

Masonic Lodges allowed the British and the Indians, in particular, to 'meet on the level' – just as they did on the cricket field (India wasn't so good at cricket back then) – offering an opportunity to flatter, cajole and negotiate in a more egalitarian setting. According to John Dickier's wonderful book *The Craft: How the Freemasons Made the Modern World*, there were at least ten Indian Freemasons in 1914 who put 'Maharajah' as their occupation in the Lodge register.

5. Liberty, Equality, Freemasonry – the first modern conspiracy theory

Catholic Europe was generally less enamoured with Freemasonry, especially during the bloody throes of the French Revolution in the 1790s. Having already been excommunicated by the Pope back in 1738, Freemasons were a convenient scapegoat for the worst elements of the revolution. Even the most innocent interpretation saw their activities as a subversive, free-thinking challenge to the supremacy of the court. So as the blood on the guillotine dried in the wake of Robespierre's Reign of Terror, it didn't take much for Augustin Barruel, a Jesuit priest living in exile on London's Edgware Road in 1797, to paint them as dangerous, heretical devil-worshippers bent on overthrowing Christianity.

The birth of the conspiracy theory in its modern form

– the alluring notion of secret elites pulling the strings behind the scenes – can therefore be traced back to the Catholic fear of Freemasonry in the eighteenth century. This fear re-emerged periodically over the next 200 years.

In 1885, the French Catholic Church was delighted when one of its fiercest critics, the anti-clerical writer Léo Taxil, supposedly had a Damascene conversion and exposed the grotesque Masonic network to which he had belonged since his teens. The worst Masons of all, he said, were the New Reformed Palladians, led by a devil-worshipping lesbian called Sister Sophia-Sapho, who would force a newly initiated sister to have sex with the sacramental bread.

This gigantic hoax fooled the Church for twelve years.

In the twentieth century, a deeply paranoid General Franco was fed fake information over three decades by a secret network claiming to be a Deep Throat inside the international Masonic conspiracy. Membership of a Masonic Lodge – or even the Rotary Club, which was perceived as a Masonic front – carried a minimum sentence of twelve years in prison in fascist Spain. No one has ever worked out who was behind the conspiracy, although it was doubtless a good way of damaging one's enemies. There is also a theory that Franco's Masonic membership was blackballed by his own brother – and that this was his elaborate revenge.

6. The Rites of Men – and mafias

Although the Honourable Fraternity of Ancient Freemasons, a British Masonic fraternity for women, can trace its origins back to 1913 and has around 800 members today, Freemasonry remains principally a male domain.*

Its hazing rituals, secretive language and bizarre titles – you begin your career as an Entered Apprentice before progressing to Master Mason via the Fellow Craft – have clubbable echoes in everything from rugby drinking societies to the Mormon Church, American campus fraternities to the Ku Klux Klan.

Freemasonry also undoubtedly inspired the Sicilian Mafia, the pairing providing a rare example of an outlandish conspiracy theory about the Freemasons that might actually be true. On 17 June 1982, Roberto Calvi, an Italian dubbed 'God's banker' owing to his close ties to the Vatican, was found hanging from Blackfriars Bridge in London. The finger of unproven suspicion has long pointed at the Mafia and Licio Gelli, the charismatic leader of Propaganda Due (P2), a breakaway, enormously influential Masonic Lodge in Rome which funded right-wing terrorism and laundered money for the Mafia.

P2 was expelled by the Grand Orient of Italy in 1976 and dissolved in 1982. Gelli was still under investigation

---

* A major source of hilarity in the eighteenth century was the story of 'le Chevalier d'Éon' – or maybe 'la Chevalière d'Éon' – a French spy who joined a Masonic Lodge in London, returned to France and either claimed to be a woman or started dressing as a woman. A huge betting market opened up about the truth until a witness claimed that he had had sex with the Chevalier and that she was definitely a woman. A post-mortem found 'male organs in every respect perfectly formed'.

for Calvi's murder when he died in 2015. Ten years earlier, when asked if he was responsible, he replied, 'It is not up to us to deliver judgments. Only God will be able to tell the truth.'

Great British Quaker Off

THE HISTORY OF CHOCOLATE IN SIX RECIPES

The global chocolate market was worth around $115 billion in 2023 – marginally more than the GDP of Kenya, Bulgaria or Guatemala. How did the humble cocoa bean take the world by storm? And what does its development tell us about the wider international and social context of the last 500 years?

Dig out your dipping forks, your sugar dredgers and your heavy moulds – let's open our **The Rest is History** *cookbook and find out.*

Marvellous Mesoamerican Mocha (Tenochtitlán, 1522)

Serves 2 (e.g. Montezuma and Cortés)*

Ingredients

Cocoa beans
Human sacrifice
A strong stomach
Absolutely no sugar

This delicious hot drink is a perfect accompaniment for ritual celebrations and peace treaties, tapping into a rich tradition that stretches back over a thousand years. When our ancestors the Olmecs weren't carving enormous stone heads, they liked to play *ollamaliztli*, a ball game that involved ritual sacrifice for the losers, who would be buried alongside crushed cocoa beans, and a cup of chocolate for the victors.

Revenge, as they say, is a bitter drink best served hot.

These days we still like to offer cocoa beans for the dead, alongside blankets, bread and chickens, even when they've perished of natural causes. And if you have any leftover beans, you can use them as barter in the great market in Tenochtitlán. It's one of our few raw products for which the Spanish don't (yet) have a sickness of the heart.

---

* The accounts of Cortés and Montezuma sipping hot chocolate together are not widely accepted, but it is a nicer image than most of the other events that unfolded during his expedition.

Bitter Blasphemous Pigswill (London, 1636)

Serves no one (unless you're Spanish)

Ingredients

Cocoa beans

Catholicism

As much honey, sugar and vanilla as possible

Chocolate does not have a great reputation in this continent, ever since Philip II of Spain turned up his nose in 1544 at a gift of cocoa seeds from one of his conquistadors. And yet the Spanish have made the Mesoamerican drink slightly more palatable by adding honey and vanilla, not to mention the copious amounts of sugar they've been producing in the Canary Islands and the Caribbean.

For the past eighty years, they've also been baffling European courts by offering this extraordinary beverage as a diplomatic gift – much to the disgust of the French, in particular.*

Here in England, we've tended to agree with Girolamo Benzoni's view that chocolate is a 'drink for pigs'.† Whenever Sir Francis Drake captured a Spanish ship in the 1570s, he threw the cocoa beans into the sea, thinking they looked like sheep droppings.

We've also watched with bemused fascination as Catholic cardinals have tied themselves in knots arguing

---

* There is a long and glorious history of awful diplomatic gifts that are far more offensive than a mug of chocolate. Highlights include: the Marquis de Lafayette giving John Quincy Adams an alligator, which the President kept in a White House bathroom; Saddam Hussein giving Donald Rumsfeld a puppy snuff video; and the Sultan of Brunei giving George W. Bush six jars of fertiliser.

† The Italian resisted drinking chocolate for a year before eventually cracking when he couldn't find any wine. He regretted it.

about the idolatrous origins of cocoa. In 1569 Pope Pius V said that he didn't need to give in to Dominican lobbying to ban the drink as it was 'so foul' that no one would be tempted to partake of it in any case. And now, as religious wars ravage continental Europe, the Catholics are arguing among themselves about whether chocolate constitutes a drink or a food substance – and whether its consumption therefore breaks an Ecclesiastical fast.*

Thanks goodness we broke from Rome.

So do try this foetid, foreign drink if you like. But frankly, we think you'd be better off sticking to beer and beef.

Rakishly Ravishing Joccolatte (London, 1693)

Serves anyone with enough money†

Ingredients
Cocoa beans
Lasciviousness
Sugar
Long red pepper
Cloves
Aniseed
Almonds
Orange water flower

---

* The first salvo in this ludicrous debate was written by Antonio de León Pinelo, a Spanish historian, in 1636. Under the catchy title, 'Does Chocolate Break an Ecclesiastical Fast, A Moral Question', he concluded that cocoa was a food, not a drink, and therefore it did. Rival clerics waded in on the opposite side of the debate. Eventually, in 1666, Pope Alexander VII proclaimed, *'Liquidum non frangit jejunum'* (Liquids do not break the fast).
† According to one historian, a pound of cocoa beans cost 50p in the seventeenth century, a week's work for a skilled tradesman.

It's the drink that's taken fashionable London by storm and now, for the first time, you can see the written recipe behind the sensation.

When Oliver Cromwell captured Jamaica from the Spanish in 1655, he was disappointed not to discover any gold, but he did inherit a huge trade in sugar and cocoa (as well as an African slave population that constituted 80 per cent of the island's people). Within two years, the first advertisements were appearing in the *Publick Advisor* praising an 'excellent West India drink called chocolate', sold from a house in South Kensington. Pepys drank a cup of 'joccolatte' in 1664 with Commissioner Pett, pronouncing it 'very good'. And earlier this year, Mrs White's Chocolate House opened in Mayfair.*

As you might imagine, it's an expensive beverage, thanks to the high import duties from the Caribbean. But if you want to have a racy, lewd conversation with other rakes, there's nothing that can beat doing so over a mug of sugary, nut-flavoured cocoa.†

If you prefer to drink alone, you can also buy ground cocoa beans, like you might buy ground coffee, pressed into a little cake and wrapped in paper. Chocolate syrup, which can be stored for up to a week before adding milk, makes for a light and wholesome breakfast.‡

---

* White's, the oldest gentlemen's club in St James's, includes the King and Prince William among its members.
† Daniel Defoe, the author of *Robinson Crusoe* (1719), said that fathers should warn their daughters of the evils of promiscuous conversations that take place in chocolate houses. Others were more concerned with the direct effect of chocolate on women. The *Virginia Almanac* warned in 1770 that the 'fair sex' should be 'careful how they meddle with romances, chocolate, novels and the like' as they were all 'inflamers' and 'very dangerous'.
‡ Maria Rundell, who wrote a cookbook in 1814 called *A New System*

The Affluent Apothecary (Bath, 1796)

Serves anyone feeling a bit under the weather

Ingredients

Cocoa beans
An unhealthy dose of credulity
~~Powders of millipedes, vipers and earthworms~~
~~Livers and galls of eels~~

'If a person fatigued with long and hard labour, or with a violent agitation of the mind, takes a good dish of chocolate, he shall perceive almost instantly that his faintness shall cease, and his strength shall be recovered,' wrote M. de Quélus, a Frenchman who had spent a lot of time in the Caribbean, in 1724.

De Quélus also suggested that you add snake powder to chocolate to enhance its medicinal effects, creating a product that matches beef for nourishment. Benjamin Franklin even recommended chocolate as a cure for smallpox.

But it has taken an Englishman to realise that you don't have to mess around with chocolate – or make ludicrous claims – to reap its health benefits. Joseph Fry, an austere, sober Quaker,* started an apothecary business in Bristol

---

of Domestic Cookery, was one such champion of a chocolate-based breakfast.
* After emerging as a radical Protestant sect in the 1650s, prone to taking their clothes off in public and shaking convulsively, the Quakers became markedly more sober over the next two centuries.

in 1753. Within a decade, he had shops in fifty towns across England, all selling drinking chocolate as a medicinal product. Today the Frys run the biggest cocoa works in the world, thanks to a new grinding process that uses a James Watt steam engine: the industrial revolution meets the culinary revolution.

Queen's Own Chocolate (Birmingham, 1878)

Serves the royal family (and other discerning customers)

Ingredients
Cocoa
Iceland moss
Potato flour
Treacle
Sago
~~Brick dust~~
~~Lead~~

John Cadbury, a Birmingham Quaker, quickly gained a reputation as a chocolatier to the stars, earning a Royal Warrant with his 'Queen's Own Chocolate', wrapped in Cadbury's distinctive royal purple. Three years ago, following endorsements from the *Lancet* and the *British Medical Journal*, Cadbury launched its first Easter egg, another upmarket product with the slogan, 'Absolutely pure, therefore best'.

Foreswearing alcohol and pushed to the margins of English society, they often opened shops or banks. Chocolate offered an acceptable alternative vice to wine or beer.

Can you reproduce their recipes at home, creating your own 'chocolate bar' which Fry and Cadbury first pioneered in the 1840s? Probably not. The chocolatiers' techniques are getting pretty sophisticated – and they don't adulterate their products with brick dust or lead like some of their competitors. But why not apply for a job at Cadbury's new Bournville factory outside Birmingham and find out for yourself?*

A Flaky Revolution (Wigan Pier, 1937)

Serves absolutely everyone

Ingredients

Closely guarded secret

Take a world war during which Cadbury provided books and clothing for the troops on the Western Front, as well as chocolates, and mix it with massive domestic shortages of milk and sugar. Add a merger with Fry's to form the British Cocoa and Chocolate Company in 1919. Stir in the Flake (1920) and the Fruit and Nut (1926). Sprinkle some technological innovations which see the price of a Dairy Milk (invented in 1905) fall by 70 per cent in ten years and simmer while sales go through the roof.†

---

* The Bournville factory became a physical embodiment of the Quaker principles espoused by the Cadbury family. One of the first companies to have a genuine company culture, they gave their workers better rights, including bank holidays, a five-and-a-half-day working week and, by 1906, pensions. They also built the village of Bournville to house around 20,000 workers, hosting evening classes and sport.
† In 1900 only one in 30 families in Britain ate chocolate regularly, given how expensive it was. By 1930, this had risen to 90 per cent of households.

Serve a product once only given to Philip II to everyone, everywhere.

Sit back, peacefully, and scoff ad nauseam.*

---

* George Orwell thought that the chocolate revolution had adverted wider social unrest. 'It is quite likely,' he wrote in *The Road to Wigan Pier*, 'that fish and chips, art-silk stockings, tinned salmon, cut-price chocolate (five two-ounce bars for sixpence), the movies, the radio, strong tea and the Football Pools have between them averted revolution.'

The Hundred Years' War

WAS EDWARD III THE BIGGEST 'LAD'* IN ENGLISH HISTORY?

The Hundred Years' War, 1337–1453, was a titanic on-off struggle between England and France, famous for chivalric knights, deadly longbows, epic battles – and actually lasting 116 years. As well as transforming medieval warfare, the conflict sharpened distinct national identities, empowered the English Parliament, consolidated the French monarchy, fuelled at least another four and a half centuries of Anglo-French rivalry and made national heroes of Joan of Arc and Henry V.

---

* 'Lad in British English, noun, a lively or dashing man or youth (esp. in the phrase "a bit of a lad") / a young man whose behaviour is characteristic of male adolescents, esp. in being rowdy, macho or immature', *Collins English Dictionary*

However, the most fascinating character in the Hundred Years' War is surely Henry V's great-grandfather, Edward III. Semi-finalist in The Rest is History's *inaugural World Cup of Kings and Queens (he narrowly lost to Athelstan, the eventual winner), Edward spent 80 per cent of his long reign (1327–1377) fighting the French, pillaging their villages and attempting to sneak away with the ultimate beer trophy of their throne.*

So, was Edward the biggest lad ever to have worn the English crown, the role model for many future generations of Englishmen behaving badly overseas?

Here is the case in his favour.

―――

1. He was a teenager with all the gear – and more than a few ideas

France was comfortably the most powerful country in Europe when the Hundred Years' War started, blessed with the soft power of chivalry and a language that was used across Europe for culture and commerce, as well as the hard power of an income that was six times larger – and a population three times bigger – than England's.

French visitors to London turned up their refined noses at its squalid backwardness. This was an era when the English were famous throughout Christendom for their xenophobia, their diplomats often pretending not to understand what the French were saying when they ran into trouble (*plus ça change*, a modern Englishman might say, if he'd bothered to remember any French).

By engineering fourteen seamless successions from one king to another, the Capetian dynasty had spent 300 years extending its royal domain across most of modern-day France, annexing tasty areas such as Champagne and Brie, while kicking their English rivals out of Normandy. In 1324 Charles IV, the last of the direct Capetian line, went one step further by invading English territories in Aquitaine, leaving the English with only a couple of vineyards in Bordeaux.

Edward II (1307–1327), a weak English king described by his biographer as an 'absolute ninny', refused to pay homage to Charles IV and sent Isabella, his French wife, and the future Edward III, his eleven-year-old son, instead. Isabella ended up shacking up with Roger Mortimer, an English exile, and invading England with him, overthrowing Edward, who ended up murdered in Berkeley Castle, allegedly with a red-hot poker up his bottom. All this left England as a French puppet state.

Somehow the young Edward III, now technically king while his mother and Mortimer held the real levers of power, took this all in his stride. Having been crowned in 1327, aged fourteen, he took part in five tournaments that year, wowing the crowds with his highly decorative armour and his gilded lances. The following year Mortimer signed the Treaty of Edinburgh-Northampton with the Scots, an agreement known in England as the 'shameful peace'. In 1330, still aged only seventeen, Edward III gathered together a group of friends, executed Mortimer and started to rule

England in his own imitable way. One of his first acts after deposing Mortimer was to pay tribute to the tomb of King Arthur in Glastonbury, modelling his laddish friendship group on Arthur's Knights of the Round Table.

Three years later, this group of lads went on their first of many tours, smashing the Scots at the Battle of Halidon Hill and setting up an unequal confrontation with the French who were bound by the terms of their Auld Alliance to restore the exiled David II to the Scottish throne.

2. He declared war on the strongest country in Europe

The French Capetian line, once so fertile and secure, was in trouble by the 1320s. Three brothers had ruled – and died – in quick succession without producing any sons. Dismissing the claim of Edward III through his mother Isabella, the French settled instead on the last king's cousin, Philip of Valois, crowning him Philip VI in 1328. In 1329, Edward III begrudgingly paid homage to his depressed, obese great-uncle.

By 1337, however, Edward was in a slightly stronger position. When Philip VI announced that he was confiscating the English Duchy of Aquitaine in revenge for the Scottish defeat at Halidon Hill, Edward issued a public manifesto accusing him of behaving unlawfully in France, stirring up trouble in Scotland and attempting to invade England. This declaration of war by a minnow on a neighbouring giant would be the twentieth-century equivalent of Belgium pre-emptively invading Germany.

Everyone in Europe expected Edward to lose.

THE HUNDRED YEARS' WAR

3. He had some really good banter

As Edward explained in a punchy letter to the Pope, his only chance of winning the war was to take the fight to the enemy, 'rather than to wait for him to batter down our front door'. In 1337 he banned English wool exports to Flanders, France's richest province, and the one nearest to England, persuading Ghent, Bruges and Ypres to declare themselves neutral in the coming conflict. This rare example of a successful economic boycott paved the way to Edward invading northern France in 1339 and boldly declaring himself King of France in January 1340, despite having failed to provoke Philip VI into any form of battle.

Edward's outlandish declaration was almost as unpopular in England, where his debts were rapidly mounting and no one was particularly interested in sharing their King with the neighbours. Undeterred at the potential collapse of his entire strategy, Edward returned home and threw his energies into winning over his subjects to his cause.

4. He smashed the French with a brand-new weapon at the Battle of Sluys

The French fleet were already posing serious problems to the English, burning Portsmouth to the ground in 1338. So when Edward was brought news in June 1340 that they were anchored in the mouth of the River Zwin, opposite the Flanders port of Sluys, he promptly packed every English ship he could find with infantrymen and longbowmen and sailed across the Channel.

Taller than a man when fully strung, made of English yew and first used effectively against the Scots at the Battle of Halidon Hill, the longbow was quicker to reload than the French crossbow and could also shoot further.* The English could therefore rain down fire on the huge, immobile French fleet before grappling with any survivors at close quarters. Helped by their Flemish allies, who attacked the French from the rear, the English turned the Battle of Sluys into a bloodbath.†

Instead of issuing the customary ransom for the sole surviving French Admiral, Edward hung him from the yardarm.

5. He took his lads on a prolonged pillaging tour across France

The significance of the naval victory at Sluys in 1340 was immense: Edward now had control of the Channel,

---

* According to Clifford Rogers, the Professor of Medieval History at West Point, the United States Military Academy, the draw strength of these exceptionally thick longbows rises proportionally with the cube of its thickness: so, for example, 30 per cent greater thickness equates to 120 per cent more power.

† The story goes that the court jester was the only person brave enough to tell Philip VI what had happened at Sluys. 'Oh, the cowardly English, the cowardly English,' cried the jester. 'Why were they cowardly?' asked the King. 'They did not jump overboard like our brave Frenchmen,' explained the jester.

giving him the ability to hit the French at will with little fear of repercussions.

Unfortunately, the French were unwilling to be hit. Aware of Edward's *force de frappe* strategy – the English King wanted to corner the French army, inflict a devastating defeat and bring the French to terms – Philip VI resisted the temptation to be drawn into battle.

So Edward and his mates went looking for trouble instead. In 1342, the Earl of Northampton, one of six lads ennobled by Edward back in 1337, captured Brest, securing the sea route from England to Gascony and Bordeaux. Meanwhile, Edward amassed an invasion force of 8,000 men and a hundred field cannon and landed in Normandy in July 1346. Boldly dedicating the invasion to the compassionate cause of the 'wretched fate of the people of France', he set about improving their situation by burning everything in a fifteen-mile radius of his marching army.

This *chevauchée* – or to use the proper English word, pillaging – continued for another month as Edward crossed the Seine and the Somme, burning and looting royal properties as he went, until finally pausing at the forest of Crécy, sixty miles south of Calais.

Aware that he could no longer avoid a battle without losing face, Philip summoned his troops from across France. Having amassed 25,000 men, he outnumbered the English three to one.

6. His own lad won his spurs – and an ostrich feather – at the Battle of Crécy

At the Battle of Crécy in August 1346, the French army had only one soldier who came close to rivalling the English in the lad stakes. His name was John, the blind King of Bohemia, placed in command of the mercenary Genoese crossbowmen because his renowned chivalry was deemed more militarily important than the ability to see.

Things went badly for King John in the battle. Rain slackened the cords on the advancing Genoese's crossbows, leading to their rout, at which point a rumour went around that the Genoese were cowards or traitors and they were run down by their allies in the French cavalry. Deciding that he'd let down France, Philip and himself, John of Bohemia ordered his squire to point him in the direction of the battle and charged towards his certain death.

Meanwhile, the English had made the most of their cannons (strapped under wagons, so the French couldn't see them coming) and their longbowmen to kill 5,000 Frenchmen, including eleven princes, two counts and an archbishop. Philip VI left the battlefield with an arrow in the face and the Oriflamme, the great royal standard, trampled in the mud.

Edward's sixteen-year-old son, who had bravely commanded the first line at Crécy, presented his father with the ostrich feather crest and the motto 'Ich dien' ('I serve') of the fallen King of Bohemia. Edward gave it back to him

– and the motto and the crest are still associated with the Prince of Wales today.*

---

7. He redefined what it meant to be a chivalric lad

Edward III built on his resounding success at Crécy in August 1346 by capturing David II, the exiled Scottish King, in October, followed by Charles de Blois, Philip VI's candidate to be Duke of Brittany, the following June and the crucial city of Calais in August. And although Philip avoided further defeat, he died in 1350 a much-diminished figure.

Philip's son, John II, looked more like a king than his father (although he was almost as thick as his beard). Hoping to restore France's reputation as the home of chivalry, he commissioned Geoffroi de Charny, the Mbappé of fourteenth-century tournaments, to write a new rulebook.

After two years twiddling his thumbs as a prisoner in London – an Italian mercenary had promised to smuggle him into Calais, only to betray him to the English – de Charny was convinced that the entry requirements for the new Order of the Star should be more rigorous than for previous chivalric orders. No longer was it sufficient to be a top jouster at tournaments while winking winningly at the ladies. After the disaster at Crécy, during which many Frenchmen had fled the field, wannabe knights should

---

* At one point during the Battle of Crécy, messages were sent by the knights around the Prince of Wales to Edward III requesting reinforcements. 'Let the boy win his spurs,' the King is said to have replied, declining the request.

now have to prove themselves in battle as well, standing their ground at all times.

Unfortunately, the first meeting of the Order of the Star, on 6 January 1352, turned out to be almost as disastrous as Crécy. Not only did few Frenchmen turn up, but one of the knights who did put in an appearance found his castle near Calais had been seized by the English in his absence.

Back at home, meanwhile, the English were redefining chivalry in far more successful terms. On St George's Day 1349, at the height of the Black Death that was plaguing Europe, Edward III ignored the advice of his physicians to socially distance by holding a massive tournament at Windsor Castle. Redesigned to look like an Arthurian fantasy of Camelot, the Castle hosted a dazzling celebration that presented Queen Philippa as a new Guinevere and introduced the Order of the Garter, a chivalric honour which is still awarded today.*

Among its twenty-six recipients that day (alongside a knight by the fine name of Sir Thomas Holland) was the Prince of Wales, now renowned across Europe as the Black Prince.

---

* The garter was a military garment in the fourteenth century. Today's members, who are still limited to twenty-six, include a former Lord Chief Justice, a former Chief of the Defence Staff, a former spymaster, Andrew Lloyd Webber and two former Prime Ministers: John Major and Tony Blair.

8. The Black Prince was as big a lad as his dad

Having won his spurs at Crécy, the Black Prince landed in Bordeaux on 20 September 1355 with 2,220 men, ready for a looting and pillaging tour across the south of France. Moving at terrifying speed and picking up 5,000 Gascon troops, they had advanced almost to the Mediterranean by the end of the autumn, loading 1,000 wagons with loot, destroying 500 villages and burning down a dozen towns.

This shattering blow to French self-confidence took a further turn for the worse when the Black Prince headed north towards the Loire, attempting to join up with the Duke of Lancaster, who was conducting a similar *chevauchée* in Normandy and Brittany. In response, John II, the French King, raised a huge force, the sacred Oriflamme borne aloft by our old friend Geoffroi de Charny.

At the resulting Battle of Poitiers, in September 1356, de Charny died with his fingers still wrapped tightly round the staff of the flag (although at least fewer Frenchmen ran away this time). The Black Prince's beer trophies included 2,000 French noblemen, John II himself, his son Philip and the French crown jewels, which John II had decided to take into battle as a token of his confidence in his forces.

On 24 May 1357, the Black Prince accompanied John II into London, riding a shorter horse in order to give the French King his dignity as the greatest monarch in Europe. The crowds viewing this medieval equivalent of an open-top bus tour were so large that it took the royal party three hours to cross the city. As the ransom negotiations began, Edward III put on endless spectacles of dancing, hunting, hawking, banquets and tournaments, including the first ever day-night tournament under blazing torches in Bristol.

In April 1358, John II signed a treaty setting his ransom at twenty times the ordinary annual revenue of the English King. Although Edward III renounced his claim to the French crown, it was agreed that he would still rule around a quarter of France.

9. He lost everything he worked for

In the absence of their ransomed King, authority in France broke down in the late 1350s with uprisings among the bourgeoisie and the peasantry spreading from Paris across the country. Although this might have seemed good news for Edward III, it meant that his quarter of France was as ungovernable as the rest.

When the French refused to honour the ransom treaty, the forty-eight-year-old King went on one last *chevauchée*, pillaging everywhere between Calais and Paris in the spring of 1360, before finally taking the advice of the Duke of Lancaster to negotiate. Although the Treaty of Brétigny had similar terms to the agreement made at Windsor eighteen months earlier, it led to the slow unravelling of Edward's authority in France.

When John II died in April 1364, his son Charles V played a long, slow (and distinctly unladdish) game of delayed gratification, reintroducing order, winning back the loyalty of the lords in English-occupied regions and carefully marshalling France's greater resources to hurt the English. The Black Prince died of dysentery in 1376, having given up his duchy of Aquitaine. His father,

Edward III, died of dementia the following year, having lost all his lands in France except Calais.

So was it all in vain? The war lasted another seventy-six years and claimed thousands more victims. And although Henry V briefly recreated his great-grandfather's glory following his victory at Agincourt in 1415, England was again reduced to holding only Calais by the end of the war in 1453 (handing it over for good 105 years later).

On the other hand, did we mention that Edward III was an absolutely massive lad?

Iron Mask

WHO WAS THE MAN IN THE IRON MASK?

During the long, dazzling reign of Louis XIV* an anonymous prisoner disappeared into the gaols of the 'Sun King', never to be seen again. The man's face was covered by a mask he couldn't remove; none of the prison authorities were allowed to speak his name; and

---

* Louis XIV's 72-year rule, from 1643 until 1715, during which he commissioned the splendours of the Palace of Versailles, is the longest confirmed reign of all time, edging Queen Elizabeth II into second place. Some believe he should be denied the top spot by an early Egyptian pharaoh, called Pepi II, who ruled for 94 years, although most historians doubt the veracity of the claim.

yet it was said that he was treated as a nobleman by the prison authorities and a visiting Minister of War.

The identity of this prisoner has fascinated people for almost 300 years. After the story was popularised by philosopher and wit Voltaire in the 1750s, the Man in the Iron Mask featured in one of Alexandre Dumas's Three Musketeers *books in the 1840s and has been the subject of half a dozen films and TV series since 1923.*

Who are the six potential candidates for the Man in the Iron Mask?

1. He was the King's illegitimate brother

In 1717, Voltaire himself spent some time locked up in the Bastille, the notorious Parisian fortress-prison, for being rude about the despotic royal family – a punishment that modern British royals can only dream about. While chatting to his guards and fellow prisoners, Voltaire heard stories about an anonymous prisoner who had died there in 1703. In 1751, after Louis XIV was safely in his grave, Voltaire published a history of his reign that included the eye-catching story of the Man in the Iron Mask.

According to Voltaire, the iron mask had been welded onto the man's head, its chin-piece operated by hinges that allowed him to eat. Voltaire saw the prisoner as the dark side of Louis XIV's glittering reign, a secret victim who had been denied not only freedom and justice, but his very identity.

Was this outlandish story true?

A seventeenth-century paper trail allows us to follow an anonymous masked prisoner being moved around French prisons, in conditions of the utmost secrecy, from 1669 until his death in the Bastille in 1703.* He was accompanied throughout by Monsieur de Saint-Mars, a gaoler who answered directly to the Minister of War.

Voltaire added two especially juicy details. While the prisoner was locked up in 1687 on an island near Cannes called Sainte-Marguerite, it was said that Saint-Mars, by now the island's Governor, himself served his meals. What's more, when the Minister of War, the Marquis de Louvois, came to the Bastille to check up on the prisoner, the Marquis stood while the lowly prisoner sat, an extraordinary reversal in hierarchy-obsessed seventeenth-century France.

So who was this secretive, sedentary, solitary, seditious inmate? Voltaire thought the most likely explanation was that he was Louis's illegitimate older brother, the result of an affair by Louis's mother. Such a child would have brought scandal and shame on the royal family, calling into question the legitimacy of her subsequent children, including Louis himself.

So instead of giving Louis's enemies an opportunity to undermine his claim to the throne, his family locked up his illegitimate brother's face in an iron mask – and threw away the key.

Fun rating: 💀💀💀💀💀💀💀
Likelihood: 💀💀💀

---

* It does seem that Voltaire tweaked at least one detail in his account. Contemporaneous accounts of the masked prisoner variously describe him wearing a mask of steel or of black velvet, not iron. 'The Man in the Black Velvet Mask' gives off a different vibe entirely.

2. He was the King's evil twin brother

Other eighteenth-century detectives went one step further: what if the prisoner was not simply Louis's illegitimate older brother, but his identical twin?

This theory was endorsed by another famous eighteenth-century writer, Denis Diderot, who produced a heroically unconvincing chain of evidence: he'd heard it from a German journalist, who'd heard it from the niece of Louis XIV, who'd heard it from her father, who'd heard it from Louis XV,* the great-grandson and heir of Louis XIV.†

Why would the royals want to lock up the King's twin brother? Well, if he tried to stir up trouble, for example by dressing up as the King, sleeping with the King's wife and/or giving orders to the court, how would people be able to tell who the real King was? In the seventeenth century, there was also a theory that the twin born second was actually conceived first. This raised troubling questions as to which brother was technically older – and therefore the rightful heir.

Fun rating: 🎭🎭🎭🎭🎭🎭🎭🎭
Likelihood: 🎭🎭

---

* This claim becomes even more implausible when you consider that Philippe of Orleans, the father of Louis XIV's niece, died several years before Louis XV was born.

† It is rare for a monarch to be succeeded immediately by their great-grandson: the British equivalent would be the throne passing directly from George VI to Prince William or from Elizabeth II to Prince George. Louis XV wasn't even the Sun King's eldest great-grandson: his older brother and his father were both killed by a family measles outbreak in 1712.

3. He was the King's gigolo father

An equally fun theory is that the Man in the Iron Mask was another of Louis's awkward relatives – his real father.

Louis's 'official' parents, Louis XIII and Anne of Austria, were married for twenty-three years before he was born, which suggests that something in the bedroom was not going swimmingly, as it were. One person who was desperate for Louis and Anne to have a child was Louis XIII's Chief Minister, Cardinal Richelieu, a bitter enemy of Louis XIII's younger brother, Gaston, the Duke of Orleans, the next in line to the throne.

In his eagerness to make sure that Anne of Austria had a child, the theory goes, Cardinal Richelieu employed a commoner to impregnate her. Once this was successful, the stud father was sworn to secrecy and dispatched to America.

This became a serious problem for Louis XIV's legitimacy when his real father returned from America and attempted to blackmail him. So the Sun King made him vanish off the face of the earth, into the bowels of the prison system.

Is this theory true? Unfortunately, there is no evidence for it whatsoever.*

Fun rating: 💀💀💀💀💀💀💀
Likelihood: 0

---

* The champion of this theory was an idiosyncratic aristocrat called Hugh Cecil, later Baron Quickswood. Son of Queen Victoria's last Prime Minister, Lord Salisbury, he was part of the great Cecil political dynasty, becoming MP for Oxford University as well as being best man at Winston Churchill's wedding. He was named Provost of Eton in 1936, despite having hated his time there as a pupil; he then spent several happy years undermining the Eton headmaster by siding with the boys in every school dispute.

4. He was a revolting English bastard

There was a contemporary rumour that the prisoner was the son of Oliver Cromwell. This is unlikely, as we know what happened to both the sons who outlived him: Henry had died in England by 1674 and Richard, who had briefly succeeded his father as Lord Protector of Britain and Ireland, was still travelling around Europe in exile. Neither had simply vanished.

Others said that the prisoner was the Duke of Monmouth, the bastard son of Charles II, who led a rebellion against his uncle, James II, in 1685. After the rebellion failed, Monmouth had his head chopped off in a very public – and very gory – execution.* But what if, in a moment of avuncular mercy, James II had had him switched with another prisoner and given him to the French to look after?

Again, there is no evidence for this theory.

Fun rating:
Likelihood: 0

---

* By all accounts, the execution of the Duke of Monmouth was pretty horrible. The executioner, Jack Ketch, took so many attempts that after several botched axe-blows, the Duke staggered up from his execution block and begged Ketch to get on with it. 'Jack Ketch' became a slang byword for a nasty death.

5. He was a pseudonymous Italian count / spy / dodgy estate agent

Next to the entry in the Bastille ledger recording the death of 'the Unknown Prisoner' in 1703, someone has added in a later hand the name 'M. de Marchiel'. Given that there are no records of a M. de Marchiel ever having existed, this was probably a pseudonym, leading some creative researchers to the conclusion that 'Marchiel' was chosen because it began with the same letter as the real name of the mysterious Man in the Iron Mask.

Their preferred candidate was an Italian count called Ercole Mattioli, a minister for the Duke of Mantua. While working for the French spy service, Mattioli had made the foolish mistake of double-crossing Louis XIV over a property deal in northern Italy.

Louis XIV had Mattioli kidnapped and delivered up as a prisoner to none other than Saint-Mars. Could 'Marchiel' and 'Mattioli' be one and the same person, the Man in the Iron Mask? Mattioli is said to have boasted in captivity that he knew secrets that could bring down the French monarchy (he is also said to have gone mad quite quickly in captivity).

Until the middle of the twentieth century, Mattioli was the leading candidate for the Man in the Iron Mask. But in the 1960s, new letters to and from Saint-Mars were discovered, revealing that Mattioli died in the 1690s and was never transferred to the Bastille.

Fun rating:
Likelihood:

6. He was a valet with a sinister secret

Some of these letters to Saint-Mars were written in 1669 by both Louis XIV and his Minister of War, telling the gaoler to expect a prisoner who was to be killed if he talked about anything other than his most basic requirements. This man was named as Eustache Dauger, a valet who had been arrested in Calais. Saint-Mars dutifully guarded him in Pignerol, then on Sainte-Marguerite, and finally in the Bastille. There is now no doubt that Eustache Dauger was the name given to the Man in the Iron Mask.

But even this revelation still leaves a lot of unanswered questions.

What if this was a cover story, with the prisoner given Dauger's identity? There are no records of Dauger before his arrest, an absence that (just about) keeps all the other theories alive. And if the prisoner really was Eustache Dauger, a simple valet, two other doubts remain: what about the clues that the prisoner was some kind of nobleman? And why was the King himself so interested in making him disappear?

It's possible – likely, even – that Voltaire was a little imaginative in his description of the Man in the Iron Mask. There are also doubts about Saint-Mars's integrity. Guarding this secret prisoner was the high point of his career, giving him a heightened sense of self-importance. In letters to friends, he even admits to exaggerating some of his stories – and he enjoyed hearing rumours that the man might be Oliver Cromwell's son. Louis never mentioned the mask, so was it Saint-Mars's own idea, to inflate the legend of the prisoner under his command?

But even if Dauger was a simple valet, whose story was exaggerated by Saint-Mars and Voltaire, why couldn't he be treated like a normal prisoner – or, failing that, executed? The less important Dauger was, the more spectacular his secret must have been.

So, was he an English spy in Calais? Did his job give him access to information he shouldn't have known? Had he made the wrong bigwig a criminally bad continental breakfast? We simply don't know – and unless more seventeenth-century clues come to light, the trail has gone cold.

Fun rating: 💀💀💀💀💀💀💀
Likelihood: 💀💀💀💀💀💀💀

Indiana Jones

THE HISTORY BEHIND *THE RAIDERS OF THE LOST ARK*

In the film Raiders of the Lost Ark, *released in 1981 and set in 1936, the American government hires Indiana Jones, an archaeologist played by Harrison Ford in his prime, to find the Ark of the Covenant before the Nazis (and a rogue French archaeologist) can harness its lethal power for themselves. And although the plot might seem enjoyably ludicrous, it actually has some basis in historical – or at least biblical – fact.**

Here is how an expert historical advisor might have responded if asked his opinion before the film went into development.

---

* Philip Kaufman, who suggested the story for *Raiders of the Lost Ark* to Lawrence Kasdan, the screenwriter, had studied history at university – as, frankly, should everyone who works in Hollywood.

Dear Mr Spielberg,
Thank you so much for your letter. It was an honour to hear from the director of *Jaws* and *Close Encounters of the Third Kind*, two of my favourite films, and I am excited to learn that you are now planning an action-adventure series about a scholarly professor of archaeology. Perhaps you will do something similar for professional historians one day? Three-day seminars on 'The Structural Inadequacies of the League of Nations, 1920–1935' are simply crying out for the old Hollywood magic.

Anyway, I read your draft synopsis for *Raiders of the Lost Ark* with great interest, especially when I realised the film was about a powerful – dare I say, sacral – box, and not Noah's boring old boat.

You asked for my thoughts on the historical context behind the narrative. They are as follows.

1. The biblical Ark was a weapon of mass destruction

Your Indiana Jones wants to stop the Nazis finding the Ark of the Covenant because he fears it will make the Wehrmacht invincible. If the experience of the Old Testament Israelites is anything to go by, Dr Jones is absolutely right to be afraid.

Glossing over the competing tradition that the Ark of the Covenant is simply a filing cabinet in which to keep the Jewish law safe (even you might struggle to make a good film out of that), the principal biblical understanding is that the Ark is the embodiment of God's power on earth. The Old Testament's Yahweh appeared to Adam in the Garden of Eden, to Moses in a bush and to Job in a whirlwind, but it is only in the Ark that he is routinely manifest, nestled between two cherubim atop a golden chest.*

It was built, of course, at the foot of Mount Sinai where the Children of Israel gathered to receive the Ten Commandments. When Moses returned with the stone tablets, he also had precise instructions about how to build a tabernacle, a tent in which to house the Ark that contained the tablets. This led to a wry observation by the aptly named Hermann Witsius, a nineteenth-century Dutch theologian (which I very much hope you will include in your script), that God created the world in six days but needed forty to instruct Moses on how to build a tent.

The Ark was kept at the back of the tabernacle, in the 'Holy of Holies', and was extremely dangerous from the outset. Only Moses could go in there: when his nephews tried to make offerings to the Ark, they were struck down.

This awesome power helped the Children of Israel in their exile, leading them across the desert,† drying the waters of the River Jordan (some great opportunities there for your special effects department) and knocking down the walls of Jericho after being paraded round the city seven times. It wasn't long before the Israelites had conquered the promised land of Canaan.

---

* Cherubim have benefited from some misleading PR in the subsequent millennia. The Bible describes them as terrifying four-headed sphinx-like angels.
† Although the Ark featured rings for inserting carrying poles, it often floated by itself, which was probably just as well given its propensity to smite anyone who got too close.

2. The power of the Ark was a double-edged sword

There is a nice irony in your film that the barbarous, anti-Semitic Nazis are desperate to get their hands on something so central to Judaism.

No doubt you will exploit the tension that the power of the Ark can backfire spectacularly in the wrong hands. 1 Samuel 4 describes how Hophni and Phinehas, the badly behaved sons of the Judge Eli, lost a battle against the Philistines, despite taking the Ark with them, so that God could make His point about their unworthiness. When Eli heard the news, he dropped dead with shock.

Having taken the captured Ark to Ashdod, where it shattered a statue of their corn god Dagon – and moved it to another town, which was promptly plagued by mice and illness – the Philistines sensibly returned the Ark to the Israelites, whereupon God 'smote of the people fifty thousand, and three score, and ten men' who looked directly at it.

I suggest Dr Jones keeps his eyes firmly shut if he doesn't want to get smitten too.

3. The Ark is (probably) gone – but definitely not forgotten

When King David captured Jerusalem in 2 Samuel 6, he was so excited that he danced in front of the Ark in the streets, embarrassing his wife (and, frankly, himself). David's son, Solomon, built the stone Temple in Jerusalem, modelled on the tabernacle, to house the Ark. The last biblical references to the Ark appear in 2 Kings 19, where King Hezekiah of Judah visits the Temple as the Assyrians try and fail to take Jerusalem by siege in 701 BC, and in 2 Chronicles 35, when a later king, Josiah, orders an end to the carrying about of the ark on special occasions, restricting it to the Temple. In 597 BC, the Babylonians successfully took the city, destroying the Temple.

Did they destroy the Ark of the Covenant too? We'll come back to that.

In some ways, however, it doesn't matter. Although other tribes in the region, including the Egyptians and the Phoenicians, had similar sacred chests, the covenant between God and his chosen Israelite people, as represented in the Ark, is unique in the context of antiquity and is still crucial to both Jewish and Christian understandings of their relationship to God.

So there should be a nice big market for your film.

This unique relationship was underpinned by an agreement that God would protect his people and only punish them periodically if they broke his covenant. The idea that an all-powerful God could bind himself contractually made it easier for Christianity to fuse with Greek philosophy, a discipline that also focused on the contractual relationships between men, gods and the universe.

By the third century AD, rabbis were arguing that the *shekhinah*, the presence of God, could be experienced by the Jewish people without need for a physical building, let alone an Ark. Similarly, St Paul had preached a second covenant, ushered in by Christ and written in the heart of each Christian's individual relationship with the Messiah.

The 'Ark' had become abstract.

Great, I hear you say. But Dr Jones can't don his fedora and bullwhip and go looking for an abstract symbol. So where is the actual Ark now?

4. The Ark might be in Egypt – or Ethiopia or the Holy Land or Ireland

I see you're going with the theory that Shishak, who was probably an Egyptian pharaoh called Sheshonq, carted the Ark of the Covenant off to Egypt after he'd sacked Jerusalem in the tenth century BC. And who's to say that you're wrong? 2 Chronicles 12 states that he took treasures from the Temple of the Lord, although it doesn't give an inventory – and the idea does conflict with the apparent interactions with the ark by Hezekiah and Josiah a couple of hundred years later.

All we know for certain is that Pompey found no Ark when he conquered Jerusalem in 63 BC and desecrated the Temple by visiting the Holy of the Holies – although his career did start to tank from there on (so be careful).

So if the Ark isn't in Jerusalem, where else might it be? The Samaritans, whom the Jews hated, claim it's hidden on their sacred Mount Gerizim, near the Palestinian city of Nablus. Others say one of the Kings of Judah hid it somewhere in the Holy Land before the Babylonians arrived. Others still think that the Babylonians took it home with them when they captured Jerusalem in 597 BC, although the inventory of the loot taken from the Temple in 2 Kings doesn't include the Ark.

So might it have been taken to Ireland by an Egyptian princess who also transported the Stone of Scone, which is the pillow on which Jacob rested his head in the Book of Genesis? That's the doubtful claim of a group of nineteenth-century British Israelites who claimed descent from the lost tribes of Israel and tried to excavate the Hill of Tara where the High Kings of Ireland were proclaimed. They were stopped only by an unlikely coalition of Arthur Griffith, a monarchist leader of Sinn Féin, and Maud Gonne MacBride, Republican revolutionary and W.B. Yeats's muse.

A marginally more plausible theory is that the Ark was taken to Ethiopia. According to the *Kebra Nagast*, a revered fourteenth-century Ethiopian text meaning 'The Glory of the Kings', Solomon welcomed the Queen of Sheba to Jerusalem, converted her and tricked her into sleeping with him. Two decades later, their son Menelik was welcomed back to Jerusalem, whereupon his Ethiopian followers stole the Ark with the help of the Archangel Michael. Solomon went mad, Menelik became very powerful and Ethiopian emperors continued to take the epic seriously into the late twentieth century.[*]

There is an Ethiopian prophecy that when Christ returns, the Ark will leave Ethiopia and go back to Jerusalem – so don't take too long making the film, in case you're caught out by the Second Coming and have to make some last-minute edits to the storyline.[†]

---

[*] Haile Selassie, the last Ethiopian Emperor, was crowned at the church in Aksum which claims to house the Ark. Graham Hancock, the excitable peddler of Atlantis theories, also thinks that the Ark came to Aksum, albeit via a different route.

[†] The Ethiopians also predicted that Menelik would defeat the Romans and conquer Constantinople, so maybe there's not too much to worry about here.

5. Indiana Jones and the Never-ending Franchise

It strikes me that, if this film does well, there is significant scope for sequels. Do let me know if you would like any historical context on holy grails, Archimedes's dials, alien crystal skulls or the normal retirement age for an academic archaeologist.

Kind regards,
Tom Holland
Aged twelve and a half

JFK

TOP 10 THEORIES FOR THE PRESIDENT'S ASSASSINATION ANALYSED

It's 7.30 a.m. on Friday 22 November 1963. President John F. Kennedy wakes up in a hotel room in Fort Worth, Texas, and struggles painfully into the heavy back brace he has worn for most of his adult life. It is a quiet news day: one of the leading items in his morning briefing is that the British Labour Party has just won the Dundee West by-election.

The President is joined for breakfast by a group of local businessmen and his wife Jackie. Having recently lost their infant son, Patrick, only two days after he was born, the couple are looking forward to his brother, John Jr's, third birthday party on Monday once they're back in Washington DC.

First, however, they have to show their faces in downtown Dallas, a chance to paper over splits in the Texas Democratic Party before the presidential *election in a year's time. Kennedy is nervous. Dallas, a hotbed of conservatism and of the Southern-based old guard of the Democratic Party, has a reputation for being a difficult place to visit. Vice President Lyndon Johnson, a Texan himself, was spat at here during the 1960 campaign. Adlai Stevenson, the Ambassador to the United Nations, was hit with a placard only a month earlier. 'We're heading into nut country today,' says Kennedy.*

But the morning gets off to a very promising start. After a fifteen-minute flight in Air Force One,* the President's entourage is met at Dallas Love Field at 11.40 by an enthusiastic crowd of around 2,000 people. It is a beautiful autumn day, so they decide to jettison the Plexiglas bubble that might have covered the President's armour-plated Lincoln Continental. By 11.55 the entire motorcade is on the move, the Kennedys sitting in raised seats so that they are more visible than their fellow passengers, Governor Connally of Texas and his wife.

The entourage stops briefly twice: once for Kennedy to shake hands with children holding a placard saying, 'Please stop and shake our hands'; a second time for him to greet a group of nuns. By 12.22 it has reached a crowded Main Street in downtown Dallas. Kennedy's staff are delighted by the enthusiastic reception. At 12.29 Governor Connally leans back to Kennedy and

---

* It would have taken only half an hour to drive from Fort Worth to Dallas, but Kennedy's entourage wanted the pictures of Air Force One on the evening news.

says, 'Mr President, they can't make you believe now that there aren't people in Dallas who love and appreciate you, can they?'

Kennedy grins. 'No, they can't,' he says.

Less than a minute later, a shot rings out, missing its target. Unable to duck due to his back corset, Kennedy is hit in the shoulder seven seconds later by a second bullet, which also catches Connally in his back. A second and a half later, a third bullet hits the President on the right side of his head, his body toppling into the arms of his wife, part of his skull coming apart in her hands.

The motorcade accelerates towards Parkland Memorial Hospital, four miles away, arriving at 12.37 p.m. But it is too late. At 1 p.m. the President is declared dead. At 1.38 p.m., the news is broken to the American public by Walter Cronkite on CBS.

―――

The assassination of President Kennedy was a generation's 9/11 and death of Princess Diana rolled into one: the unforgettable moment when the optimism of the early 1960s began to turn towards a darker iconoclasm. Conspiracy theories gathered pace almost immediately, fuelled by the undisputed fact that Lee Harvey Oswald, the twenty-four-year-old suspect swiftly arrested by the Dallas police on 22 November, was himself shot dead by a Dallas nightclub owner two days later. In the absence of a confession or a trial, numerous theories continue to swirl around the internet today. In his 1,632-page book, *Reclaiming History: The Assassination of President John F. Kennedy*, published in 2007, Vincent Bugliosi listed forty-four organisations, from the Nazis to dissident French paramilitaries, as well as 214 individuals, from Richard Nixon to J. Edgar Hoover to Frank Sinatra's drummer, who have been accused of involvement.

Some of the more outlandish theories analysed by Bugliosi include: Governor Connally shot himself, as well as the president; Kennedy was impersonated by a police officer and survived to attend a birthday party for Truman Capote a year later; and Kennedy was murdered by a group including Henry Kissinger, David Rockefeller and George Bush Senior because he had discovered their deal with aliens to build a base on the moon. As Bugliosi dryly notes: 'With at least eighty-two [alleged] gunmen shooting at Kennedy in Dealey Plaza that day, it's remarkable that his body was sufficiently intact to make it to the autopsy table.'

Here, however, are the top ten theories that have gained the most traction over the last sixty years.

1. Kennedy was assassinated by the Russians

Evidence for

Having been wrongfooted by the Russians during the Vienna Summit in June 1961 and again by the construction of the Berlin Wall two months later, President Kennedy got his own back during the Cuban Missile Crisis the following October, emerging (at least in the Western media) as the stronger statesman who forced Khrushchev back from the brink of nuclear confrontation. Assassinating Kennedy was, therefore, the Russians' chance to avenge that humiliation.

What's more, Lee Harvey Oswald himself identified as a socialist as a teenager, taking this autodidactic flirtation into adulthood by reading Russian dictionaries during his time in the US Marines and travelling to Moscow in October 1959 in an attempt to renounce his American citizenship and settle down in Russia.

Evidence against

More than anything, the Soviet leadership craved stability in the global system. Killing the US President would, therefore, be an irrational gamble of extraordinary magnitude, especially given that the Test Ban Treaty signed in October 1963, a month before Kennedy's death, was leading to a thawing of Cold War relations.

The facts of Oswald's sojourn in the USSR also make him a very unlikely Soviet assassin. After a spell in a psychiatric hospital, he was sent to an electronics factory in Minsk, Belarus, where he spent a miserable few years as a lathe operator. In May 1962, having married (and fathered a daughter), he begged the American embassy to allow him to return home.

There is absolutely no evidence linking the Soviets with the assassination – or indeed Oswald with the Soviet government. Indeed, die-hard conspiracy theorists tend to shy away from the Russian angle as it doesn't satisfy their deeply held need to uncover a secret cabal controlling American politics.

Popularity of theory:

Likelihood of theory: 0

2. It was Castro and the Cubans

Evidence for

In April 1961, only a few months after becoming President, Kennedy launched the disastrous Bay of Pigs operation, a CIA-led attempt to overthrow Fidel Castro, the Soviet-backed Cuban President who had himself overthrown the pro-American dictator, Fulgencio Batista, in 1959. Fearing a second, more successful invasion, Castro had asked Khrushchev for more Soviet support to shore up the Cuban Revolution, leading to the Cuban Missile Crisis in October 1962.

The CIA made hundreds of doomed attempts to assassinate Castro, involving everything from poisonous cigars to exploding seashells. So who is to say that the Cubans didn't orchestrate a more successful operation on the American leader?

This theory is given further credence by Oswald's passion for Cuba. Having failed to make a life for himself in Russia, he travelled to Mexico City in September 1963 and attempted to get a Cuban visa.

Evidence against

Two good sources – a French journalist accompanying Castro on 22 November 1963 and US National Security Agency intercepts – agree that the Cubans were terrified that they would be framed for Kennedy's assassination and that his successor would be even more hardline. Despite having a vested interest in blaming Cuba – the House Select Committee on Assassinations even interviewed Castro personally in the 1970s – the Americans never found any evidence linking Castro to Kennedy's death.

Popularity of theory: 🙂🙂
Likelihood of theory: 0

---

3. It was Cuban exiles

Evidence for

Unsurprisingly, Cuban exiles blamed Kennedy for the failure of the Bay of Pigs, a botched operation that doomed them to a very long exile. So what if they got their own back by killing the American President and pointing the finger of suspicion at Castro, thereby killing two birds (and potentially two leaders they despised) with one stone?

Evidence against

Cuban exiles were predominantly middle-class doctors, intellectuals and businessmen – not the most likely group to employ assassins. And why would Oswald, a man who hated Cuban exiles and loved Castro, want to work with them anyway?

Not only was Kennedy still determined to get rid of Castro (viz. exploding seashells, etc.), his relationship with the Cuban exile community was actually quite positive by the end of his life. Following the Missile Crisis, he attended an event in Miami to welcome freed prisoners who had been detained during the Bay of Pigs. Tens of thousands of enthusiastic people lined the streets. When

Kennedy was presented with a flag, he said, 'One day, this flag will be returned to a free Havana.' The crowd went wild.

Popularity of theory: 🙂🙂🙂🙂🙂
Likelihood of theory: 🙂

---

4. It was the CIA, in league with the military-industrial complex

Evidence for

After the Bay of Pigs, Kennedy said that he wanted to 'splinter the CIA into a thousand pieces and scatter it to the wind' – and even if he didn't actually say this (historians struggle to find the exact quote), perhaps that doesn't matter if he was widely thought to have said it.

So either Kennedy went or the CIA went, runs the theory.

Furthermore, Kennedy's apparent reluctance to commit troops to Vietnam threatened the CIA's powerful allies in the military-industrial complex. So they clubbed together and bumped him off. That's a rough synopsis of Oliver Stone's 1991 film, *JFK*, anyway.

Could Lee Harvey Oswald have been a CIA agent? Why not? After all, the American Embassy in Moscow did give him a loan of $435 in repatriation expenses in 1962.

Evidence against

Far from smashing up the CIA, Kennedy brought in a new person to run it, with whom he had a friendly lunch once a week. And although the CIA has a history of complicity in the assassination of foreign leaders, it doesn't have a history of murdering American politicians on American soil (at least, officially).

Kennedy, a passionate internationalist who had come to power promising to 'pay any price, bear any burden, in the defence of liberty', was an asset, not a threat, to the CIA's worldview. A Cold War hawk, he radically increased the number of military advisors in Vietnam.

If the CIA and the military-industrial complex had wanted to assassinate Kennedy, would they not have tried something similar with Johnson, who passed sweeping civil rights reforms, with Nixon, who went to Beijing, and with Trump, who relentlessly attacked the CIA and NATO?

Neither was Oswald, one of 2,343 destitute US nationals repatriated between 1959 and 1963 thanks to a State Department loan, a very convincing CIA assassin. The KGB, the world's most suspicious people, kept him under constant surveillance during his time in the USSR, concluding that he was an incompetent, inept loner.

Popularity of theory: 🙂🙂🙂🙂🙂🙂
Likelihood of theory: 🙂

5. It was the FBI

Evidence for

J. Edgar Hoover, the Director of the FBI, had an awkward relationship with the Kennedys, resenting the influence of the President's brother, Robert, who was Attorney

General, and fearing that he would be made to retire by the President when he turned 70 in 1965. (In fact, Hoover ended up serving under two more presidents, finally stepping down in 1972.)

On 24 November 1963, two days after Kennedy's death, Hoover called one of President Johnson's aides and said that they needed to convince the public that Oswald was the real assassin.

Separately, Oswald's mother had told newspapers back in 1961 that her son was an FBI agent in the Soviet Union.

Evidence against

A more generous explanation of Hoover's phone call on 24 November is that he was worried about the swirl of rumours and allegations surrounding the murders of Kennedy and Oswald – and wanted to get a grip on the narrative before lurid conspiracy theories competed for the truth. Evidently, he didn't succeed.

The FBI, a domestic intelligence agency, was aware of Oswald due to his strange behaviour in Russia, but they have no history of employing undercover agents overseas, nor indeed of assassinating American political figures. They also have a deep, institutional rivalry with the CIA.

And how likely is it that the involvement of either the FBI or the CIA – government departments generally staffed with intelligent, public-spirited people – would have been kept quiet for so long?

As for Hoover's retirement plans, he had worked closely with Kennedy for three years, amassing a huge file on the President's extramarital affairs. Threatening to reveal these details would have been a far more effective way of securing an extension to his directorship than killing Kennedy in broad daylight.

Meanwhile, Oswald's mother, a self-absorbed woman whose parenting was so haphazard that her son was almost put in care in the 1950s, was hardly the most reliable of witnesses.

Popularity of theory: 🙂🙂🙂
Likelihood of theory: 🙂

6. It was right-wing businessmen

Evidence for

On the morning of his death, Kennedy was shown an advertisement in the *Dallas Morning News*, funded by a right-wing political advocacy group, which sardonically welcomed the President to Dallas and accused him of being a communist.

Evidence against

Kennedy oversaw a growing economy in all three years of his administration, making average tax cuts of around 20 per cent.

Squarely in the pragmatic centre of the Democratic Party, his administration included a number of Washington lifers who had also worked for his Republican predecessor Eisenhower. He was not nearly as left-wing as, say, President Franklin D. Roosevelt, whom right-wing businessmen (also) didn't assassinate.

Right-wing businessmen had no links to Lee Harvey Oswald, a socialist.

Popularity of theory: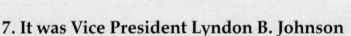

Likelihood of theory: 0

---

7. It was Vice President Lyndon B. Johnson

Evidence for

Who benefits – *cui bono* – from the assassination of President Kennedy? His Vice President, of course, Lyndon Johnson, who was immediately sworn in as the 36th President.

And can it be a coincidence that Kennedy was assassinated in Texas, Johnson's home state, and that Johnson led the USA deeper into Vietnam?

Evidence against

Yes, it is a coincidence. Why would Johnson, a canny political operator, run the risk of assassinating his boss in broad daylight in his home state when it would have been far easier to bump him off in Washington?

Johnson was visibly distraught in the aftermath of Kennedy's assassination. His first act on entering the White House was to write moving letters to Kennedy's two children. Before the end of the month, he had set up the Warren Commission to investigate their father's assassination, staffed by many of his own political opponents.

Johnson had never heard of Lee Harvey Oswald until 22 November 1963.

Popularity of theory: 🙂🙂🙂
Likelihood of theory: 0

8. It was the Ku Klux Klan

Evidence for

President Kennedy's support for civil rights in the summer of 1963 had angered racists in the American South. TASS, the Soviet news agency, blamed ultra-right-wing fascist and racist circles for the President's murder.

Evidence against

TASS was not exactly the most reliable news source.

The Klan was a crude, shambolic and incompetent organisation under intense investigation by the authorities. It is implausible that they would have masterminded a sophisticated assassination without the Dallas Police Department, the FBI and the Warren Commission unearthing any evidence.

It is also unlikely that they would have worked with Lee Harvey Oswald, a communist.

Popularity of theory: 🙂🙂
Likelihood of theory: 0

9. The Mafia killed JFK – and then employed Jack Ruby to silence Oswald

Evidence for

The Mafia loathed Robert Kennedy, who had led a big crackdown on racketeering and corruption, and we know from FBI wiretaps that some mobsters were gleeful about JFK's death. Some also believe that Joe Kennedy, an ambassador to Britain at the outbreak of the Second World War, bought the 1960 presidential election for his son on behalf of the Mafia. When President Kennedy failed to deliver, they assassinated him.

The Mafia angle that really excites conspiracy theorists, however, is the undisputed fact that Lee Harvey Oswald was assassinated on 24 November in police custody by Jack Ruby, a local nightclub owner who often bought drinks for people involved in organised crime. Was Ruby employed to silence Oswald so he wouldn't talk? It was certainly a huge embarrassment for the Dallas police that their prize prisoner was shot in front of seventy officers – and the world's media – while being transported to a more secure location.

Evidence against

Almost every conspiracy theory involves the Mafia, which became powerful during the prohibition era in the 1920s and continued to attract popular interest thanks to the *Godfather* films released in the 1970s. However, the American Mafia were very different from their Sicilian counterparts in that they went out of their way to avoid targeting judges or politicians. Yes, they loathed Robert

Kennedy, but would they try to blunt his investigations by targeting his brother? We know from FBI wiretaps of a Philadelphia Mafia boss that they feared Kennedy's successors being even more hardline.

Neither is there any evidence of systematic corruption in the 1960 presidential election.

Similarly, it's difficult to say whether Jack Ruby or Lee Harvey Oswald is the more unlikely Mafia assassin. Oswald was so inept that he didn't even have a getaway car. Ruby, the killer supposedly sent to neutralise a killer, spent the two days in which Oswald was being interrogated wandering around the city in tears and telling everyone how much he loved the Kennedys. Three minutes before he shot Oswald, he was in a queue at a bank, paying one of his strippers. It was only chance that saw him pass the police station at the same moment that Oswald was being transferred.

Although Ruby often bought drinks for Mafia members, he also gave drinks (his favourite was a celery tonic) to the Dallas police department. There is no evidence that he was involved in organised crime.

Popularity of theory:

Likelihood of theory:

10. Lee Harvey Oswald was a crank who operated alone

Evidence for

Born in New Orleans, Louisiana, in 1939 to a tempestuous mother and a father who had died two months previously,

Lee Harvey Oswald was a lonely, sullen and troubled boy. Having moved to the Bronx in New York aged twelve, he was sent to a reformatory, where a psychiatrist diagnosed personality pattern disturbance and schizoid features.

He joined the Marines aged seventeen in 1956, where his shooting scores were sufficiently high to qualify as a sharpshooter.

Tiring of military life, he left the Marines three years later, spent time in Russia and returned with his wife, whom he regularly beat, and their young daughter to Texas. On 12 March 1963 he bought a mail-order rifle under the false name of A.J. Hidell. The following month he used this rifle to try to kill Major General Edwin Walker, a segregationist living in Dallas, scuttling away into the darkness when the bullet missed its mark. In October he got a job in the Texas School Book Depository, a warehouse in downtown Dallas. The President's route was announced in the newspapers on 19 November.

On Thursday 21 November, the night before Kennedy's death, Oswald took the unusual step of visiting his wife (they lived separately during the week), leaving his wedding ring behind and collecting a package that he described as curtain rods. The following morning, he took a lift with a neighbour into Dallas, carrying a long package wrapped up in brown paper. At midday, half an hour before Kennedy's death, Oswald was seen on the sixth floor by his colleagues, refusing to join them for lunch and asking for the elevator gate to be closed. No one else was on the sixth floor and no one else left the building after the shooting. At 1.06 p.m., six minutes after Kennedy was proclaimed dead, the Dallas police found a sniper's nest by a window on the sixth floor. Sixteen minutes later, they found the murder weapon, an infantry rifle.

Meanwhile, Oswald had taken a bus, which got stuck in traffic, and then ordered a taxi, which he never normally did. He got out in the Oak Cliff district of Dallas and was spoken to by a policeman called J.D. Tippit who had spotted him acting suspiciously. At 1.11 p.m., at the junction of East 10th Street and South Patton Avenue, an eyewitness saw Oswald shoot Tippit dead. He was arrested just over half an hour later in a theatre, telling the arresting officer, 'I hear they burn for murder.' The police found two ID cards in his wallet: one in the name of Lee Harvey Oswald; the other in the name of A.J. Hidell.

Under interrogation by Captain J.W. Fritz, Oswald denied two perfectly legal activities: bringing curtain rods to work and buying a mail-order gun under the name of A.J. Hidell. By the end of 23 November, the FBI had managed to match the rifle to a mail-order shop in Chicago; the handwriting on the money order to Oswald's own; and a photograph of Oswald in his backyard with the rifle.

The following day, he was visited by his mother, his wife and his brother, all of whom thought he'd murdered Kennedy.

Ten months later, the Warren Commission, chaired by the Chief Justice, delivered an 888-page report concluding that Lee Harvey Oswald acted alone and that there was no conspiracy.

Evidence against

Lee Harvey Oswald denied killing President Kennedy, claiming that he was a 'patsy'.

When he was shot by Jack Ruby on 24 November, detectives tried desperately to save Oswald's life. One of them stood over him, asking again and again, 'Is there anything you want to say now?'

Oswald took his secrets to the grave. He was declared dead in the same hospital as Kennedy, two days and seven minutes after the President.

Popularity of theory: 🙂🙂🙂🙂🙂
Likelihood of theory: 🙂🙂🙂🙂🙂🙂🙂🙂🙂🙂

Martin Luther King Jr.:
The Biblical Book of Martin the Baptist

Regularly voted the greatest speech of all time, Martin Luther King Jr.'s twelve-minute address on 28 August 1963 was viewed by a crowd of 250,000 civil rights campaigners in Washington, DC – and by millions more on television. It has continued to resonate long after his assassination in 1968: protestors in Tiananmen Square in 1989 held up placards with the words 'I have a dream' and extracts can be seen on the Palestinian side of the wall surrounding the West Bank.

King was a third-generation Baptist preacher who would recite biblical extracts from memory while still at kindergarten, and his Christian faith is central to understanding the tone, timbre and resonance of his speech. So here is how a missing book from the New Testament Apocrypha might describe the context and impact of that summer's day in 1963.

A BUS BOYCOTT IS BEGOTTEN

1 BEHOLD, there was a man sent by God, whose name was Martin, born in the first year of the reign of President Hoover (1929) in Atlanta, Georgia.

2 And lo, Georgia was a divided land where the law of Jim Crow prevented black men and women from the breaking of bread – or even the sharing of schools, universities and the same part of a bus – with their white brethren.

3 Martin pondered these laws in his heart and was filled with righteous anger. Was it not written that God created Man in His own image? Did the Founding Fathers of the United States of America not give a new commandment that all men were created equal?

4 Martin waxed strong in spirit, and so did a whole multitude of others, who put on the full armour of God – the breastplate of righteousness, the belt of truth and the shield of faith – to stand against the government's decrees (and police brutality).

5 Now it came to pass that a Civil Rights movement, which started in the 1890s, began to bear fruit and multiply in the 1950s. African Americans spake with ever-louder voices about their service in the Second World War.

6 Others pondered verily about the merits of segregation at a time when America claimed to stand as a flinty rock of faith and freedom against Soviet communism.

7 Brown v Board of Education decreed that segregated schools were detestable in the sight of God and Man (and the constitution).

8 A woman named Rosa Parks refused to take her place at the back of a Montgomery bus.

9 Rosa's actions begat a year-long bus boycott led by Martin. Segregationists smote his dwelling place with bombs in January 1956. A woman tried to slay him in the chest in September 1958.

10 But Martin was strong and of good courage.

11 'It's all right,' he said unto the people. 'Everything is going to be all right.'

MARTIN GOES TO BIRMINGHAM

2 AND it came to pass that there was a man named George Wallace, the Governor of Alabama, who was sore troubled by the Civil Rights movement in the third year of the reign of President Kennedy. He said unto the people in January 1963, 'In the name of the greatest people that have ever trod this earth, I draw the line in the dust and toss the gauntlet before the feet of tyranny. We stand for segregation now, segregation tomorrow, segregation for ever.'*

2 Many people were amazed that Governor Wallace did not share the glad tidings of the 1960s.

3 But while some white brethren believed they were taking up the cross for states' rights in the face of oppressive decrees from the federal government, a multitude of black brethren were taking up the cross for the right not to be smitten with dogs and water cannons while protesting peacefully to be treated as equal citizens.

4 Martin, knowing their thoughts, walked among his brethren and said unto them, 'We must rise to the majestic heights of meeting physical force with soul force.'

5 He went on to say, 'Injustice anywhere is a threat to justice everywhere.'

6 Now it came to pass that in April he went to Birmingham, Alabama, a town named Bombingham after all the smiting of civil rights activists' dwelling places by white supremacists.

7 Martin said, 'Just as the Apostle Paul left his village of Tarsus and carried the gospel of Jesus Christ to the far corners of the Greco-Roman world, so am I compelled to carry the gospel of freedom beyond my own home town.'

8 Now Birmingham was a violent, segregationist city controlled by a police chief named Eugene 'Bull' Connor who greatly disdained the civil rights brethren. Martin was apprehended on Good Friday, but he was not dismayed. In prison he wrote a letter on a parchment of toilet paper calling Jesus of Nazareth 'an extremist for love'.

---

* Governor Wallace's infamous inauguration speech, which he regretted in later years, propelled him into the national limelight. He ran unsuccessfully for president three times.

9 On the eleventh day he was released and suffered the little children to come unto him – and be placed on the front line of the protests.

10 It made for extraordinary scenes on the television.

11 But it did not calm the exceeding disciples of the Black Power activist Malcolm X who argued that Man could not live on non-violence alone.

12 Martin said unto them, 'We adopt the means of non-violence because our end is a community at peace with itself.'

13 He also desired to incite the shame of white liberals, especially among the Kennedy elders, who feared the wrath of their southern base if they were exceedingly consumed with zeal for civil rights.

MARTIN MARCHES ON WASHINGTON

3 NOW in the days of the 1960s, it was not natural to march forth peaceably on the nation's capital. But A. Philip Randolph was not a natural man.

2 While leader of the Brotherhood of Sleeping Car Porters in 1941, he had tried to gather a march to protest against segregation in the military.

3 'I will desegregate the war industries instead,' President Roosevelt said unto him.

4 'Okay,' said Randolph unto the President.

5 Now in his threescore and fourteenth year, Randolph wanted to organise another march on Washington. Martin was of one mind as 1963 was the centenary of the Emancipation Proclamation by Abraham Lincoln.

6 And they were aided by a man less stricken in years called Bayard Rustin, a tall, gay, communist Quaker.

7 President Kennedy, who had pledged his troth to the cause of civil rights after the protests in Birmingham, was filled with fear by young Bayard's communism.

8 So it was decreed that Bayard would organise the march without exceeding pomp.*

9 And although many white brethren were sore afraid that there would be smiting in the capital, it came to pass that there was no violence at all (although Marlon Brando carried an electric

---

* Bayard Rustin was a brilliant organiser, even focusing on such minutiae as advising protestors not to put mayonnaise in their sandwiches as it would spoil in the sun and cause diarrhoea.

cattle prod to symbolise police brutality).*

10 There were more children, more elderly people and more black people than were prophesied, many dressed as though they were worshipping the Lord on the Sabbath.†

THE SERMON ON THE MEMORIAL

4 NOW when Martin saw the multitudes gathered around Lincoln's Memorial on 28 August, he first listened to the fifteen speakers who prepared the way for him, since no one wanted to speak after the greatest orator of the Civil Rights movement.

2 Martin would give 350 sermons a year, aided by a company of men who had been working on this sermon for three or four days.

3 'Don't use your "I have a dream" riff,' said Wyatt Tee Walker, one of his disciples, unto Martin in their room at an inn the night before the sermon.

4 For Martin had already spoken some of his 'dream' material in Georgia and North Carolina in 1962, and at a fundraiser in Chicago seven days earlier.

5 So in the fourth watch of the night, on the day of the sermon, he told his disciples that he would go upstairs at the inn to counsel with his Lord. Having done so, he decided that they were right and that he would not recycle his greatest hits.

6 Now when the time came, he looked out on the multitudes, some of them sheltering from the sun under the trees, others starting their departures unto their dwelling places at the end of a long day.

7 And lo, the TV networks interrupted their regular programming to broadcast his sermon live.

8 Now, it had been decreed that Martin had only ten minutes until he would be cut off from his microphone.

9 He began to speak unto the multitudes in his slow, rolling baritone.

10 The protestors were there, he said unto them, to cash a cheque

---

* In Washington DC, all elective operations were cancelled in anticipation of the hospitals being overrun with victims of violence, judges prepared for criminal hearings to run through the night and the Pentagon put 19,000 troops on standby.
† The organisers expected a black:white ratio of 50:50, but it ended up being closer to 80:20.

MARTIN 5

on the defaulted promissory note that all men were created equal.*

11 He spake of the 'fierce urgency of now'.

12 He spake from the Book of Amos, justice rolling down like waters, and righteousness like a mighty stream.

13 There was a polite clapping of hands. Maybe this would be another solid – but unmemorable – sermon.

14 Martin was about to move unto his peroration when the Lord caused a woman to call out from the crowd.

15 'Tell them about the dream, Martin,' she said unto him.

16 The spirit of the Lord fell upon Martin.

17 Like Joseph, son of Jacob, he decided to tell his brothers about his dream.

18 That one day on the red hills of Georgia, the sons of former slaves and the sons of former slave owners would be able to sit down together at the table of brotherhood.

19 That his four little children would one day live in a nation where they would not be judged by the colour of their skin but by the content of their character.

20 Martin had many other dreams, some borrowed of his previous sermons, some borrowed of the Book of Isaiah, some brand new.† And lo, the multitudes rose to their feet to praise him.

21 'From every mountainside, let freedom ring,' he said unto them, making mention of states from New Hampshire to New York, Colorado to California.

22 And Martin finished with the prophecy of a day when 'all God's children, black men and white men, Jews and Gentiles, Protestants and Catholics, will be able to join hands and sing in the words of the old negro spiritual: free at last, free at last. Thank God Almighty we're free at last.'

23 'He is damned good,' President Kennedy said unto his aides as he watched Martin for the first time on a television in the Oval Office.

---

* Whereas Malcolm X argued that black Americans should emancipate themselves from the entire structures of white America, King's strategy was to shame white America into fulfilling its promises to all its citizens. This division continues to reverberate among contemporary campaigners for black rights, split between those asking America to live up to its professed ideals and those arguing that the country was fatally poisoned by its original sin of slavery.

† Gary Younge points out in his brilliant book *The Speech* that the 'dream' sequence for which King's speech is principally remembered was just 301 words long (less than a fifth of the total) and delivered in two minutes and forty seconds. He also notes that King spoke at 77 words a minute, around half the speed of an average audiobook.

THE ASCENSION

5 AND it came to pass that Martin was named *Time*'s 'Man of the Year' in 1963. In the year that followed, he was the youngest person to be recompensed by the Lord according to his righteousness with the Nobel Peace Prize.

2 But the day after his speech the headline in the Jackson, Mississippi *Clarion-Ledger* read: 'Washington is clean again with negro trash removed.'

3 And by 1966, he was being mocked with boos in Chicago by young black brethren.

4 And when Martin heard that, he said, 'I had preached to them about my dream, but they were hostile watching the dream that they had so readily accepted turn into a frustrating nightmare.'

5 In 1968 an escaped racist captive slew him.

6 Many of his disciples thought Martin should be remembered for his more radical sermons attacking imperialism, capitalism and Vietnam – instead of a 1963 sermon that presents a sanitised, less confrontational figure, more palatable to conservative America.

7 Since 1986 he has been remembered at the appointed time every year on Martin Luther King Jr. Day, an honour suggesting that a prophet can sometimes be honoured in his own country.

Library of Alexandria

WHO DESTROYED THE GREATEST LIBRARY IN THE WORLD?

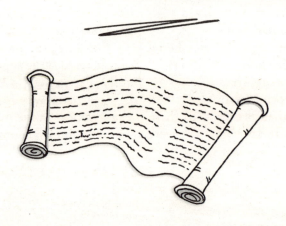

It was the greatest library ever built, with a huge collection that contained all the learning of the ancient world – and when it burned down, the world lost a vast store of knowledge. That's what everyone knows about the Great Library of Alexandria, which was established around 300 BC. But when, exactly, was it destroyed – and who burned it down? With theories spanning almost 700 years, from 48 BC to AD 642, it's a more complicated mystery than one might expect.

Theory 1: It was accidentally destroyed by a randy Julius Caesar in 48 BC

Evidence for

When Ptolemy, Alexander the Great's one-time general, became Pharaoh of Egypt in around 305 BC, he established a thrusting new regime, with Alexandria as its dynamic new capital on the shores of the Mediterranean. Amid all the architectural splendour of Alexandria, Ptolemy – a cultivated man, who had been taught by Aristotle alongside Alexander – wanted to preserve everything that was best about Greek culture.

Ptolemy's plan was to create a prestigious collection of all the best thinkers in the Greek world, preserved in scrolls written on thin papyrus and covering topics from philosophy and Athenian tragedy to mathematics and geography.* He also wanted a fun new hobby now that his days of marching across Asia were behind him.

Arriving in Egypt 250 years later, in 48 BC, Julius Caesar met Ptolemy's descendant Cleopatra, and began what he no doubt thought was the greatest love story in the history of Rome.† He'd be disappointed to know that it wasn't

---

* It was scholars working in the Great Library who ironed out the inconsistencies in rival texts to form the standard versions of works like the *Iliad*. Even more spectacularly, one of the Library's scholars, a geographer and mathematician called Eratosthenes, first calculated the circumference of the earth around 200 BC. His calculations were so accurate that flat-earth theory should have died out there and then.
† Egypt was the only part of the Mediterranean still outside the Roman Empire. Caesar hadn't planned to get involved in Egyptian affairs – he was instead in hot pursuit of his great enemy, Pompey. But when it turned out that the Egyptians had already cut off Pompey's head, he got sidetracked by Cleopatra and her own political problems. It took Caesar several months to extricate himself and rejoin his civil war.

even the greatest love story in the history of Cleopatra's Roman boyfriends – his lieutenant Mark Antony later took that prize. As a keen author,* he'd be even more disappointed to discover that he later got blamed for destroying Alexandria's Great Library on the same trip.

The case for the prosecution? Caesar's forces found themselves attacked by Cleopatra's brother and political enemy, Ptolemy XIII (the Ptolemies believed that variety was good on a bookshelf, but less good for baby names). In the course of the battle, Caesar burned some of his own ships to stop the other side capturing them. This fire spread to Alexandria's warehouses, where Roman historians recorded that thousands of scrolls stored in the warehouses were lost. One historian, Plutarch, goes so far as to say that the Great Library of Alexandria itself was destroyed in this fire.

Evidence against

Did Caesar's tactical gamble really come at such a devastating cost? It does seem like an implausible piece of bad luck. After all, the Library was part of the palace complex, which was a safe distance from the dockside warehouses.

And although historians now think that 'the Great Library of Alexandria' referred to the collection, not the rooms it occupied (so it could conceivably have been stored in the warehouses), it is much more likely that Plutarch is wrong and that a different set of scrolls were destroyed.

---

* Like modern politicians, Caesar liked to write self-referential, self-justifying books (although he did have the good grace not to call any of them *A Journey*). His book about his conquest of Gaul begins with the famously no-nonsense phrase, 'All of Gaul is divided into three parts.'

The evidence for this counter-theory? More than a hundred years later, during the reign of the Emperor Domitian, a fire in Rome destroyed a number of libraries – whereupon Domitian sent copyists to Alexandria to replace the books Rome had lost. Clearly, the scroll collection in Alexandria remained the best in the ancient world.

Theory 2: The Emperor Aurelian banished the barbarians – and then burned the books

Evidence for

During the third and fourth centuries AD, the Roman Empire had a pretty rotten time of it. In the 270s, after four decades of continuous civil war, the Emperor Aurelian unexpectedly won a series of astonishing victories against various barbarian invaders and breakaway provinces.

His efforts rescued the disintegrating empire and led the Senate to award him the title *'Restitutor Orbis'* (Restorer of the World). But you don't reconquer the Roman Empire by being soft and cuddly: as part of his tough-love programme of reunification, he sacked Alexandria in 273 and destroyed the Ptolemies' old palace complex, which had contained the library.

Evidence against

No sources explicitly state that the Great Library was destroyed in this period (although we have very few written sources at all from this tumultuous era because fragile papyrus scrolls don't tend to fare well in the upheavals of war).

If the Library survived Aurelian's wars of the 270s, there were other rounds of civil war – especially in the 290s – that brought their own catastrophes to the streets of Alexandria. The Great Library's chances of making it unscathed to the end of the century are therefore fairly small.

However, there are still two other theories about the nature and the timing of its destruction.

Theory 3: The 'People of the Book' burned the books

Evidence for

The arrival of Christianity and – later – of Islam have both been gleefully blamed for the Library's disappearance by historians who think that monotheism took all the fun out of ancient history and ushered in the Dark Ages.

Edward Gibbon, the eighteenth-century author of *The History of the Decline and Fall of the Roman Empire*, was the person most responsible for popularising this narrative, claiming that the Great Library – or at any rate *a* library – was destroyed by a Christian mob that looted the Temple of Serapis in Alexandria in 391 AD.

Similarly, there's a thirteenth-century Arab legend that when their ancestors captured Alexandria in 642 AD, they destroyed the Great Library because the Caliph said that the only book they needed was the Quran.

Evidence against

Although lots of historians believed Gibbon's version of events, it seems that he was sexing-up his sources (it was easier to get away with that sort of behaviour in the 1780s, when history hadn't yet been established as a proper academic discipline/a worthy topic for popular podcasts). There are five separate written accounts of the riot that ransacked the Temple of Serapis, and none of them mention any libraries being damaged.

Similarly, the early Muslims treated Greek learning with respect: many Greek texts have survived precisely because they were so carefully looked after throughout the Middle Ages by Christian and Muslim scholars.

Theory 4: Of mice and myths

Evidence for

Sometimes, there is a disappointingly banal explanation for glamorous historical mysteries.

Yes, the Roman Empire became less and less stable from the third century onwards, leading to constant violence, even in its greatest cities such as Alexandria.

But even if the Library was never burned in a single, great event, its contents would not have lasted more than a few hundred years anyway. Papyrus is fragile, and it decays. For the texts to be preserved, they needed to be laboriously copied out onto fresh papyrus, a process that would have become much rarer as the third- and fourth-century civil wars shrank the number of scholars in Alexandria.

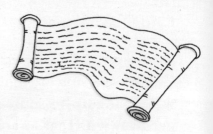

In the absence of these efforts, the texts would have slowly succumbed to mildew, mites and mice.

We are fortunate that some of the works have survived to this day, thanks to copies made in Alexandria and shipped around the Roman Empire where they were preserved in palaces and monasteries in places like Constantinople.

And in the absence of any concrete evidence, the very fact that the Library was destroyed continues to give it such a powerful hold over our imaginations. The Great Library of Alexandria is ultimately most potent as a myth. We can fantasise over what it might have contained and imagine the perfect universal library, the Bodleian, the British Library – and maybe even Wikipedia – all rolled into one.*

---

* A quick glance at the latter (confirmed by a second, more reliable source) tells us that the 'Bibliotheca Alexandria' was opened (or reopened) in Alexandria in 2002 at a cost of $220 million, its Latin name a conscious nod to its inheritance. It is still building its collection, but has shelf space for eight million books.

Historical Love Island

THIS YEAR'S WINNERS

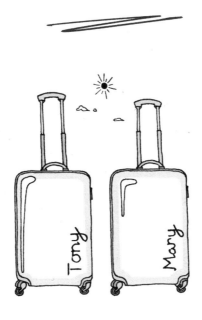

Love Island, *a hugely successful reality TV show in which good-looking young people are dispatched to a Spanish villa in order to 'get to know each other better', has attracted mixed reviews since it first aired in 2015. To its legions of fans, it is a harmless piece of titillation, gripping the nation every summer with its dramatic twists, short-lived romances and often shorter-lived influencer careers. To its detractors, it is a sign of everything that is wrong with Britain today.*

But what if the show simultaneously told us something about the past? After our popular inaugural episode of Historical Love Island *was won by the unlikely combination of Stanley Baldwin, the inter-war British Prime Minister, and Theodora, the sixth-century Byzantine Empress, we decided to risk the wrath of the critics and send eight more historical figures to the villa: Charles II and Empress Zoe; Sir William Hamilton and Catherine Howard; Peter the Great and Poppaea Sabina; Tony Benn and Mary Fisher.*

Only two of those couples made it through to the closely fought final round. Here is what a 'serious' newspaper editorial might have made of the surprising result of the public vote.

God Rest Ye Serious, Gentle Benn

As this year's series of *Historical Love Island* comes to a close on *The Rest is History*, the public appears to have shunned the ruthless, the cruel and the flippant, in favour of a seventeenth-century Quaker and a twentieth-century British Secretary of State for Industry.

Yes, they were impressed by the way in which Peter the Great, one of the four finalists, had expanded Russia's frontiers from the Baltics to the Black Sea in the eighteenth century, building a navy, founding St Petersburg and modernising the country by drawing heavily upon western European culture and science. But they were less impressed by the fact that Vladimir Putin has openly compared himself to the ruthlessly expansionist autocrat.

There were also objections to the manner in which Peter the Great impaled his ex-wife's lover on a stake, deliberately avoiding his vital organs and forcing his soldiers to watch his long death agonies. Neither did the audience warm to the way in which he beheaded his mistress, using her severed head to lecture the crowd on anatomy before kissing her bloody lips.

Both anecdotes went down badly on *Love Island*'s talent night when Peter the Great tried to recreate the gruesome scenes using a colourful beanbag and a branded water bottle – although Charles II, Peter the Great's closest ally on the show, declared it 'absolutely brilliant banter'. We live in serious times, and this does not appear to be the ideal moment for a 6'8" Russian who once hosted a wedding in St Petersburg for his favourite dwarf, forcing every other dwarf in Russia to attend, drinking goblets of vodka and dancing until they fell over.

The producers mischievously paired the Russian roué with the equally ruthless Poppaea Sabina, the most fashionable woman in first-century Rome,* who once insisted that her husband Nero present her with the severed head of his exiled wife Octavia – and was delighted to make it to the final.

Life ended badly for both of them: a pregnant Poppaea Sabina was probably kicked to death in 65 AD by Nero;† Peter the Great died from a gangrenous bladder blocked

---

* Nero was so impressed by Poppaea Sabina's strawberry-blonde hair that he sent to Denmark for amber, decorating his place with the stones as a tribute to her.

† There is no consensus about how exactly Poppaea Sabina died, or what might have triggered the fatal round of brutality, although Nero was notoriously unstable. Tacitus describes it as a 'chance fit of anger', whereas Suetonius, another Roman historian, writes that 'she had scolded him for coming home late from the races'. Later writers point out that neither historian was a fan of Nero and that she might have died in childbirth.

with two litres of urine his doctors tried to extract. And although some viewers continued to take the mickey centuries later, almost voting this blood-stained, dwarf-tossing, murderous couple to victory, we can ultimately be thankful that the great British public saw sense and rejected their toxic micro- and macro-aggressions in favour of a more popular couple.

The public also showed an unusual ability to see through any hint of insincerity in the contestants. Poppaea Sabina unleashed an X storm (formerly known as a Twitter storm), when she confessed in the beach hut that she had deliberately dumped her first two husbands en route to snaring Nero. And not even her incredible branding potential, including viral Instagram photos of ass's milk baths and mules shod with gold, could save her from an increasingly puritan public.

Viewers were equally unimpressed by Catherine Howard, Henry VIII's fifth wife, whose infidelities were brought to an abrupt end by Archbishop Thomas Cramner leaving an anonymous note on Henry's church pew.* She behaved similarly in the show, 'mugging off' her first partner Sir William Howard, the cuckolded husband of Nelson's mistress,† before losing her head all over again

---

* The powerful Howard family had pushed their 17-year-old daughter in front of a 49-year-old king with a 52-inch waist and a leg ulcer. Perhaps unsurprisingly, Catherine continued her affair with Thomas Culpeper, one of Henry's hunting friends. Cranmer's note led to a treason charge and her execution on 13 February 1542 after only eighteen months of marriage.
† The British ambassador to Naples for much of the second half of the eighteenth century, Sir William Hamilton became the most famous cuckold in Britain when his young second wife, Emma Hamilton, took up with the married Horatio Nelson in 1798. Sir William gamely tolerated the public humiliation, dying in Emma's arms in 1803 and leaving her all his money.

and shamelessly shacking up with Nelson himself. Charles II, who had twelve children by seven mistresses, including last year's contestant, Louise de Kéroualle, was also undone by his infidelities, as well as a lack of seriousness. None of them lasted long in the villa.

So if the viewers didn't rally to the rogues and the rascals, who did they root for?

Zoe, the eleventh-century Byzantine Empress, almost repeated last year's winning streak by Theodora, the sixth-century Empress. No stranger to public acclaim – when Zoe's nephew tried to banish her to a monastery in 1042, sympathetic rioters gouged out his eyes – she won over a modern audience with a heart-rending backstory, artfully leaked to the tabloids by her PR team. The public feasted on tales of a woman who, needing a husband to rule, found herself pre-deceased by the first, imprisoned by the third (a 'fake grafter' whom she'd persuaded to murder the second) and cheated on by the fourth.

But although the cuckolds were more popular than the cads, this year's undoubted winners were a wonderful couple who combined seriousness of purpose with commendable devotion to their marriages – a heady cocktail for these times.

Resisting all attempts by Poppaea Sabina to 'pull him for a chat to see where his head was at', Tony Benn, the teetotal, tea-drinking, pipe-smoking British Minister of Technology and Secretary of State for Energy in the 1970s – and the voice of the Labour Left for decades – wowed younger viewers with his campaign to nationalise the villa from the rapaciously capitalist ITV and replace the contestants' swimwear with donkey jackets.

They also warmed to a man described by the *Guardian*'s obituary in 2014 as 'the Home Counties' favourite revolutionary', by his party leader Harold Wilson as 'immaturing with age' and by the right-wing press as 'the most dangerous man in Britain'. In a world of ephemeral social media, they were particularly touched by his charming habit of writing down his thoughts – with pen and paper – in a daily diary that he had kept since 1964.*

Viewers' heartstrings were also tugged by a politician who had met his beloved wife, a wealthy, socialist American called Caroline Middleton DeCamp, on a park bench in Oxford University in 1949, proposed nine days later and installed the park bench in the garden of their London house, where they remained happily married for over fifty years.

Mr Benn's devotion to his cause and his marriage found its match in Mary Fisher, a relatively unknown seventeenth-century Quaker, who is also buried alongside her beloved spouse.

'He had me at Trotskyite Militant Tendency,' she said after Mr Benn's talent night performance of 'The Red Flag', accompanied by a tearful miners' choir.

Mrs Fisher endeared herself to *Love Island* fans with her unswerving commitment to her faith, as well as her habit of stripping off to make religious pronouncements (many of them censored by Ofcom). Undeterred by being

---

* After Benn failed to win the deputy leadership of his party in 1981, his arguments for democratic socialism were increasingly drowned out by a growing Thatcherite consensus and the rise of New Labour. He retired from Parliament in 2001, 51 years after first becoming an MP, in order 'to devote more time to politics', and remained relevant as President of the Stop the War coalition and a fierce critic of Tony Blair. 'He will be remembered as a great parliamentarian, a great radical and a great diarist,' wrote the *Guardian*. 'He will be forgotten as a practical politician and a political thinker.'

the first Quaker to be whipped for her ministry (she had protested in 1653 against Cambridge students becoming vicars, a position of which Quakers disapproved), she converted the Governor of Barbados in 1655 and spent five weeks in a Boston prison in 1655, where she was stripped naked and searched for signs of witchcraft, before being deported back to England.

Undeterred, she set off in 1657 with six fellow Quakers to attempt to convert the Ottoman Sultan. Remarkably, the Sultan, who didn't speak English, received Mary Fisher, an English housemaid, who didn't speak Turkish, listening politely to what she had to say. 'He was very noble unto me,' said Mary, despite failing to convert him.

This anecdote led to one of the most memorable moments in this *Love Island* series: the half-naked contestants exchanging robust views around the swimming pool about whether it was more difficult for a British housemaid to convert a Turkish Muslim to non-conformist Christianity in the seventeenth century or for a British MP who had renounced his hereditary title to campaign for democratic socialism at the end of the twentieth century.

Dumbing down in the media? Not here.

Love Island Personality Test

Historical fish-out-of-water at the villa? Take the quiz to find out which of Tom and Dominic's residents you'd be.

What would be your ideal first date?

A. A banquet. Followed by a party. Followed by a banquet.
B. Preaching. Rebuking priests.
C. Political rally, followed by a walk along a river.
D. Watching a joust. Being read romantic poetry.

If you were an animal what would you be?

A. A lion. Loud, dominant, great hair.
B. A border collie. Bright, learns quickly. Loud bark when required.
C. An elephant. Intelligent, loyal and strong.
D. A white-tailed deer. Slight and fast with bright eyes.

What is your favourite genre of film?

A. Gross-out comedy
B. Biopics
C. Drama
D. Romance

LOVE ISLAND PERSONALITY TEST

When planning something with others, which of these would you be?

A. Galvaniser. Being enthusiastic and making sure everyone is on board.
B. Listener. Takes information and gets on with it.
C. Leader. Good at delegating and playing to everyone's strengths.
D. Joker. Making sure nobody takes things too seriously.

And finally, which of the following are most important to you?

A. Parties
B. Preaching
C. Politics
D. Privacy

See page 415 for ratings.

Mitfords

THE FAMILY'S CHRISTMAS ROUND-ROBIN LETTERS FROM THE 1930s

The glamorous and aristocratic Mitford sisters, infamous in the 1930s and 1940s for embracing variously Nazism, Communism, home-grown British fascism and novel writing, continue to exert a powerful grip on the imagination of publishers and the heritage industry.

Even more interesting than a walking tour around their Cotswold gravestones, however, is the insight the family provides into the rise and fall of fascism in Britain. Unity Mitford, the fourth of six girls, met Adolf Hitler more than 140 times in the 1930s, introducing the Führer to most of the rest of her family. There were even rumours that she gave birth to his child. Meanwhile, Diana, her older sister, married Sir Oswald Mosley, leader of the British Union of Fascists, in Goebbels's drawing room in October 1936.

What might their parents, Lord and Lady Redesdale, have made of all this? Fortunately, we have access to some of the Christmas round-robin letters written by their mother, covering the more eventful years of that most eventful decade, the 1930s.*

1932

Dear Friends,

I hope this Christmas card finds you well.

Unity is cutting a wonderful dash as a debutante at court, having turned eighteen in August. The Daily Express called her 'the prettiest girl', which was kind of them, as we have often thought her somewhat galumphing and big-boned compared to Diana. Still, at least she's not like some of those dreadful flappers we saw so much of last decade, all narrow hips, short hair and shorter skirts. The London social scene suits Unity more than school,

---

* The much-maligned Christmas round-robin letter, in which middle-class families humble-brag to their nearest and dearest about Laetitia's merit in grade four flute, probably hit its peak in the 1990s. Nancy, the eldest Mitford sister and author of the well-received novels *The Pursuit of Love* and *Love in a Cold Climate*, would probably have considered them as 'non-U' (a tongue-in-cheek moniker for anything that wasn't upper class) as saying 'Pardon me, where is the toilet?'

which we finally gave up on last year.* She shows a great deal of interest in art, for which she has some talent, and in handsome young men, for which she has even more talent. Thankfully, she is entirely apolitical.

Unity is enjoying spending more time in London with Diana, although sadly her oldest sister is in the early stages of a messy divorce. I must say: I really don't understand what she is playing at. Diana has everything that matters in life: beauty, connections, an estate in Hampshire, houses in London and Dublin – and a rich husband.† And she appears to be throwing it all away for a silly fling with the fascist leader Sir Oswald Mosley.

Now, I have nothing against fascism per se. It strikes me as a jolly good alternative to some of the world's worst evils: communism, egalitarianism, Stanley Baldwin. If he's the best

---

* Like many aristocratic families, the Mitfords disapproved of sending their daughters to school. Not only did they consider such fripperies as organised education vulgar, but Lord Redesdale also worried that their calves might grow too thick from playing hockey. They made an exception, however, when it came to Unity, whom they found too stressful to educate at home. Unity's schools felt similarly, expelling her twice.

† Diana, whose many admirers included her second cousin, Randolph Churchill, was married to the fabulously wealthy Bryan Guinness, scion of the brewing empire. Evelyn Waugh dedicated his 1930 novel *Vile Bodies* to the couple.

that parliamentary democracy can produce, maybe it has run its course.

But I can't help wondering: isn't fascism a bit, well, common, just a teeny bit _foreign_?

It reminds one of all those ghastly people in the 1920s who styled themselves on Benito Mussolini, that frightful Italian. What was it they called themselves? The British Fascisti? The National Fascisti? Imagine! Even when the Imperial Fascist League was set up in 1928, a group with a decent Anglo-Saxon name, they were led by a vet best known for writing a Treatise on the One-Humped Camel in Health and Disease.

Sir Oswald Mosley, an Old Wykehamist with a glamorous war wound, is, I admit, cut from a different cloth. He seems to have slept with half my friends before, during and after his courtship of Lady Cynthia, Lord Curzon's daughter – another reason for Diana to steer well clear.* But he has hopped political parties almost as often as he has hopped beds, leaving the Conservatives and then Labour to found the doomed New Party last year.

---

* In 1933, Mosley told Robert Boothby, another rakish MP, that he had come clean to his wife about his affairs. 'All of them?' asked Boothby. 'All except her stepmother and her sister,' replied Mosley.

I can't see his latest incarnation, the British Union of Fascists, catching on either. He's attracting all the wrong sorts of people. Women. The working classes. Ex-servicemen called Sid or something, drinking the wrong sort of tea, out of mugs, can you imagine, at the wrong time of day, reminiscing about the Battle of Loos.

Much as I admire Germany, we didn't lose the Great War, we don't have fighting on the streets between Nazis and Communists and we don't have six million unemployed (I mean, honestly, it's almost impossible to hire decent servants these days, so surely everyone who actually wants a job can get one?).

Happy Christmas.

Sydney

1933

Dear Friends,

It has been lovely to spend time with so many of you during the course of another eventful year.

Those of you we haven't managed to see in person

might not know that the dreadful Mosley has now corrupted not one, but two, of our daughters.

His wife Lady Cynthia passed away from peritonitis in May, which was jolly sad for her, of course, but also rather inconvenient for me. I had hoped that Diana might see sense, having thrown in her lot with a womaniser who showed no inclination of leaving his wife. But now the path is clear for them both to remarry if they ever grow tired of living in sin.

Needless to say, Diana and I are not on speaking terms.

To make matters worse, Unity has become rather political this year, idolising her older sister's new man by selling his ghastly black shirts on the streets of Oxford. In August, she went to Nuremberg as part of a delegation of British fascists, becoming besotted (from a distance, thankfully) with that common little corporal, Adolf Hitler. Now back in England, she greets everyone with clicked heels and the Hitler salute, causing some raised eyebrows in the local post office.

Meanwhile, Unity's younger sister Jessica, whom we call our 'red sheep', has become a communist, much to their father's annoyance.

A dear chap from the Foreign Office came for dinner at Swinbrook earlier this year.

'Are you a fascist or a communist?' they asked him.

'Neither,' he said. 'I believe in democracy.'

'How wet,' they roared in unison.

How we laughed. Such larks!

Happy Christmas.

Sydney

1934

Dear Friends,

Would you believe it: Unity has taken her obsession with fascism to another level, spending the entire summer and autumn in Germany. She has even met Hitler, describing the encounter in a letter to her father as 'the most wonderful and beautiful day of my life'. Her copy of Mein Kampf has pride of place on her bookshelf (adjacent, I think, to the last book she read, in 1924, An ABC for Baby Patriots), signed by the Führer and pretty much every other luminary in the Third Reich.

'All those men,' says Nanny Blor. 'I do wish you wouldn't keep going to Germany.'

But Unity won't be deterred, mooning over the Stormtroopers as her 'Darling Storms'.

Meanwhile, I'm beginning to wonder whether the British Union of Fascists might have something about them after all. Their new January Club dinners are attracting some proper people – Earl Jellicoe, the Marquis of Tavistock, Lord Londonderry and so on. Even in somewhere called 'Leeds' (Nanny Blor had to fetch me a map), they have members such as Viscountess Downe and Lady Howard. They have also set up branches in schools such as Winchester, Marlborough and Stowe.

So I wasn't sure what to make of the rally in Kensington Olympia in June this year. There were 12,000 people in the audience, including 150 MPs, numerous aristocrats and blackshirted thugs. You can imagine the scene: floodlights; flags; loudspeakers piping Mosley's voice throughout the arena. Every time someone heckled, Mosley would stop speaking, the searchlights would be trained on the heckler and he would be beaten on the spot with knuckledusters and truncheons.

You can't make an omelette without breaking eggs, as Diana likes to say.* But can't they be violent in their privacy of their own homes?

In any case, all this déclassé thuggery appears to be coming back to bite them. Having started the year with 50,000 members, the British Union of Fascists now has only 5,000. They have also lost the support of Lord Rothermere, owner of the Daily Mail.†

Maybe Diana will take up with someone more successful now. Let's hope so.

Happy Christmas.

Sydney

---

* When Diana Mitford married Bryan Guinness in 1929, her new mother-in-law was astounded at her ability to fry eggs. 'I've never heard of such a thing,' she said. 'It's too clever.'
† Lord Rothermere regretted the infamous 'Hurrah for the Black Shirts' column he wrote in January 1934, especially after Hitler's violent 'Night of the Long Knives' purge further tainted the fascist cause in June.

1936

Dear Friends,

Well, what a year! Where to start?! With Unity's visit to the Berlin Olympics? With the 'Battle of Cable Street' in London in October? With Diana's marriage to Sir Oswald Mosley two days later? Or with the family's meeting in November with the darling Führer (I admit it: I'm a fan)?

In the summer, as a thank you for the spectacularly anti-Semitic letter she sent to Der Stürmer last year (now there's a newspaper that doesn't flip-flop around like the Daily Mail),* Unity was given a box at the Berlin Olympics, where she was seated next to Eva Braun, Hitler's girlfriend.†

The "blissful Führer", as Unity calls him, really seems to relax in her company, doing

---

* Unity Mitford's friendship with Julius Streicher, the shaven-headed editor of *Der Stürmer*, the Nazi rag, was even more extraordinary than her relationship with Hitler. Even other Nazis avoided Streicher during the Nuremberg trials, viewing him as a vulgar monster.
† Eva Braun was so affronted by the presence of Unity Mitford at the Berlin Olympics that she staged a suicide attempt to regain Hitler's attention.

hilarious impressions of Mussolini and showering her with tasteful gifts such as gold swastikas with his signature engraved on the back.* I remember Unity once telling a school friend that she hoped to become the power behind a mighty throne when she grew up, so it is wonderful to see her realising her ambition. She is establishing herself as quite the helpful diplomatic go-between for our two great nations, sharing harmless titbits with the dear Führer, such as the fact that London has no air defences.

How prescient that we gave her the middle name of Valkyrie when she was born in Swastika, Canada, back in 1914!

Unity has also achieved some remarkable familial diplomacy, introducing Diana to Hitler, with the result that the Führer attended Diana's secret wedding to Sir Oswald in Goebbels's drawing room (although I imagine he called it his 'lounge') in October.

---

* 'She was highly in love with Hitler,' wrote Rudolf Hess, the deputy Führer, about Unity Mitford. 'We could see it easily, her face brightened up, her eyes gleaming, staring at Hitler. Hero-worship.' And the feeling appears to have been mutual, despite their relationship never being consummated. 'He behaved,' wrote Hess, 'as a 17-year-old would.'

It must have been a blessed relief for the two of them, only two days after the so-called 'Battle of Cable Street', during which hundreds of thousands of perfectly dreadful East End Londoners, Jews and socialists aggressively picked a fight with the police for no reason at all and Mosley's Blackshirts bravely ran away.*

At least the membership of the British Union of Fascists has risen in the aftermath. I'm rather warming to them, I must say, especially after they became more anti-Semitic last year to stir up trouble in areas such as London, Leeds and Manchester.

Of course, this is all coming straight out of Hitler's playbook, whom we were lucky enough to meet in November, thanks to an introduction by Unity. Pamela, our second daughter, described him as 'an old farmer in a brown suit', and Jessica and Nancy refused to meet him. But the rest of us were completely bowled over, my

---

* In October 1936, some 77,000 people signed a petition asking for the Home Secretary to ban Mosley's provocative march through the East End of London. When he refused on the grounds of political liberty, a huge number of people turned out to confront Mosley's Blackshirts. However, the myth that Cable Street 'defeated' British fascism has gathered momentum over the reality. The only fighting occurred between police and elements of the anti-fascist groups. And some of the worst anti-Semitic violence in London took place the following weekend, in Stepney.

husband vowing to speak up enthusiastically in favour of the Anschluss in the House of Lords if Mussolini ever stops blocking Hitler's intentions in Austria. Meanwhile, the Führer listened most attentively, while I described the best way of making bread. And in return, he inspired me to look up the 'recipe' for global Jewish domination. The Protocols of the Elders of Zion is such a convincing text, don't you think?*

The only dark cloud in an otherwise glorious year was the abdication of King Edward VIII this month, despite the Blackshirts jogging round Newcastle chanting, 'Two, four, six, eight, the King must not abdicate'. Such a shame. He could have been almost as useful as Unity in fostering harmonious understanding with Germany.

May the ~~peace~~ iron will of the Christ child be yours this Christmas.

Sydney

---

* Despite being conclusively shown as a hoax by *The Times* in 1921, *The Protocols of the Elders of Zion,* which was largely cooked up by Russian Tsarist security services in the late 19th century, continued to excite conspiracy theorists throughout the 20th (and 21st) century. Lady Redesdale inherited her anti-Semitism from her father, and it was turbocharged by her meeting with Hitler in 1936.

1939

Dear Friends (if we have any left),

Well, frankly, it's been an absolutely dreadful year. For a while, it seemed as if the stars were finally aligning for the British Union of Fascists, whose principled support of appeasement saw their membership climb back to 30,000 by the beginning of the year. Why bother about Czechoslovakia, they argued? It's just a contrived country. Why guarantee the borders of Poland? It's rotten and corrupt. Give Germany room, they said. Don't strangle or embattle the poor Nazis.

Did those warmongers Neville Chamberlain and Clement Attlee listen to these small, calm voices of reason? Did they heck!

Diana was sensible enough to return home from Germany before war was declared, the better to support her husband in his ongoing campaign for peace.

Poor Unity wasn't so lucky. On 3 September, the day Britain foolishly declared war on Germany, she left the Munich flat that had been taken from a Jewish couple and given to her by the Führer, walked to the Englischer Garten in the city centre and shot herself in the head with a pearl-handled pistol. She is made of such strong stuff that she survived the small calibre bullet. Hitler, Goebbels and Ribbentrop all sent the most delightful flowers while she recuperated in hospital. And when she came to, she tried and failed to commit suicide a second time by swallowing her swastika badge.

On 8 November, the darling Führer visited and arranged for Unity to return home to England via Switzerland. I met her in Bern and took her to hospital in Oxford. Unable to extract the bullet from her brain, the doctors say that the poor thing will remain incontinent, with the mental age of a bright ten-year-old, for the rest of her life.

I am sharing these unpleasant details to dampen

rumours that Unity was bearing the Führer's child, in which there is (sadly) no truth.*

I will write again next year, if I have happier news.

Sydney

Unity's injury in 1939 was the first in a series of misfortunes for the Mitford family. The following May, Churchill's amendment of the Emergency Powers Act led to the arrest of Sir Oswald and Lady Diana Mosley, alongside almost 750 fellow fascists. Diana remained interned with her husband for three years, by which time her parents' marriage had broken down. Fundamentally a patriot, Lord Redesdale had immediately swung behind the British war effort in 1939, whereas his wife's fascism saw her remain an enthusiast for Hitler. The strain was too much for their relationship to bear.

Family divisions also saw Jessica, the communist, emigrate to America, and Nancy, the novelist, to France. Tom, the only son, was killed in action in Burma in 1945 (having been posted to Asia after refusing to fight against the Germans), and Unity died in 1948 from meningitis relating to her bullet wound.

Sir Oswald, a Holocaust denier, stood once more for

---

* Serious biographers treat the notion that Unity Mitford was carrying Hitler's child with as much respect as the idea that the Führer escaped his Berlin bunker in 1945 for a peaceful retirement in Argentina.

election, in 1959, on a racist ticket in riot-torn North Kensington. He received only 8 per cent of the vote and emigrated to France, where he died in 1980. Lady Diana outlived her husband by another decade, still expressing her admiration for Hitler in a controversial appearance on the BBC's *Desert Island Discs* in 1989.

Her musical choices included two pieces by Wagner – and the Procol Harum song 'A Whiter Shade of Pale'.

Monkeys

TOP TEN MONKEYS IN HISTORY

After the (mainly) ecstatic feedback about our episode on 'Top Ten Dogs', we decided to repeat the feat for the monkeys and apes who have made the largest impact on their primate cousins over the last 2,000 years. From rock stars to the railway, mascots to the military, here is the definitive list, in chronological order.

An Anonymous Middle-Class Mediterranean Macaque

Era: End of the fifth century AD

Owner: Unknown

Claim to fame: In 2001, archaeologists in the Spanish town of Llívia, on the Pyrenean border with France, discovered the skeleton of a five-and-a-half-year-old macaque with bad teeth, buried alongside food, ornaments and assorted military kit. So who was this mysterious macaque? Was the Roman Empire in such a perilous state by the fifth century that it was recruiting monkeys into its legions? Or was this a Visigothic monkey who had helped to depose Romulus Augustus, the last Roman Emperor of the West, in AD 476? The latter is *slightly* more likely – belt buckles are associated with barbarian burials because the Romans didn't bury people with funerary goods – but a more plausible explanation is that it was a mascot for a regiment. The macaque could also have been a pet: monkeys were domesticated across the Roman Empire, with similar burial sites found in Pompeii, Poitiers – and Yorkshire. It is thought that, when the Empire fell, some barbarians continued to, well, *ape* the Roman custom as a marker of abandoned imperial class. But the simple – delicious – truth is that *no one* is entirely sure, allowing *everyone* to project their own narrative onto this mystery monkey.

Abu Qais, the Horse-Riding Monkey

Era: Seventh-century Syria

Owner: Yazid, the second Umayyad Caliph, a man hated by the Shi'a for killing Husayn, the grandson of the prophet Muhammad, at the Battle of Karbala; and hated by other Muslims for drinking too much and owning a monkey (another way in which the Umayyads were accused of copying the Caesars).

Claim to fame: Yazid trained Abu Qais, his favourite monkey, as a jockey, entering him in horse races. Unfortunately, Abu Qais fell from his horse and died.

Legacy: Yazid ordered that Abu Qais be wrapped in a white shroud and mourned by his subjects. Few of them were impressed by the instruction. 'Curses be on the one who became our caliph while his closest friends were monkeys,' wrote the Muslim scholar al-Tabari.

The Hanged Hartlepool Monkey

Era: Napoleonic Wars, 1803–1815

Owner: The French navy

Claim to fame: During England's epic struggle with Napoleonic France at the beginning of the nineteenth century, a French ship was dashed against the rocks off the coast of Hartlepool in County Durham. Everyone drowned except a single survivor, a monkey in French naval uniform. Having never seen a monkey or a Frenchman before, the locals struggled to tell the difference between a hairy, ill-groomed creature spouting gibberish – and a monkey. So they hanged it as a spy.

The twist in the tail: How true is this story? A similar tale is told along the length of England's isolated fishing communities, from Cornwall to Tyneside. There is also some suggestion that the story was retrofitted to suit a mid-nineteenth-century song – 'In former times, 'mid war and strife / When French invasion threatened life / And all was armoured to the knife / The fishermen hung the monkey.'

Monkey for mayor: Regardless, the people of Hartlepool have decided to double down on the slur against their ancestors. In 1999, Hartlepool United Football Club adopted the hanged monkey as their mascot. Wittily, they called him H'Angus. Three years later, when Tony Blair's government decided to introduce elected mayors, Stuart Drummond, the man inside the mascot, campaigned as the monkey. Running on the slogan, 'Vote for H'Angus – he gives a monkey's', and the promise to give every schoolchild a banana, he beat the Labour candidate by 500 votes. Drummond won two further terms before the Labour councillors got so fed up that they abolished the position of directly elected mayor. H'Angus is, therefore, the only non-human primate to date to have held elected office.

Jacco Macacco, the Victorian Sporting Star

Era: 1820s London

Owner: Charles Aistrop, who ran the Westminster pit, a hugely popular arena for Victorian blood-sports such as dog-fighting and badger-baiting.

Origin story: It is disputed how Jacco Macacco, a rhesus macaque, actually ended up in Westminster. According to William Pitt Lennox, the author of the 1860 book *Pictures of Sporting Life and Character*, he worked his way through the lower fighting divisions of the Chick Lane and Tottenham Court Road pits, where he was known as the Hoxton Ape, before being sold to Aistrop. However, Aistrop himself said that Jacco belonged to a Hoxton silversmith who had to buy a sheet of iron to protect himself from an aggressive pet who had taken three fingers off his previous owner during a dispute over a saucer of milk. Tired of being attacked, the silversmith set a dog on Jacco – who promptly defeated the dog. Spotting an opportunity, the silversmith sold him directly to Aistrop.

Claim to fame: However Jacco ended up at the Westminster pit, he quickly became one of its biggest stars, eclipsing a dog called Billy who had famously killed a hundred rats in six minutes and twenty-five seconds in October 1822. Weighing around 5.5kg, Jacco would challenge a dog of up to twice his weight, overcoming fourteen opponents in cruel, brutal bouts.* 'His mode of attack,' wrote Lennox, 'was first to present his back or neck to the dog and to

---

* George Charles Grantley FitzHardinge Berkeley, a Whig MP, wrote in his memoir that he believed these fights were rigged, the dogs injured before the bouts in order to engineer a more dramatic spectacle.

shift and tumble about until he could lay hold on the arm or chest when he ascended to the windpipe, clawing and biting away, which usually occupied him for a minute and a half... after every bout, the monkey exhibited a frightful appearance, being deluged with blood. But it was that of his opponent alone.'

Death: The cause of Jacco's death is disputed. According to one account, he died following a fight against a dog with the confusing name of Puss, an obsolete breed of bull-and-terrier (confusingly, not a bullterrier) owned by Tom Cribb, the All England boxing champion. In June 1821, with the sizeable sum of £50 at stake, Puss severed Jacco's carotid artery in a fight lasting thirty minutes and ripped off his jaw. Jacco lingered for a further two hours and then died. That, at least, was the story of Richard Martin, the MP for Galway and a passionate campaigner against cruelty to animals. Aistrop, the owner of the Westminster pit, made the radically different claim that Jacco defeated Puss (who survived) in two and a half minutes before dying fifteen months later of an unrelated illness.

Legacy: According to Aistrop, an uninjured Jacco was stuffed and mounted on an admirer's mantelpiece. Richard Martin, who called Jacco's fight with Puss the nadir of British cruelty to animals, set up the Society for the Prevention of Cruelty to Animals three years later, the precursor to the RSPCA.*

---

* George IV thought this woke tosh, nicknaming Richard Martin 'Humanity Dick', so it fell to Queen Victoria to give the society royal approval.

Jenny, Darwin's Orangutan

Era: 1830s London

Owner: London Zoo, the world's oldest scientific zoo, founded by Sir Stamford Raffles, who was also the founder of Singapore. The three-year-old Jenny arrived there in 1837, having been sold by a sailor called Mr Moss for £150.

Claim to fame: Kept in a heated giraffe house, where she wore human clothes and drank tea, Jenny was visited on 28 March 1838 by Charles Darwin, who had returned from his five-year voyage on the *Beagle* two years earlier. Jenny clearly made a profound impression on Darwin who visited her regularly, writing in his notebook, 'Let man visit orang-utan in domestication, hear expressive whine, see its intelligence when spoken to, as if it understands every word said. See its affection. See its passion and rage. Sulkiness and very reactions of despair. And then let man boast of his proud pre-eminence. Man in his arrogance thinks himself a great work, worthy of the interposition of a deity. More humble, and I believe true, to consider him created from animals.'

Legacy: Jenny died a year later, in 1839, replaced by another orangutan also called Jenny, who was visited by Queen Victoria. Two decades later, Darwin published *On the Origin of Species*, advancing his theory of natural selection.

Jack, the South African Signal-Baboon

Era: 1880s Cape Town

Owner: James Wide, a railway signalman on the Cape Town to Port Elizabeth Railway whose nickname was Jumper, because he used to jump between the railway carriages.

Claim to fame: One day Wide mistimed his jump and lost both legs. So he bought a baboon called Jack to act as his carer, pushing him around in a wheelchair. Wide also taught Jack how to use the railway signals, training him to such perfection, according to a 1908 report in the periodical *The Railway Signal*, that 'he was able to sit in his cabin while the animal, which was chained up outside, pulled all the levers and points'. When someone complained to the railway authorities, they sent an investigator called George B. Howe who wrote in his report: 'Jack knows the signal whistle as well as I do and every one of the levers. It was very touching to see his fondness for his master. As I drew near, they were both sitting on the trolley, the baboon's arms around his master's neck, the other stroking Wide's face.' Jack became an official railway employee, paid 20 cents a day and a half bottle of beer a week. In nine years, he never made a single mistake.

Legacy: Hopefully, someone who runs the British railways is reading this.

Corporal Jackie, the Infantry Mascot

Era: First World War, Western Front

Owner: A South African farmer called Albert Marr who took Jackie, a baboon, with him when he was drafted into the Great War in 1915.

Claim to fame: Jackie became a mascot for the 3rd South African Infantry Regiment, who gave him a uniform, rations and a pay book. In return, he saluted officers, lit cigarettes for the men and used a knife and fork at the mess table. Having survived the Somme in 1916, the pair were sent to Egypt, where Marr was shot in the shoulder, Jackie licking his wound while others went to get help. Back in Belgium in April 1918, Jackie was hit by shrapnel and saved by a doctor who amputated and dressed his leg. While convalescing in England, he became a much-loved celebrity, marching/hopping in the Lord Mayor's Show and raising huge sums for the Red Cross. People paid half a crown to shake his hand or five shillings to kiss him.

Death: Returning to South Africa, where he was awarded a medal in Pretoria on 31 July 1920, Jackie went back to Marr's family farm. Tragically, the baboon remained affected by shellshock, dying of a heart attack in May 1921 in the belief that a thunderstorm over the high veld heralded the return of the Germans.

Scatter, the Scatological Film Star

Era: 1960s Memphis, USA

Owner: Elvis Presley

Claim to fame: Much like Rin Tin Tin, the Hollywood star who featured in our episode on History's Top Dogs, primates have also made waves on the large and small screen. Perhaps the most famous is Scatter, a baby chimpanzee, who starred in a show called *Scatter's World* on a Memphis TV channel. As he grew up, Scatter became increasingly aggressive and disruptive, with a fondness for throwing faecal matter. Undeterred, Elvis Presley offered to give him the run of Graceland, where Scatter added ripping down curtains and looking up women's skirts (something Elvis found hilarious) to his repertoire.

Death: There are conflicting accounts of Scatter's demise. According to one narrative, he was banished by Elvis to a climate-controlled room, where he died of a broken heart. Others say that he bit a maid, who poisoned him. And others probably think he is still alive, living on the moon with his owner.

Peter, the Swedish Chimp Artist

Era: Gothenburg, Sweden, 1964

Owner: Borås Zoo

Claim to fame: In 1964 an art gallery in Gothenburg put on an exhibition of modern art, including four works by an unknown, avant-garde French artist called Pierre

Brassau. The erudite *Göteborgs-Posten* sent its top critic, Rolf Anderberg, to survey the artwork. 'Brassau paints with powerful strokes but also a clear determination,' wrote Anderberg. 'His brushstrokes twist with furious fastidiousness. He's an artist who performs with the delicacy of a ballet dancer.' To the universal delight of modern art sceptics, it was later revealed that Brassau was actually a four-year-old chimpanzee from Borås Zoo, put up to the prank by a tabloid journalist on the rival *Göteborgs-Tidningen*. To Anderberg's credit, the critic retorted that 'they're still the best pictures in the exhibition'.

Bubbles, the Moonwalking Survivor

Era: 1980s Neverland, California, USA

Owner: Directly inspired by Elvis and Scatter, Michael Jackson clearly believed that no pop star's entourage was complete without the addition of a baby chimp. He sourced Bubbles from a Texas research facility in 1988 when the chimp was eight months old, moving him to Neverland, where he wore a nappy, slept in a crib in Jackson's room and watched films with the star. Emblematic of the singer's weirdness and infantilism, Bubbles featured in films, TV shows and music videos and accompanied his owner to Japan to have tea with the Mayor of Osaka. There are also unverified rumours that Bubbles had his own bodyguard; that Jackson taught him to moonwalk; and that Freddie Mercury was so annoyed with Jackson asking his chimpanzee for his opinion during the recording of a duet that he stormed off.

Legacy: We do, however, know that Bubbles copied Scatters' rock star behaviour, becoming increasingly aggressive and disruptive as he grew up. In 2005 he was sent to a sanctuary for apes in Florida where he remains to this day, 'occasionally spitting water or throwing sand (with amazing accuracy) at strangers, just to see how they react'. Considered 'artistic, gentle and shy' by his caregivers, he often turns his back when he sees a camera.

Napoleon

WHAT SORT OF MAN WAS THE YOUNG NAPOLEON?

Hero of France, transformer of the political map of Europe, begetter of a civil code that is still largely extant today and emphatic victor of Austerlitz, Jena-Auerstedt and Borodino (if not Waterloo), Napoleon Bonaparte is one of the greatest men in all of great-men history.

The general's well-known journey from First Consul to Emperor of France to master of Europe ended in exile on the remote island of St Helena in 1815, where he was brought low by a combination of the Russian winter, the British navy and the Duke of Wellington. But where did it all begin?

As the French Revolution was kicking off in July 1789, young Napoleon, not quite twenty years old, was enrolled as a junior artillery officer at the military college in Auxonne, in eastern France. Join our intrepid time traveller as he interviews Napoleon a day after the fall of the Bastille to see if we can get under the skin of a moody, unimpressive teenager from an obscure Corsican family.

15 July 1789

TIME TRAVELLER: My God, it worked! You there, young man, are you Napoleon Bonaparte?

NAPOLEONE: Who are you calling *Napoleon*? Bah! What an ugly, French-sounding way of pronouncing my name. I'm *Napoleone Buonaparte* the Corsican, with an E and a U, and don't you forget it. I've been called *Nabuleone*. I'll even accept *Nabulio*. But don't ever mistake me for a Frenchman again.

TIME TRAVELLER: Gosh, they told me you were touchy but—

NAPOLEONE: Who told you that? Who are you?

TIME TRAVELLER: I'm from the future.

NAPOLEONE: *Dio mio.* Well, maybe that explains your baggy blue breeches and your strange hat... unless this is another one of those jokes like the French boys liked to play on me at school? I'll make you regret it with my fists if it is.

NAPOLEON

TIME TRAVELLER: No, I'm the real deal, I promise.

NAPOLEONE: So you can tell me all about the future?

TIME TRAVELLER: I can't tell you much. I don't want to change the course of history – that's your job. But I'm interested in finding out a bit more about your early life. Some Hollywood executives are making a film about you and—

NAPOLEONE: Some Hollywood what-nows are doing what-now?

TIME TRAVELLER: They're making a film. It's a bit like a play, but the seats are more comfortable and no one minds if you fiddle with your phone. Anyway, they want to know if it's worth having a few scenes set when you're a teenager.

NAPOLEONE: Hold on – there's going to be a play about me? Am I important?

TIME TRAVELLER: You make the cut for a few fantasy dinner parties.

NAPOLEONE: I knew it! I shall be written in the pages of history as Signor Buonaparte, the great Corsican who liberated my beloved homeland from the tyranny of France.

TIME TRAVELLER: The great Corsican what-now?

NAPOLEONE: When the day comes, I'll be ready to fight for the freedom of my fatherland.*

TIME TRAVELLER: I'm going to level with you: our film

---

* Corsican freedom fighters had long campaigned for independence from Genoa, their masters for five centuries. In 1768, the year before Napoleon was born, Genoa sold Corsica to France, which violently crushed the Corsican independence movement and made the islanders French subjects. This wasn't the outcome for which the Corsicans had fought the Genoese.

isn't about Corsican nationalism. We don't want a *Matrix Resurrections* flop on our hands.

NAPOLEONE: A what *Resurrections*? Okay, never mind. This… film must be about my writings, then. Sometimes I wonder which will be more famous, my political tracts or my fiction.

TIME TRAVELLER: You write fiction?

NAPOLEONE: You haven't read my Gothic novels set on Corsica? *Le Comte d'Essex* is my best – full of blood and horror. I also like stories that involve vengeful Corsicans massacring French soldiers. But my dream is to write a great history of Corsica. Tell me – will I ever finish my Corsican history book?

TIME TRAVELLER: I really don't know.

NAPOLEONE: What's the use of you, then, you imbecile? I'm not going to help with your stupid research unless I can find out something about my future.

TIME TRAVELLER: Fine. I'll let you know about the next seven years – up until 1796.

NAPOLEONE: I'll be twenty-seven by then. Will I have achieved anything?

TIME TRAVELLER: Have you heard the news about the Storming of the Bastille?

NAPOLEONE: Yes. The people rose up in Paris just yesterday against the tyranny of King Louis XVI. The French state has repressed them for too long – just like it's repressed us Corsicans. And now the Bastille – the very symbol of the *ancien régime* – has fallen.* Perhaps it's the start of great things for my beloved Corsica.

TIME TRAVELLER: You're in favour of the storming of the Bastille, then?

NAPOLEONE: Oh, yes – unlike my comrades in the artillery corps. They think the riots will lead to anarchy. But they are stupid Frenchmen, and they fear change, whereas like a proud Corsican I can see what an opportunity it might bring.

TIME TRAVELLER: What kind of opportunity?

NAPOLEONE: The King will have no choice but to meet the people's demands. I'm off to Corsica as soon as I can get leave, to see how I can take advantage of this great moment.

TIME TRAVELLER: But what are you doing in the French army if you feel so strongly about Corsica?

NAPOLEONE: Well, my father wanted the best for me, so he sent me to French military academies from the age of nine. After a horrible school in Brienne-le-Château, I entered the École Militaire in Paris five years ago. It was miserable. Those French brutes sneered at me for reading so many books about ancient Rome. They mocked my accent, they laughed at me, they said I was too serious. They called me humourless, moody and unfriendly. But how could I not be so? I've seen the bodies of brave Corsican rebels, strung up as a warning by French occupiers. I've seen—

---

* The annual celebration of the Storming of the Bastille, which triggered the French Revolution, involves fireworks and revelry, just like Britain's Bonfire Night, which celebrates the *failure* of a violent action against the status quo. Feel free to draw your own conclusions about national character from this.

TIME TRAVELLER: And yet you still joined the French artillery?

NAPOLEONE: I had to get on in life, didn't I? Four years ago, when I sat the exam for the artillery, I came forty-second out of fifty-eight candidates – a pretty good result, you have to admit. I'm the first Corsican ever to graduate from the École Militaire. What? You look at me like I'm a fool for coming forty-second.

TIME TRAVELLER: I didn't say anything. There's no need to be so defensive.

NAPOLEONE: Who are you calling defensive? Insult me again and I'll beat you right out of the eighteenth century.

TIME TRAVELLER: Sorry. So, are you going to see your family in Corsica?

NAPOLEONE: Yes, they're all there. I've got three sisters, four brothers, and five others who died in infancy. Now, look – are you going to tell me about my future or not?

TIME TRAVELLER: Okay, well, to be perfectly honest, you're walking into a huge mess. While you spend the next three years on Corsica, the Corsicans are going to fight one another constantly.

NAPOLEONE: Typical.

TIME TRAVELLER: There will be riots and murders and factionalism as the island responds to the events in Paris, trying to work out if it is more in favour of independence or revolution. Next year your great hero, the Corsican nationalist Pasquale Paoli, will return to the island—

NAPOLEONE: Paoli! Paoli is the hero of my whole family. He calls himself the General of the Corsican Nation. It is he who will strike the first decisive blow against the hated French!

TIME TRAVELLER: Well, he does get rid of them – briefly – but then he ends up in exile in London. And you also have to leave Corsica in 1792, to defend yourself in Paris against accusations of treachery.

NAPOLEONE: A traitor to the cause of Corsican nationalism? Never.

TIME TRAVELLER: No, a traitor to France. You remain in the French army and they're worried about your activities in Corsica. But Paris is in such turmoil that no one really cares.

NAPOLEONE: If there is one thing I cannot stand, it is disorder. If only there was a strong leader who could give this new revolutionary era some firm direction.

TIME TRAVELLER: Funny you should say that.

NAPOLEONE: What? Why?

TIME TRAVELLER: No reason. You're in Paris in September 1792 when the monarchy finally falls and the revolutionaries take over the government entirely. You start writing firebrand political pamphlets in support of the Revolution.

NAPOLEONE: I bet I write excellent firebrand political pamphlets.

TIME TRAVELLER: You do. You're still part of the French army, so when the Revolution's military leaders decide to launch an attack on Sardinia, you get sent there in 1793. It's meant to be an easy, morale-boosting victory, but it's a disaster and you're defeated in just a few weeks. You return briefly to Corsica, where you're arrested and dramatically rescued at gunpoint by your relatives. Paoli views the Bonapartes as prone to street violence and too closely aligned with the revolution. Your whole family ends up fleeing the island before you're murdered.

NAPOLEONE: This gets worse and worse. Will my siblings be okay?

TIME TRAVELLER: Very much so – you'll see to that.*

TIME TRAVELLER: And now begins your journey towards identifying as a Frenchman.

NAPOLEONE: My journey towards *what*?

TIME TRAVELLER: It's not so bad, I promise. After Louis XVI is executed in January 1793, there's a chance to build a new kind of state, where everyone – even you – can feel included. And the French Revolution will leave so many gaps in the military chain of command that there's a real chance for a promising young soldier to rise rapidly through the ranks. And that's what happens to you.

NAPOLEONE: Finally, some encouraging news.

TIME TRAVELLER: France's neighbours declare war in an effort to re-establish the French monarchy. In August 1793, the British navy captures the crucial port of Toulon. You're part of the army sent to recapture the town. When the artillery commander is wounded, you're promoted because the generals think that all your over-the-top pamphlets—

NAPOLEONE: Hey!

---

* Napoleon's siblings did very well indeed out of his nepotism. His four brothers became King of Spain, King of Holland, King of Westphalia and Prince of Canino and Musignano; his three sisters became Grand Duchess of Tuscany, Princess of Guastalla and Queen of Naples.

TIME TRAVELLER: —prove that you're a sound revolutionary. So you take command of the artillery, and you do a brilliant job. You have the tactical vision to see that it's a better idea to capture the heights outside Toulon, which will force the British ships to retreat, than to attempt a direct attack on Toulon itself. You're the hero of the hour, wounded in the leg by a bayonet while leading your men.* In December 1793, the British general surrenders, and Toulon is liberated.†

NAPOLEONE: Ha. Didn't I tell those good-for-nothings at school that I'd show them what kind of man I am?

TIME TRAVELLER: And then you have another lucky escape. You make a good friend during the siege, called Augustin Robespierre. His brother Maximilien has become one of the key men running the show in Paris, and he's trying to 'purify' the Revolution by executing his political enemies. Unfortunately, everyone seems like a potential political enemy. Tens of thousands of people are executed by the summer of 1794.

NAPOLEONE: Sounds messy.

TIME TRAVELLER: It's unbelievably messy. And you're lucky to avoid this Terror yourself, because it ends up turning on itself. After the surrender of Toulon, Augustin Robespierre invites you to Paris with him, but you decline because you want more military adventures. If you'd gone

---

* When an artilleryman was killed near him in the heat of battle, Napoleon seized the ramrod for the dead man's cannon and loaded it himself. Unfortunately the ramrod gave him scabies, a condition that afflicted him for years.
† General Charles O'Hara had also surrendered at the Battle of Yorktown during the American Revolutionary War. As such, he has the dubious distinction of being the only man to surrender personally to both George Washington and Napoleon.

to Paris to join the Robespierre faction, you would probably have ended up executed along with the brothers.

NAPOLEONE: I like men who are lucky.

TIME TRAVELLER: So instead of having your head cut off in 1794, you're promoted to Brigadier General, at the age of twenty-four. You go to Paris as it's recovering from the Terror, and all the Parisians are having decadent orgiastic parties.

NAPOLEONE: That doesn't sound like my scene at all.

TIME TRAVELLER: It's not. You're a fish out of water. But you befriend a corrupt, cynical man called Paul Barras, who has his finger in every pie. In October 1795, when the mob rises up in one of the Parisian districts, Barras gives you the job of suppressing it. You do so with brutal effectiveness. Hundreds of people are killed, Barras's regime is secured, and your reward is to be appointed Commander of the Army of the Interior.

NAPOLEONE: You know what, I'm starting to like you.

TIME TRAVELLER: And now that you're established as one of the key players in Paris, you begin your great love affair with the woman you will marry.

NAPOLEONE: Now we're talking.

TIME TRAVELLER: Have you had much luck with the ladies yet?

NAPOLEONE: My stupid French comrades are always chasing girls. I think it's very undignified.

TIME TRAVELLER: I'll take that as a no.

NAPOLEONE: I'm not sure the girls take much notice of me.

NAPOLEON

TIME TRAVELLER: I can imagine. I knew you'd be short, but you're a bit scrawnier and scruffier than I expected.

NAPOLEONE: You knew I'd be short? What *exactly* do you mean by that?

TIME TRAVELLER: Well, to be perfectly honest, you're well known for overcompensating for your height.

NAPOLEONE: How dare you!

TIME TRAVELLER: You've got a bit of a Napoleon complex, which – oh God –

NAPOLEONE: I have no idea what you're talking about. I don't need to compensate for anything. I had a wonderful evening of amorous triumph with a prostitute two years ago. I met her in the street and talked about all the things that matter between two young people: the mingling of souls, the philosophical implications of the conjoining of two youthful bodies—

TIME TRAVELLER: I bet she loved that.

NAPOLEONE: Actually she said that she was cold, and that she wanted to go back to her flat to get on with it.

TIME TRAVELLER: Don't worry. You will fall in love properly one day. Her name is Josephine.

NAPOLEONE: Tell me about her.

TIME TRAVELLER: She's from Martinique, she's six years older than you, and her first husband gets executed during the Revolution. She's been Barras's girlfriend, but he wants to offload her onto you. You meet her at a society ball in 1795. Also, she doesn't have any teeth.

NAPOLEONE: She sounds perfect. Is she a good lover?

TIME TRAVELLER: She's phenomenal. She's especially good at the zig-zags.

NAPOLEONE: What are the zig-zags?

TIME TRAVELLER: Nobody knows. But you like them.*

NAPOLEONE: *Dio mio.* I'm excited.

TIME TRAVELLER: You're also very keen on her not washing.

NAPOLEONE: Oh, stop. I'm getting all hot and bothered.

TIME TRAVELLER: By this point you've come up with a plan to invade France's great enemy, Austria, which wants to restore the French monarchy. Before heading off on this expedition in 1796 via Italy, you decide to make an honest woman of Josephine.

NAPOLEONE: I marry her?

TIME TRAVELLER: Kind of. You're two hours late to the ceremony, so the guy who was meant to conduct it has gone home. The replacement isn't legally qualified, so technically the wedding is invalid. And that, I'm afraid, is all I'm allowed to tell you.

NAPOLEONE: Well, it's better than nothing. And have I given you good material for this play of yours? Have you learned lots of important things about my unswerving passion for a Corsica that will soon be free?†

---

* The only tantalising clue we have about Josephine's bedroom zig-zags is that Napoleon enjoyed them a lot.
† Corsica was occupied by the British between 1794 and 1796 – and by the Italians and Germans between 1942 and 1943. Otherwise, it has remained a French territory to this day.

TIME TRAVELLER: To be completely honest, I'm not sure the studio will want to include many scenes about Corsican nationalism. The film is already several hours too long. But I've given you some good news, haven't I? By March 1796, you'll have made a name for yourself, you'll have married Josephine (sort of), and history will beckon you and your army to Italy for the start of the Napoleonic Wars.

NAPOLEONE: The start of what?

TIME TRAVELLER: Er, nothing.

New York City

'WELCOME TO THE JUNGLE': A TOURIST BOARD LEAFLET FROM 1978

Welcome, brave traveller, to New York City, the Big ~~Rotting~~ Apple, the City So ~~Full of Vice~~ Nice They Named It Twice, the City That Never Sleeps ~~(with its windows open in case one of its 20,000 gang members murders you in your bed)~~.

Are you sure you want to visit? You're not just transiting through JFK to get to Florida? Okay, great. Step this way. You're in for a real treat.

Shall we start by addressing the elephant in the room?

If you'd arrived at this airport three years ago, you'd have been met by members of the police union handing out leaflets entitled, 'Welcome to Fear City'. And perhaps they weren't exaggerating. When Mayor Abraham Beame took office in January 1974, he had to borrow money at interest rates of 10 per cent just to pay the city's workers. He ended up firing 63,000 people, including thousands of teachers, hospital staff, firefighters and police officers.

This didn't help a murder rate that had risen 173 per cent – or a rape rate that had risen 112 per cent – between 1966 and 1973.

And then the police didn't help themselves by handing out those scaremongering leaflets, blocking the Brooklyn Bridge with barricades and throwing beer bottles at people's cars.

Four years on, we're confident that things are slowly improving in the NYPD. We have been acting on the recommendations of the Knapp Commission, 1972, which found systematic corruption in the force, including reports of officers selling cocaine, taking bribes from pornographers and betraying informants to the mob.

Maybe don't ask anyone in uniform for directions, though. Or for the time. Or for help.

Now, some of you might also have read about the great blackout that lasted over twenty-four hours last July, plunging all five boroughs of New York City into darkness as subway trains, elevators, air conditioners, televisions and refrigerators suddenly wheezed to a halt.

Perhaps you saw a copy of Rupert Murdoch's *New York Post*, emblazoned with the headline '24 Hours of Terror'. The tabloid newspaper gained tens of thousands of extra readers thanks to its descriptions of 'scum' and 'animal' looters who broke into 2,000 stores, set off 1,000 fires and caused hundreds of millions of dollars of damage.

Or maybe you read the *New York Times*'s more sober reporting, echoing President Carter's opinion that the looting was principally a protest against unemployment, which ran at 70 per cent among African Americans and 80 per cent among New York's Hispanic population.

Wherever you get your news, you might be worried that something similar could happen again this summer during your visit. Will there be another freak lightning strike on an electricity substation in the Hudson River, blacking out the city? The scenes that followed were astonishing. Will we, once more, see an affluent shopper in Midtown Manhattan stuffing a bag of ice into her Louis Vuitton handbag? Or dozens of people driving up to hi-fi stores on Broadway, just south of Columbia University, and filling their trucks? Will fifty brand-new cars be driven brazenly out of a showroom in the Bronx? Numerous neighborhoods in Brooklyn be ransacked by their own communities? Fire crews be bombarded with rocks by jeering looters? Four thousand people be arrested – until the police have to resort to cracking their skulls instead because they can't fit them in the cells any more?

We certainly hope not – although maybe buy a flashlight and some batteries just in case. And if it does all kick off again (and you don't fancy filling your own boots), why not head to the Metropolitan Opera, where the harpist spontaneously struck up 'Dancing in the Dark' last summer, or the Upper East Side, where waiters moved the tables into the street and illuminated them with car headlights?

In any case, there is a strong feeling that New York City is finally turning a corner after several decades of decline from its 1950s heyday.

Whatever Robert de Niro's Travis Bickle said in *Taxi Driver* two years ago, this city is not 'an open sewer full of filth and scum' any more.

A serial killer, who killed six people in Queens and the Bronx between 1976 and 1977, has just been caught and sentenced to life imprisonment.* Mr Beame lost the mayoral election last November to Ed Koch, a fellow Democrat who has vowed to crack down on crime, take on the unions and allow private developers a freer hand when it comes to developing the city.

This approach is already reaping dividends, with work recently starting on an exciting new hotel near Grand Central Station, spearheaded by an ambitious young developer called Donald J. Trump.

Mr Trump is just the kind of glamorous, sophisticated and squeaky-clean resident who will make this city the envy of the world once more.

Have a great stay (and don't forget to bolt your door)!

The New York City Tourist Board

---

* Just as Jack the Ripper, the nineteenth-century British serial killer, used to write letters to the police, David Berkowitz, the serial killer known as 'Son of Sam', wrote regular updates to a columnist on the *Daily News*. 'Hello from the gutters of N.Y.C. which are filled with dog manure, vomit, stale wine, urine and blood,' read one of them.

Oppenheimer
THE FBI'S OPPENHEIMER FILES

J. Robert Oppenheimer's development of the first atomic bomb ended the Second World War, kickstarted a Cold War and ushered in a nuclear age under whose shadow we continue to live today.

Was the Manhattan Project, which Oppenheimer oversaw in the Los Alamos desert between 1942 and 1945, a scientific marvel that saved hundreds of thousands of lives, bringing the war against Japan to an early end? Or had the scientist unleashed a terrible technology that will for ever hang over the entire human race? Oppenheimer himself struggled to answer these questions – a struggle beautifully illustrated in the eponymous film released in the summer of 2023.*

---

* *Oppenheimer* narrowly lost to *Barbie* in the titanic #barbenheimer box office struggle, but ultimately won more awards.

Later, Oppenheimer famously became one the most prominent victim of America's anti-communist purges of the 1940s and 1950s after the FBI compiled a staggering 1,000 pages of files on him. Here is what some of them might have looked like.

Document 12-4167, March 1941

TO: Headquarters, Federal Bureau of Investigation

INFORMATION CONCERNING: Julius Robert Oppenheimer

During our routine monitoring of suspected communist operatives, we've come across a curious individual. Name of Oppenheimer – we found his numberplate on a car parked outside a gathering of known commies. We're opening a file on him, and we're adding him to the list of suspicious persons to be arrested in the case of a national emergency. The passing of the Lend-Lease Act earlier this month means that we are no longer neutral with regards to Hitler's war in Europe. So we have to be very careful about who our friends are – and who they aren't.

Oppenheimer's birth certificate says that he was born in New York in April 1904. Parents: German-Jewish immigrants. The father, Julius, made a lot of money from a clothing company, and likes collecting art: Rembrandt, Picasso, van Gogh – he's done very well for himself. The mother is a painter called Ella. House on Upper West Side, a summer house in Long Island – nice, comfortable childhood. Every reason in the world to be satisfied with capitalism.

Our inquiries have revealed that little Oppenheimer was a smart kid – he loved poetry and geology at school – and was by all accounts a bit of a loner. He had an unfortunate experience at summer camp when he was fourteen and ratted on his campmates for telling him the facts of life. Our source says that they stripped him, painted his buttocks and genitals in green paint – and locked him overnight in an icehouse.

He turned up at Harvard a hard worker, but still no social skills. Wrote alarming erotic poetry in his spare time and taught himself Sanskrit for fun. Went off to Cambridge, where he made himself unpopular by being clumsy with the test tubes and trying to kill his tutor with a poisoned apple. Studied theoretical physics at Göttingen, Germany, where his questions were so unpopular that the other students said they'd boycott the course unless he was kicked off.

Definitely had some hangups over the ladies. In a third-class railway carriage with a kissing couple, Oppenheimer threw himself on the woman when the man stepped outside and tried to carry on where he'd left off. On another occasion, when his friend told him he was engaged, Oppenheimer leaped on him with a strap and tried to strangle him.

The subject is now back in the States, getting a reputation as one of America's top scientists.

He works at the Berkeley Radiation Lab, a new cutting-edge research center in California. They call it the Rad Lab, which is neat because in our opinion they're all a bit… radical. Lots of commies, lots of secret Stalinists masquerading as 'do-gooders'.

There is no question that Oppenheimer has been mixing with a troubling set of associates. His ex-girlfriend is a commie, his brother's a commie, his wife's first husband was a commie, even his landlady's a commie. Above all, Oppenheimer has gotten very friendly with a dangerous leftist professor called Haakon Chevalier.

We'll be keeping a close eye on all of them.

Document 12-4183, August 1942

TO: Headquarters, Federal Bureau of Investigation

INFORMATION CONCERNING: Julius Robert Oppenheimer

Our office wishes to register serious alarm about the plan to appoint J. Robert Oppenheimer to lead the Manhattan Project. In addition to our concerns about his communist sympathies and associations (see Document 12-4167), we also believe him to be a highly erratic and unstable personality. What's more, he has no leadership experience.

We're struggling to reason with Colonel Groves, the military director of the Manhattan

Project, who is desperate to have Oppenheimer at any cost. This is despite the military top brass sharing our concerns that he's an extremely risky horse to back on a project this sensitive.

In our opinion, they're both single-minded obsessives – and this concerns us.

Document 12-4262, August 1943

TO: Headquarters, Federal Bureau of Investigation

INFORMATION CONCERNING: Julius Robert Oppenheimer

There has been a very worrying development in our ongoing monitoring operation of Oppenheimer. He recently reported to us that he had a conversation with his old friend Haakon Chevalier, Professor of French Literature at the University of California, Berkeley, in which Chevalier sounded him out about passing nuclear information to the Soviets. Oppenheimer claims he turned Chevalier down. The problem is that this conversation happened in January or February of this year – and he waited more than six months to tell us. This strikes us as highly suspicious.

To make matters worse, when an agent interviewed him about this conversation, Oppenheimer was vague, rambling, inconsistent – and, we're sure, intentionally misleading. Is he protecting Chevalier? Or does he have a guilty conscience?

Colonel Groves has, once again, stepped in to protect Oppenheimer. So for now, there is nothing we can do except keep tabs on him. We have wiretapped his phone and his office in Los Alamos, we are reading all his letters, and his chauffeur is a counterintelligence agent. We even straight-up told him that we'd be tailing him whenever he left Los Alamos, just to make sure he knows not to try anything.

If we distrusted Oppenheimer before all this, it's nothing compared to how we feel about him now.

Document 12-4354, November 1945

TO: J. Edgar Hoover, Director, Federal Bureau of Investigation

INFORMATION CONCERNING: Julius Robert Oppenheimer

Sir, we have received your personal request for the Oppenheimer documents in light of the subject's new notoriety. You will find them in the (rather heavy) box accompanying this letter.

Since Oppenheimer's nuclear bomb was dropped on Hiroshima on 6 August this year, he has been acting stranger than ever – sometimes playing the hero, sometimes moping around like it's weighing on him.

On the day of the Hiroshima bombing, his 6,000-strong staff greeted him with cheers and he clasped his hands above his head like some kind of boxing champion. But our wiretaps tell a different story. He's a nervous wreck – morose and withdrawn. One of our sources tells us that a few days later, Oppenheimer was found muttering to himself, 'Those poor little people, those poor little people.'

Now that Japan has surrendered and the war has ended, Oppenheimer has become a national hero to many Americans. This is a serious concern to the Bureau, as we have more reason than ever to doubt his loyalty. He has started to talk about using this moment in history to create a united world – all of us coming together, free Americans and commie Soviets alike. We believe he's finally showing his true colors. If it was up to him, he'd share the secrets of the bomb with the Soviets – and everyone else for that matter. We know, sir, that this is a matter of grave concern to you personally.

Last month, you will have heard that he was invited to the White House for a meeting with President Truman. It was a disaster. The President hated it when Oppenheimer said, 'Mr President, I feel I have blood on my hands.' As soon as he'd left, the President told his aides, 'I don't want ever to see that son of a bitch in this office again. Damn it, he hasn't half as much blood on his hands as I have.'

So at least this unpredictable commie-sympathiser no longer has the ear of the President. But he remains on various governmental Atomic Energy committees. And when he makes another mistake, we'll be ready.

OPPENHEIMER

Document 12-4786, April 1954

TO: Headquarters, Federal Bureau of Investigation

INFORMATION CONCERNING: Julius Robert Oppenheimer

Finally, we think we've got Oppenheimer.
  Our suspicions have grown exponentially in the decade since 1945, as the Cold War has forced us to take a harder position against the enemies within. The Soviet Union got the atom bomb much faster than we had expected. Did they get the information from Oppenheimer? He keeps calling for an end to nuclear secrecy – openly saying that we couldn't win a nuclear war. Did the Soviets tell him to say that?
  He has also locked horns with his new boss at Princeton, where Oppenheimer is Director of the Institute for Advanced Study. Like Colonel Groves, Lewis Strauss is another obsessive. But unlike Groves, he hates Oppenheimer's guts.*
A Washington power broker and a member of the Atomic Energy Commission, Strauss was behind the creation of the H-bomb in 1952. Oppenheimer said this was going too far: he thinks a bomb that kills hundreds of thousands of people at once is

---

* The Strauss-Oppenheimer feud seems to have been fuelled by extraordinarily petty disputes, starting with Strauss asking a question and Oppenheimer answering in a mocking tone – a warning, perhaps, about the dangers of crossing one's colleagues. Tom Holland should take note.

already powerful enough, which seems a bit soft as far as we're concerned.

However, our surveillance revealed no clinching proof until Oppenheimer finally crossed a line last year. We were tailing him around Paris, as we do, and we caught him having dinner with his old commie friend Haakon Chevalier. There's no way he can justify meeting up with Chevalier, having reported to us that Chevalier had once tried to recruit him to be a Soviet spy.

The White House is finally listening to us, and we've suspended Oppenheimer's security clearance. He's chosen to appeal, as we knew he would – so now we'll publicly destroy him. Strauss has handpicked the judges for the hearing, so there's only one way this hearing will end next week. We're going to make an example of him – by crushing a high-profile figure like Oppenheimer, we'll prove to the whole country that every single communist in our great nation will be rooted out.

Document 12-4790, May 1954

TO: Headquarters, Federal Bureau of Investigation

INFORMATION CONCERNING: Julius Robert Oppenheimer

The Bureau is delighted to note that Oppenheimer's appeal has failed, and he has officially lost his security clearance. The result of the hearing is a total humiliation for him. He was accused of employing communists at Los Alamos, as well as enjoying other dangerously left-wing connections. He also had to admit that he hadn't been totally honest with us about his dealings with Haakon Chevalier in 1943.

The best bit was when Edward Teller, an old colleague of Oppenheimer's, said his behaviour at Los Alamos had often been inexplicable. When Teller was asked whether he thought Oppenheimer's security clearance should be withdrawn, he said that he thought US interests should be in much better hands. It was a devastating moment.

Admittedly, one of Strauss's three judges disagreed with the decision, so it only passed 2-1. In the third judge's dissent, he said that the hearing had revealed nothing that hadn't been known in the 1940s, and that the ruling against Oppenheimer was 'a black mark on the escutcheon of our country'. But never mind. It's just a minor detail. The bottom line is, the FBI has succeeded in its efforts to bring Oppenheimer down, and we should congratulate ourselves on a job well done.

Document 12-4825, February 1967

TO: Headquarters, Federal Bureau of Investigation

INFORMATION CONCERNING: Julius Robert Oppenheimer

Upon the death from throat cancer of J. Robert Oppenheimer, a man haunted until the end by his sense of responsibility for Hiroshima, we are reviewing his file in order to close it.

To be honest, we never did find any evidence that he was a commie. And considering how closely we watched him, we hate to say it, but it does begin to look like we might have been, well, wrong.

Strauss continued to be obsessed with Oppenheimer and made sure that we kept tabs on him. But a few years after the hearing, the Senate blocked Strauss's nomination as Secretary of Commerce, because lots of Senators didn't like his treatment of Oppenheimer. The scientist had become a martyr for everyone who thought that our brave anti-communist efforts were a witch-hunt that went too far. In 1963, he was even invited to the White House for dinner by JFK (whom we definitely didn't murder).

Still, at least Oppenheimer never regained access to the precious nuclear secrets he'd done so much to create in the first place.

Job done.

File closed.

Paris in 1968
THE STUDENTS ARE REVOLTING

1968 was one of the most extraordinary years in post-war history, featuring the assassinations of Martin Luther King Jr. and Robert Kennedy, the Soviet invasion of Czechoslovakia, the Tet Offensive in Vietnam, the first manned orbit of the moon, a Black Power salute at the Summer Olympics – and to round it all off, the election of Richard Nixon in November.

In the middle of this eventful year, the world's eyes turned to Paris, which appeared to be on the brink of a revolution to rival the events of 1789. 'Soyons réalistes, demandons l'impossible,' read one of the students' famous slogans.* But what exactly did the students want? And how realistic or impossible were their demands? Let's join our budding columnist on the Sorbonne's student newspaper and find out.

---

* 'Be realistic – demand the impossible'

I have something to say, but I don't know what

23 March 1968

Yesterday, your columnist was part of a group of sociology, poetry and theatre students (I think the fascist medics and engineers were all at lectures) who dressed up as clowns and occupied a university administration building in Nanterre, in the suburbs of Paris.

Why did we do so? Because we are the *enragés*. And why are we enraged? Let me count the ways.

But the youth of France has been quiescent for too long. In Washington, they march for civil rights at home and peace in Vietnam. In London, they grow their hair long[*] and openly mock their leaders in satirical magazines and television shows. And here in Paris, you can be fined 500 francs for shouting 'retire' at de Gaulle's car as the elderly General passes.[†]

When the Beatles played in the French capital in 1964, they were amazed that there was no screaming.

'French people are bored,' wrote a journalist in *Le Monde* earlier this month. 'They are not involved in the great convulsions that are shaking the world.'

But the French youngsters are screaming inside. We are

---

[*] Englishmen sporting long hair was one of de Gaulle's particular bugbears. In 1966, the French President complained that Britain had lost all sense of moral discipline. He didn't repeat the same observation after 1968.
[†] This was the fate of a 22-year-old law student on 1 April 1963.

angry, not bored. *In a society that has abolished all adventures, the only adventure left is to abolish society.**

Yes, some of our grievances are local and prosaic. The boom in the student population has left 12,000 of us living in a building site seven miles outside Paris. These grim tower blocks have few facilities and all the academic atmosphere of a railway station.† We are taught by hastily recruited lecturers whom we rarely see, let alone speak to.

What's worse, boys and girls aren't allowed to visit each other's halls of residence at night.

But our concerns are also global. We want to talk about class discrimination and oppression and situationist theatre and Foucault‡ and Artaud and Derrida and Lacan and...

Well, I haven't finished reading all the introductions to their books as I've been too busy dressing up as a clown. *Read less, live more*, as the graffiti says. But maybe I'll have more time now as the university authorities have massively overacted and suspended all the occupiers, even though we willingly vacated the building.

---

* This was one of many gnomic slogans adopted by French students in 1968. All the italicised slogans (and most of the headlines) in this chapter were widely used – if not widely understood – at the time.

† The post-war baby boom was even bigger in France than in Britain. By 1968, the number of students in French universities had doubled since 1960 and trebled since 1950. In the face of grim accommodation and crammed lecture halls that had to resort to loudspeakers for everyone to hear, it is not surprising that three-quarters of French students didn't see their course through to graduation.

‡ Although widely associated with some of the political thought behind the *événements* of 1968, Michel Foucault actually spent the year in North Africa, writing to friends to complain that he didn't understand what was going on in Paris. He later became very interested in attempting to explain why the protests were unsuccessful. In *Discipline and Punish*, published in 1975, he argued that the state exists to geld the revolutionary spirit, creating docile bodies. Although regarded as something of a charlatan in France, he became very popular in America in the 1970s.

I have something to say, but I don't know what.
More next week – thank you for reading.

We will take, we will occupy

4 May 1968

Two days ago, the Rector of the Sorbonne shut down the entire Nanterre campus, hoping to halt the momentum of the many protests that had gathered steam after our suspensions. But our focus simply shifted to the centre of Paris, where hundreds of students occupied a lecture theatre yesterday until the riot police were called in. The Sorbonne has just been shut for the first time in a 700-year history that has withstood plagues, occupations and revolutions – but not a bunch of angry teenagers.

Professors, you are as old as your culture.
To be free is to participate.

Under the paving stones, the beach

11 May 1968

I am filing this column from hospital, having been badly beaten by the Compagnies Républicaines de Sécurité (CRS), the riot police led by Maurice Papon, a Vichy-era collaborator who deported Jews to their death from Bordeaux during the war. We knew the CRS had a bad reputation, killing hundreds of Algerians at Pont Saint-Michel in 1961 and massacring nine trade unionists at the Charonne metro station in 1962.

But we never thought they'd pick on middle-class sociology students in this way. 'CRS SS', as we like to chant.*

And it's not as if we did much to provoke them. Sure, we joined forces with the lecturers' union and formed a march of tens of thousands of protestors chanting, 'Long Live the Paris Commune'† while the authorities were simultaneously trying to hold a Vietnam peace conference. We built barricades, overturned cars, smashed shop windows and ripped up cobbles to throw at policemen's heads in the Latin Quarter.

But if you think for others, others will think for you.
Poetry is in the street.
I find my orgasms among the paving stones.

De Gaulle has been sent a petition by a gang of Nobel Prize winners telling him to go easy on the students and give us what we want.‡

If only we knew exactly what that was.

---

* De Gaulle's response to this chant was that, if the CRS were really the SS, nobody would be around to chant about them for very long.
† After France's defeat by the Prussians in 1870, the Paris Commune saw left-wing communards attempt to set up their own revolutionary administration in 1871. It was crushed by the French army.
‡ De Gaulle's initial reaction to the protests was to veer between conciliation and repression. After telling his Minister of the Interior that he should be prepared to give the order to fire on the students (he likened them to an angry child who needed to be calmed down with a smack), he suggested publicly that the main reason for their rioting was because they were afraid of taking their exams.

Workers (and students) of the world unite

23 May 1968

I was out of hospital in time to see de Gaulle reopen the Sorbonne on 13 May – and I joined the group of students occupying it the following day, driving the police out of large parts of the Left Bank and running the university on behalf of a revolutionary committee.

On the television news, they've been showing how the revolution has now spread well beyond the university to workers in the rest of France. The first strike took place in an aviation plant near Nantes on 14 May. Then it spread to huge Renault factories in the Seine and near Paris. By 18 May, two million workers were on strike. Today, it's reached ten million – two-thirds of the French workforce.

What do the workers want? An invitation to address the revolutionary committees in the Sorbonne's faculty buildings, of course.

A docker came yesterday and we tried out some of our slogans on him.

Workers of the world, have fun!
Don't negotiate with the bosses, abolish them!

He didn't seem that impressed, arguing that you needed someone to negotiate with if you wanted shorter hours, longer lunch breaks and better health and safety.*

I got the distinct impression he knew even less about alienation, false consciousness and dialectical materialism than I do.

Meanwhile, de Gaulle has returned from his five-day trip cosying up to Ceaușescu. He gave a rambling speech yesterday which has provoked more protests and more cries of 'Adieu, De Gaulle' in the streets. He also appeared to call us all bedwetters.†

The young make love, the old make obscene gestures.

Run, comrade, the old world is behind you

28 May 1968

I told you that the workers wanted more than simple improvements to their working conditions. Earlier this week, the government negotiated the Grenelle Accords, a great deal on paper that included a 35 per cent increase in the minimum wage. But when Georges Séguy, the head of the CGT, the communist union, presented it to the workers at a Renault plant, they promptly rejected it.

Like us, the workers have (rightly) become intoxicated

---

* One of the reasons that the post-war economic boom in France and Italy outstripped Britain is because large numbers of rural workers moved into the cities, a process that had already taken place in Britain in the nineteenth century. Here they often found themselves living in grim, grey, miserable places – not unlike the students in Nanterre. As many students found, however, when they tried to speak to the workers, the two groups didn't have that much else in common.

† De Gaulle's actual phrase was, '*La réforme oui, la chie-en-lit non.*'

by protest. In Paris, the violence has spread to the Right Bank of the Seine, getting closer and closer to the Elysée Palace. Two people have died. François Mitterrand, who lost the last presidential election to De Gaulle in 1965, has just declared that there is no longer a state – while offering to take it over himself. Pierre Mendès-France, his rival on the Left, is saying something similar, while offering to share power with the communists, who are planning a massive demonstration tomorrow, having previously dismissed the protests as bourgeois nonsense.

Will de Gaulle ape his autocratic predecessors, Louis XVI and Louis Philippe, and run away? And will he lose his head – or just his job?

Run, comrade, the old world is behind you.

Adieu, de Gaulle (or is it au revoir?)

30 May 1968

Your correspondent joined some 400,000 people marching through Paris yesterday chanting, 'Adieu, de Gaulle'. And where was the old general? Not in the Elysée, that's for sure. We saw his helicopter taking off and had no idea where he was going. Back to north London where he skulked for most of a war he never stops banging on about? Or to his retirement home in 'a certain sense of France' in Colombey?* No one knew. But there were

---

* Although he told Pompidou and his staff that he was going to his house in Colombey, de Gaulle directed the pilot to fly to Baden-Baden in West Germany, where the French army had a large base. Having checked that

rumours flying around of absolute chaos in the Elysée: Pompidou, the Prime Minister, had armed himself with a pistol; documents were being burned; and aides were trying to find fake ID cards in case the palace was stormed in a repeat of 1789.

Meanwhile, the atmosphere on the street was much more serene – partly because we didn't try to occupy any buildings. Instead, we had a lovely time shouting profound things like *'It is forbidden to forbid'* and *'The boss needs you, you don't need him'*.

Be young and shut up

31 May 1968

Well, how did that happen? In advance of a planned Gaullist counter-revolutionary march – a response to the communist protest the day before – de Gaulle gave a four-minute speech at 4.30 p.m. yesterday afternoon. Gone was his rambling indecision of 24 May. 'Go back to work,' he told us. 'Go back to the universities.' He would settle this now by dissolving Parliament, holding elections and offering a clear choice between the 'intimidation, intoxication and tyranny of a party that is a totalitarian enterprise' – and himself.

---

he had the army's backing with General Massu, a veteran of Suez, Indochina and the Second World War, de Gaulle revised his opinion that *'tout est foutu'* (we're absolutely screwed). He returned to Colombey the same day, leaving the family jewels in Baden-Baden just in case.

He spoke on the radio, just as he had done in the 1940s in London. And somehow people seemed to have rallied to the memory and fallen for it.

As many as 800,000 people, the largest demonstration in Parisian history, filled the Champs-Elysées, the street de Gaulle had 'liberated' in August 1944, listening to him on their cheap little radios.

Is it possible that there are more conservative students than we imagined?* Is there perhaps a 'silent majority' who don't want their windows smashed and their petrol stations closed?

I'm going to need to take some time to think all this through – and work out who to vote for in the elections next month.† Fortunately, it's the Whitsun weekend soon and Daddy's got time off from the bank to join the rest of the family in our holiday villa on the Île de Ré.

---

* Sir Roger Scruton, the British philosopher, was a student in Paris in 1968. 'What I saw was an unruly mob of middle-class hooligans,' he wrote in his essay *Why I Became a Conservative*. 'When I asked my friends what they wanted, all I got back was ludicrous Marxist gobbledygook.'
† The first round of voting on 23 June 1968 saw the largest legislative landslide in French history. Out of 486 seats, de Gaulle's party won 353, the communists 34. When de Gaulle stepped down the following year, he was succeeded by a former Rothschild banker and a man whose grandfather had added d'Estaing to the family name to make them appear more aristocratic. *Vive la révolution!*

Patagonia
LAND OF THEIR FATHERS: THE WELSH IN PATAGONIA

The two countries with the largest Welsh-speaking communities are, of course, the UK (i.e. Wales plus the 100,000 or so Welsh-speakers who've ended up living elsewhere in the islands) – and, 7,561 miles away, Argentina. The size of Spain and France put together (and don't ask how many Waleses, the traditional currency of size), Argentina's sparsely populated southern region of Patagonia hosts a tiny population that includes a few thousand native Welsh speakers luxuriating in their own Welsh traditions and teahouses.

How did this happen? How did a group of nineteenth-century Welsh speakers leave Britain for Patagonia, a

South American region named by a Portuguese explorer in the sixteenth century?*

Perhaps some 'recently uncovered' letters can shed some light on the place they call 'Y Wladfa' (The Colony).

Liverpool, 27 May 1865

My dearest sister Sara,

Well, tomorrow's the big day! We've been shown to our cabins on the *Mimosa*, and we're soon setting sail for our new lives in Patagonia. It's going to be a little Welsh slice of paradise in southern Argentina, free from English influence – or any other influence, for that matter. Apparently the Argentinian government is very keen to have us in the area (partly so Chile doesn't claim it themselves) and they've had some trouble getting their own citizens to move there. I can't imagine why, as the advertising pamphlets say that Patagonia is the nicest, greenest land in the whole world. I suppose we're very lucky that nobody else has thought of moving there before.

The Reverend Michael Jones is here to see us off, looking thrilled that his dream of a Welsh colony, where we can preserve our language and our religion, is finally going to

---

* Patagonia was first named in 1520 by Ferdinand Magellan on his voyage to complete the first circumnavigation of the globe, inspired by a monstrous character called Patagon, who does battle with a hero called Primaleon in a sixteenth-century novel. For centuries it was rumoured that a race of giants, called Patagones, had lived in Patagonia. In 2010, gigantic dinosaur fossils were discovered near the Colony; the new species was later named *Patagotitan*.

be realised. That beard of his is bushier than ever, and he keeps thanking God for this chance to save Welsh culture after years of hard work.* He's not coming himself – but from everything he's told us about Patagonia's rolling hills and lush valleys, he's missing out. He says he's needed here in Britain, to continue his work for the cause of Welsh nationalism. I'm sure he'll join us later.

One of the poshest organisers, a Welsh nationalist called Captain Love Jones-Parry, has already been on a reconnaissance trip to Patagonia. He went with an enthusiastic young man called Lewis Jones, who's always brimming with entrepreneurial ideas and schemes. They've both come back saying it's absolutely marvellous. They've even picked the spot where we'll build our first town – called Porth Madryn, after Madryn Castle, which is Captain Jones-Parry's family home.

Between Jones, the absent reverend, Jones, the entrepreneur, and Jones-Parry, the landed gentlemen (I hope you're keeping up with these Joneses, none of whom are related to each other), I suppose we have our de facto leaders for the whole adventure.

Reverend Jones and Captain Jones-Parry say that if we moved somewhere populated, like America, we would just assimilate and lose our Welsh identity. But in Patagonia,

---

* In 1847 the British Government published a report into Welsh education, bound in three blue volumes. The gist was that the Welsh were an immoral people whose language and religious practices ought to be stamped out in schools. As can be imagined, this went down so well in Wales that the report became known as the 'Treachery of the Blue Books', and it remains resented to this day. One way in which Welsh-speakers were penalised in school was a grim classroom game called the 'Welsh Not'. If a child spoke Welsh, a wooden sign was hung round their neck with the letters 'WN' carved into it. The pupil had to wear the sign until the teacher heard another child speak Welsh. Whoever was wearing it at the end of the day was punished. Or so runs the myth, anyway.

it'll just be us and the beautiful fjords. I very much hope you'll come and join us in the near future.

Hwyl am rwan!

Ellen

Porth Madryn, 28 July 1866

My beloved Sara,

Do not, under any circumstances, come and join us in the near future.

We've made it through our first year here – well, most of us have. It turns out that Patagonia is a cold, harsh, rugged landscape, not the verdant valleys we were promised. We arrived exactly a year ago, in the heart of a bleak southern hemisphere midwinter: the whole land was icy-cold, with bitter winds and scarcely a speck of grass. There's almost no drinking water, and there's very little rain. People were pretty furious with Captain Jones-Parry and Lewis Jones for telling us how great Patagonia was. There was such a row that Lewis Jones, the so-called great entrepreneur, has moved to Buenos Aires to be safely out of our way.

Our group was originally made up of 153 volunteers, with lots of different trades to help us establish our colony: cobblers, brickmakers, miners and so on – but in a rather glaring oversight by the organisers, we've got next to no farmers. The rest of us would struggle to grow a crop at the best of times, let alone in this bleak, desert-like landscape.

At the start, we had so little wood that we had to live in caves. Then we built a fort and planted some crops, but they got washed away by a flash flood. The only reason we're still alive is that we've recently made friends with some very nice natives who have helped us. (It turns out that Patagonia isn't quite as empty as we'd been told.) They're called the Tehuelche (I'm not sure how to say their name in Welsh), and they've taught some of the men how to hunt guanacos, which are a kind of wild llama.

Frankly, it's been the longest twelve months of my life.

We had hoped that everything would get better in the summer. It didn't. We're clustered around our fires by the banks of the Chubut River, discussing what precisely we'd like to say to the Reverend Michael Jones when we see him next.

It's true that we'd be saying it to him in Welsh, which is nice, but is it worth it?

Tan y tro nesa!

Ellen

Trelew, 12 December 1889

My dearest Sara,

Merry Christmas (although I doubt this will reach you in time)! I can't believe it's now been twenty-four years since I last saw you. I hope my nephews and nieces are well – my sons are both grown up now. When are you finally coming to join us in the Chubut Valley? I know I've given mixed messages in the past, but I really think you should all move here. We've built some lovely chapels with some lovely choirs, and we're generally living the Welsh dream. Now that we've figured out an irrigation system, we've actually developed the valley into Argentina's most fertile wheatlands, despite the almost complete lack of rainfall. Our wheat has even won prizes in Paris and Chicago (although its success has attracted so many newcomers that there are now more Spanish-speakers than Welsh-speakers).

Captain Love Jones-Parry was one of the first members of the colony to return to Britain, where he's been a Liberal MP twice now. But that entrepreneurial chap, Lewis Jones, is back from Buenos Aires – now that the colony's affairs are going better, we've mostly forgiven him for exaggerating (well, lying about) how easy life in Patagonia was going to be. He also stood up to the Argentine government who decided they gave us too good a deal in the first place.* They gave him a spell in prison for his troubles.

When he was released, Jones was determined to build a railway, to help us transport all our wheat to the harbour at Porth Madryn (or Puerto Madryn, as the Spanish-speakers call it). In 1886, we had our biggest-ever shipload of new arrivals from Wales – more than 450 of them! – who had heard about the jobs building the railway.

The bad news is that we aren't getting on quite so well with the native Patagonians any more. When we ran out of viable farmland, some of the men went out west, trying to open up routes all the way to the Andes. The Tehuelche didn't seem keen on this. Five years ago, they ambushed four of our explorers and killed three of them, at a place we call the *Dyffryn y Merthyron* – the Valley of the Martyrs.

---

* Having previously been so welcoming to the Welsh, the Argentine government became increasingly nationalist towards the end of the century. In the 1890s, they even banned the teaching of Welsh in schools, much to the chagrin of the settlers who had left Britain for exactly that reason.

But generally the colony is growing stronger every year, even if all the Argentine arrivals have meant that we all find ourselves speaking more Spanish than I'd have hoped.

Saludos cordiales,

Ellen

Puerto Madryn, 28 July 1915

Dearest Sara,

Well, here we are – *Y Wladfa* has reached its fiftieth birthday and I am an old woman! Patagonia has transformed since we first got here. Instead of a vast empty space with no Europeans, it's now a vast empty space with small handfuls of Europeans. My seventh grandchild was born last month – we've called him Llewellyn.

I'm beginning to suspect you're never going to move here. But you really should. We still have Eisteddfod festivals every year, and old Lewis Jones founded a newspaper, *Y Drafod*, which has been going strong for years now. When a visitor walks into one of the Welsh tea shops or Methodist churches, they can forget for twenty – even thirty – seconds that they're not in Wales at all.

Wela i di cyn bo hir! (but probably not),

Ellen

*

Following the creation of a devolved Welsh Assembly in 1999, an upsurge in proud Welshness has resulted in growing ties among the Welsh diaspora. In 2001 the Welsh Archdruid,

Meirion Evans, attended Y Wladfa's Eisteddfod, attracting international media coverage. And when Y Wladfa celebrated its 150th birthday in 2015, Wales's First Minister, the appropriately surnamed Carwyn Jones, marked the occasion by visiting Patagonia in person.

Since 1997, the British Council has recruited three teachers every year to spend nine months teaching Welsh in Patagonia. Enthusiasts of the 'Treachery of the Blue Books' or the 'Welsh Not' need not apply.

Pregnant Pope

THE FEMALE POPE WHO WAS STONED TO DEATH

Have you heard the tale of the medieval Pope who was secretly a woman? Her cover held until she mounted a horse – and gave birth. Everyone was

horrified – a female, pregnant Pope! – and she was hastily killed and struck off the official list of the Bishops of Rome.

At least, that's the scandalous story. But is this a remarkable moment in the history of the Catholic Church? Or is it untrue? And if the latter (spoiler alert: it was the latter), what does this strange folk tale tell us about gender, authority and faith in medieval Christianity?

Theory One: it's a true story

The story of the female Pope was established by two Dominicans writing in the thirteenth century. The first chronicler, Jean de Mailly, dates the Pregnant Pope's unmasking to 1099, explaining that she quickly met a fate even worse than giving birth in public. 'Immediately,' he wrote, 'in accordance with the dictates of Roman justices, she was bound by her feet to a horse's tail and dragged for half a league while the people stoned her.'

The second chronicler, Bishop Martin of Poland, included the purported Popess on an influential list of popes that remained unchallenged for centuries. According to Bishop Martin, the Pregnant Pope's name was Joan, which she disguised under the cunning alias of John, and she had actually become Pope in AD 855. Joan was an Englishwoman who had dressed as a male clerk to pursue her lover. Through scholarly brilliance, she rose through the ranks to become a student in Athens, a teacher of science in Rome and, for two and a half years until the day of the fateful horse ride, the Pope herself.*

Perhaps surprisingly, there is some circumstantial evidence to support Bishop Martin's theory.

He specifies that Joan went into labour during a public procession along the Sacred Way, the road from St Peter's in the Vatican to the Lateran Palace, in the heart of ancient Rome. For centuries, he claims, medieval popes avoided that road, even though it's the most direct route from the Vatican to the Lateran. Why would they do that, unless the story was true, especially given that the many Gregories, Benedicts and Clements who followed Popess Joan were unlikely to fear going into labour?

What's more, an alluringly alliterative piece of papal propaganda was placed on the Sacred Way in the fifteenth century or earlier: *'Petre, Pater Patrum, Papisse Prodito Partum'* ('Peter, Father of Fathers, make known the child-bearing of the Popess').

Sadly, there are some problems with the existence of Popess Joan.

1) The two Dominican accounts give dates 244 years apart.
2) There is no contemporary evidence for Popess Joan.
3) There *is* sufficient contemporary evidence for a complete list of popes and there simply isn't space for another pope, let alone a pregnant one.
4) The sacred/shunned street is documented only in stories about Pope Joan: the real *via sacra* in Rome was

---

* Fans of Popess Joan will be relieved to hear that Bishop Martin gives a slightly more upbeat resolution to the story, which is that Joan wasn't killed but deposed. Her son got over the embarrassment of his public birth to become Bishop of Ostia.

a route through the ancient Roman forum, not one used in Catholic ceremonies

Theory Two: Popess Joan was a distorted memory of the pornocracy

Pornocracy – Greek for 'rule of the prostitutes' – was a term used by later generations of church historians to describe the sorry state of the papacy in the tenth century. It was a time when the popes were especially corrupt and sinful (and frequently murdered). It was also a time when the papacy was the plaything of mighty rival dynasties in Rome, particularly Roman women.

One such remarkable woman was Marozia, the most powerful person in Rome in her lifetime. Perhaps inevitably, she was viewed by outraged clerics in the most disobliging terms. One chronicler described her as 'a shameless whore... who ruled the Roman people as though she were a man' – which sounds somewhat Joan-like. Not only did Marozia ensure that her twenty-one-year-old son became Pope John XI, the young Pope was also rumoured to be himself the son of another pope with whom she'd had an affair.

Perhaps the worst behaved pope of the pornocracy was Marozia's grandson, John XII, who ruled between 955 and 964. Having become Pope when he was only a teenager, he kept the youthquake alive by ordaining a ten-year-old bishop. He also blinded and castrated priests who offended him, toasted the Devil and died in the midst of sexual congress (either from apoplexy or at the hands of the vengeful husband of one of his many mistresses).

So maybe clerics looked back on the depraved era of the pornocracy, when the Church was being steered by powerful women, and came up with the story of the Pregnant Pope as a warning.

Or maybe the truth is more complicated.

Theory Three: it was a ballsy just-so story

From 1099 onwards, we know that popes were crowned while sitting on one of two grand chairs in the Lateran Palace, both featuring a hole in the middle, like a lavatory seat. So what might have happened in 1099 that resulted in popes allowing access to their nether regions?

Perhaps, suggested some chroniclers, the shocking story of Popess Joan had made it vital to check that each new pope was indeed a man. As part of the coronation rite, somebody had to reach under the chair, have a feel, and then announce in Latin, *'Habet duos testiculos et bene pendentes'* ('He has a pair of testicles and they are hanging down very nicely.')*

Sadly, this ritual never actually existed, but from the late thirteenth century, chroniclers liked to think it had. Popess Joan, they reasoned, was the explanation.

---

* It is debatable whether the second half of that sentence is entirely necessary.

Theory Four: it was about Gregorian Reform

Another theory involving the holy holey chair is that the hole is a red herring – we should instead focus on the crucial fact that the chair was one of a pair. The popes called them curule chairs, which was the name of the chairs used by the two Roman consuls in the days before the emperors. The papal coronation in 1099 was right in the middle of the process whereby the popes were making it clear that they were fed up with interference from the Holy Roman Emperor. The Gregorian reform movement was named after Pope Gregory VII. After his death in 1085, the cardinals started electing their own candidates instead of allowing grubby, materialistic emperors to make the appointment – a change that has endured until today.

So perhaps Joan was an allegory for everything that was wrong with the Church before the Gregorian Reforms.

Theory Five: it was about the tensions around women's role in the church

The notion of a female pope challenges the very foundations of a Catholic Church that still doesn't allow female priests today. The simple reason, according to Catholic doctrine, is that Christ was a man, his apostles were all men, and when priests handle the sacraments, they do so in the image of Christ himself. Women, on the other hand, are viewed as the image of the Church, the bride of Christ.

Of course, it's more complicated than that: medieval misogyny often came up against the Bible's teaching that women are also images of the divine. Women were simultaneously seen as godly and temptresses, while influential preachers muddied the waters further by associating Christ with motherly qualities.* How was the medieval Catholic Church supposed to navigate all these confusing paradoxes? No wonder the story of the Pregnant Pope caught on, reflecting an obsessional concern with the masculinity of the pope.

Interestingly, there does seem to have been a genuine medieval movement to instal an all-female College of Cardinals and even a female pope. Near Milan, followers of a local saint called Guglielma claimed she was 'the Holy Spirit made flesh for the redemption of women'. Guglielma died in 1280, too late to be the original Joan, but the existence of her cult showed that a world could be imagined in which the Church was run by women.

It didn't last long. In 1300, the papacy squashed the Guglielma cult and burned the abbess who led it.

---

* Bernard of Clairvaux, the great preacher who inspired the Second Crusade, compared himself to a nursing mother with breasts filled with the milk of doctrine.

Quick-fire Quiz

SEEN ON SCREEN

1. Which actress played Empress Josephine to Joaquin Phoenix's *Napoleon*?
2. Timothée Chalamet and Zendaya star in the film adaptations of which Frank Herbert novel?
3. Leonardo DiCaprio and John Malkovich star in a 1998 film about which mysterious figure?
4. Harrison Ford plays the eponymous Henry 'Indiana' Jones Jr. Who plays Henry Jones Sr?
5. Daniel Day-Lewis and Winona Ryder star in a film adaptation of which Arthur Miller play about witch trials?

SOUNDS INTERESTING

1. *Pompeii* is a song by which English band?
2. Which musical features the songs *My Shot* and *Guns and Ships*?
3. Which Billy Joel song references major events across the 20th century?
4. Who wrote the *1812 Overture*?
5. Which castle was the inspiration for Ed Sheeran's song *Castle on the Hill*?

GRIM AND GRISLY

1. Which Russian ruler died from a gangrenous bladder?
2. How many blows did it take to execute Margaret Pole, Countess of Salisbury?

3. Which English king died as a result of eating too many lampreys?
4. Where was Thomas Becket murdered?
5. Which French king died after his eye was pierced during a joust?

GOOD SPORTS

1. In what year did the 'Open era' in tennis begin?
2. In cricket, how often is the Ashes series played between England and Australia?
3. The Roman emperors played which sport?
4. At which Olympic Games were women allowed to compete for the first time?
5. In men's football, which country was the first to win a second World Cup?

THE REST IS...

1. Who was British prime minister at the time of the Apollo 11 moon landing?
2. The battle of Bunker Hill took place during which war?
3. Which of Henry VIII's wives were alive at the time of his death in 1547?
4. What type of building in Alexandria was an ancient wonder of the world?
5. Nicholas Breakspear is the only Englishman to have been elected to what position?

Answers on page 416.

Romans and Sci-Fi

WHY HAVE THE ROMANS INSPIRED SO MUCH AMERICAN SCIENCE FICTION?

In 2023, thanks to a viral campaign started by a Swedish Instagram influencer, we learned that the average man thinks about the Roman Empire several times a week. These 'statistics' might have been skewed by science fiction's enthusiasm for the Roman era, a period that has inspired everything from *Star Wars* to *Star Trek*, and from *The Hunger Games* to Isaac Asimov's *Foundation* series.

Why is a film, television and literary genre obsessed with the future so interested in the distant past? Here are five potential explanations.

1. The fall of the Roman Republic makes for good sci-fi story lines that reflect contemporary American concerns

In 1787, Benjamin Franklin famously left the Constitutional Convention in Philadelphia and told the crowd that they had 'a republic, if you can keep it'. By the early 1970s, when George Lucas came up with the idea for *Star Wars*, this grip seemed increasingly tenuous. American politics was embroiled in Nixon's Watergate scandal and a great deal of soul-searching about the so-called 'imperial presidency', the failures in Vietnam and the vanishing promises of President Johnson's Great Society.

An American republic that was consciously modelled on its Roman predecessor – in its architecture, its separation of powers and even in its Senate – has always feared that it might descend into the chaos and the tyranny of first century BC Rome as it transformed from a republic to an empire. Was an eighteenth-century constitution sufficiently rigorous to withstand an over-mighty twentieth century executive? Might a republic founded on the principles of freedom and self-determination ever be prone to throw its weight around overseas in the name of liberty?

Many of these subconscious concerns made their way into the first *Star Wars* film, which came out in the US in 1977 and Britain in 1978.

When Obi-Wan Kenobi, a Jedi master played by Alec Guinness,* meets Luke Skywalker, he tells him that Jedi Knights were the guardians of peace and justice for over

---

* Among the many previous roles played by Guinness was Marcus Aurelius in the 1964 film *The Fall of the Roman Empire*, a direct inspiration for the 2000 film *Gladiator*.

a thousand generations. Sounding a bit like a senator in the time of Caligula, a notorious first-century AD Roman Emperor who declared war on the Senate (as well as – supposedly – on Neptune, the god of the sea), he tells Luke about the endemic corruption, repression and fear under an Emperor who has dissolved the council and swept away the last remnants of the old Republic.

George Lucas, a suburban, slightly disaffected nerd, was not a Roman Empire obsessive who sat up late reading Tacitus's histories. He had studied film at the University of Southern California, where he was close friends with Francis Ford Coppola, who made *The Godfather*. But when Lucas revisited the *Star Wars* universe at the turn of the millennium for the prequels, the allusions to Rome were even clearer. In particular, the story of Emperor Palpatine, the series' antagonist (whom many Americans thought was based on President Nixon), echoes the rise of Augustus, the first Roman Emperor, who also 'reluctantly' accepted emergency powers in order to deal with unrest he had done so much to stoke.

In *Revenge of the Sith*, the third film in the prequel trilogy, Palpatine orchestrates a series of proscriptions against his enemies, similar to those issued by Augustus in the first century BC. 'So this is how liberty dies,' says Queen Amidala, Natalie Portman's character and the Cicero of the *Star Wars* world.

2. The decline of the Roman Empire also reflects contemporary American concerns about rival powers

'It was the rise of Athens and the fear that this instilled in Sparta that made war inevitable,' wrote Thucydides, the Athenian historian and general, in the fifth century BC. Three hundred years later, Thucydides, who was widely read in Rome, had been proven right again when the Romans conquered the same Greek city states that had once fought the Spartans. In 2012, the idea of the 'Thucydides Trap' was popularised by an American political scientist to describe the threat posed to a major ruling power (such as the USA) by a major rising power (such as China).* Many American historians love the idea that you can draw immutable lessons for the future from the past.

Science-fiction writers have been equally enamoured of the idea of creating dramatic tension in their plots by mapping the decline of the Roman Empire from the fourth century AD onto futuristic, inter-galactic rivalries.

Isaac Asimov, the most celebrated science-fiction writer (and mutton-chop wearer) of the twentieth century, modelled his *Foundation* series on Edward Gibbon's *Decline and Fall of the Roman Empire*. Using 'psychohistory', a fusion of sociology and statistics that can predict the future, the hero Hari Seldon (no relation to Sir Anthony) tries to forestall the collapse of an Empire that encompasses the entire Milky Way† before a 30,000-year Dark Age sets in.

---

* Graham Allison's Harvard study concluded that twelve of these sixteen rivalries ended in war, boding badly for the current competition between the USA and China.
† And there were the Romans thinking they did well to stretch their

In Asimov's second novel, Seldon's reading of history takes a wrong turn when 'The Mule', an unexpected mutant telepath, ends up conquering the galaxy – an unflattering portrayal of the Muslim conquests in the seventh century that finished off the remnants of the Roman Empire.

Dune, a 1960s novel by the American author Frank Herbert that has sold almost 20 million copies, drew upon similar themes. Set on the desert planet of Arrakis, the main character becomes a *muad'dib* (Arabic for teacher) who launches a jihad that ends up consuming the militaristic but decadent galactic Empire.*

3. The Roman Empire had great visuals

As well as representing an excellent allegory for threats from within and without, the Roman Empire also offers unrivalled visuals for filmmakers. *The Phantom Menace*, the first in the *Star Wars* prequel trilogy, borrows liberally from the architecture of Ancient Rome for its depiction of the planet Naboo, as does the original film in its closing medal ceremony. Similarly, many of the 'good' characters in *Star Wars* (i.e. those not wearing large, black plastic helmets) in *Star Wars* are dressed like extras from a Roman market scene or as vestal virgins, making them

---

empire to the Farasan Islands.
* The toga epics, such as *Ben Hur* and *Spartacus*, which preceded the wave of sci-fi films, were shot in a Cold War era in which the Roman Empire could stand in as a proxy for Soviet totalitarianism. Whereas the freedom-loving heroes, such as Charlton Heston and Kirk Douglas, were always American, the villainous imperialists were inevitably played as stuffy Brits by Peter Ustinov and Laurence Olivier.

simultaneously familiar and exotic to modern audiences.

4. Rome remains simultaneously unsettling and thrilling

If you're looking for a futuristic, dystopian setting, Ancient Rome provides an ideal template. It doesn't take a huge leap of imagination to transpose a world of gladiatorial combat and civil disorder to a modern backdrop.

Perhaps the best example of this is *The Hunger Games*, a young adult novel and film set in a world where the United States has imploded and all the outlying districts have to send a tribute of boys and girls to fight to the death. Most of the characters have classical names, including the President, Coriolanus Snow; the capital is called Capitol; and the country itself is called Panem, an oblique reference to the *panem et circenses* ('bread and circuses') with which Roman emperors kept the masses happy.

5. A hint of the Roman gives any show the patina of class

Whereas classical interpretations of the early *Star Wars* films probably outstripped George Lucas's original intentions, other sci-fi writers have been more ostentatious in wearing their classical educations on their sleeves.

Star Trek, which has grossed more than $10 billion since 1966, probably owes some of its cult following to its overt classical references to Romulans, Vulcans and Orion, as well as an enterprising starship captain whose middle name is Tiberius. The title of the 166th episode, 'Inter Arma Enim Silent Leges', is a direct quotation from Cicero, normally translated as, 'In time of wars, the law falls silent.'

All this allows sci-fi fans to convince themselves that theirs is a serious intellectual genre, worthy of a two-hour film, a ten-hour book – or indeed an episode of a historical podcast.

Saigon

APOCALYPSE THEN: OUR MAN IN SAIGON IN 1975

On 30 April 1975, after two decades of pouring money, advisers and eventually combat troops into the embattled, divided republic of South Vietnam, the United States finally withdrew its remaining personnel and abandoned the country to the communist North Vietnamese forces. The chaotic scenes, beamed around the world, marked the nadir of American fortunes in the Cold War. Having spent US$140 billion and

lost 58,000 American lives, Washington's strategy of containment in Asia was in tatters. The debacle also foreshadowed the shambolic evacuation of Kabul forty-six years later.

One of the last Westerners out of the South Vietnamese capital was the US Ambassador, Graham Martin, a career diplomat who frequently tangled with his Washington masters and refused to believe that South Vietnam was on the verge of collapse.* Here is what his diaries 'might' have looked like.

---

23 June 1973, Saigon

Just arrived in Saigon, which is something of a culture shock after my last posting in Rome, although it's good to be back in Asia again. I'm not sure how much I'll be able to travel outside Saigon – or whether I'll even want to. Despite the Paris Peace Accords signed in January to pull the US out of direct combat involvement in the war – an agreement laughably called 'Peace with Honor' by President Nixon – the country is in a mess. The aerial war limps on in the north and the policy of 'Vietnamisation' – building up the South Vietnamese army to get them to fight the communist north on our behalf – is proving ineffective.

Meanwhile, the southern economy has tanked since we pulled out our final combat troops on 29 March. A huge

---

* An older generation might have accused Ambassador Martin of 'going native'. He was certainly referred to as 'our man from Saigon', as opposed to 'our man in Saigon'.

market had sprung up to service the needs of half a million US servicemen – there were said to be half a million prostitutes here – and that has vanished at a stroke. Much of the countryside is ravaged by Agent Orange and aerial bombing campaigns.

My job is focused on the remaining 6,000 American advisors, as well as their many dependants, collaborators and informers. We must not let them down, and we must let them do their job of keeping South Vietnam independent. Despite the mistakes so far, I am certain this war is winnable and we will stay here until the job is done.*

Washington is providing little strategic leadership. Kissinger, I'm sure, is looking for a way out that keeps his own nose clean.† And all that anyone at home will talk about is the Senate hearings into Nixon's so-called Watergate scandal.

20 August 1974, Saigon

Nixon has finally resigned and I don't hold much hope for his successor, Vice President Gerald Ford. He enters office with his room to manoeuvre significantly limited by a Congress that has grown tired of the so-called Imperial Presidency.‡ Clearly the Soviets have been following all the

---

* Martin's commitment to winning the war was partly driven by the death of his nephew, killed in action in Vietnam in 1965.
† Henry Kissinger, US Secretary of State to Presidents Nixon and Ford, had told the Chinese Premier Zhou Enlai in 1971 that he wanted a sufficient interval between American withdrawal and anything that happened afterwards, thereby distancing the USA from any blame for South Vietnam's collapse.
‡ The War Powers Resolution, passed in November 1973, limited presidential power to intervene overseas without first notifying Congress.

chaos in the *Washington Post*: they've just given their North Vietnamese allies the green light for a ground offensive.

Sources close to President Thiệu, the South Vietnamese leader, say that this is a precursor to a much larger offensive in 1976. At least that gives the south plenty of time to defend itself – although the communists have already made some alarming gains.

---

30 March 1975, Saigon

President Thiệu, of whom I've previously been a great admirer, made a catastrophic mistake earlier this month, withdrawing troops from the north in order to lure the communists into a trap near Saigon. You can't fight a military campaign when you're going backwards – as the Germans discovered in 1918. In the space of a few months, the south has lost the city of Phước Long; Pleiku, a crucial city in the Central Highland; and Huế, the country's ancient capital. In total, the north has taken more than a quarter of South Vietnam's territory, leading to millions of terrified refugees blocking the roads.

Yesterday we also lost Da Nang, site of one of the USA's main bases from 1962 to 1972 and the fifth largest city in the country. There were awful scenes of South Vietnamese soldiers shoving women and children out of the way in order to get on the planes before the communists arrived. Some of them fell off the undercarriage into the sea as the plane took off.

If only the USA showed some backbone and gave South Vietnam proper support, I'm sure we could see off the communists once and for all.

But what did President Ford make of all this? Tackled by reporters this morning while playing golf in Palm Springs, he was asked for his opinion on the situation in Da Nang. 'Ho ho ho ho ho,' he chuckled, apparently lost for words.

I'm not sure I find it quite so funny.

---

11 April 1975, Saigon

To be fair to Ford, he has been trying to formulate some kind of policy on Vietnam in the last fortnight. After the fall of Da Nang, the CIA station chief here in Saigon wired Washington warning that this war would end in disaster, galvanising the President into action.

But the problem is that Ford, who hasn't been elected, wants to run for President next year, so he is worried about alienating the massive anti-war vote at home. Some 80 per cent of the American public now want South Vietnam to be left to its fate.

Congress knows which way the wind is blowing. At the end of last month, Ford sent General Frederick C. Weyand, the last commander of US military operations in Vietnam, out here to see what it would take to keep the North Vietnamese at bay. $700 million, Weyand reported back, and more B-52s.* Ford took this suggestion to Congress. Today they said no.

---

* General Weyand was accompanied to Vietnam in April 1975 by David Kennerly, a plain-speaking *Time* magazine photographer whom Ford kept as his own personal photographer in the White House. 'Whatever the generals tell you, they are bullshitting you if they say that Vietnam has got more than three or four weeks left,' the bearded, jeans-wearing photographer told the President on his return.

16 April 1975, Saigon

Now we've had some unforgettable insight into what happens when you leave an Asian country to its fate. Cambodia, a peaceful kingdom ripped apart by the war in neighbouring Vietnam, has just been completely overrun by the Khmer Rouge. As this group of largely illiterate and rural young men, commanded by fanatical university-educated communists, descended on the capital Phnom Penh four days ago, we evacuated 82 Americans and 152 Cambodians. My counterpart, John Gunther Dean, was the last to go, folding up the American flag as he went.

Millions of Cambodians are now being forced to leave the city, their destination unknown.* Meanwhile, Ambassador Dean told me about a devastating letter given to him by Prince Sirik Matak, a former Prime Minister of Cambodia.

'I thank you very sincerely for your offer to transport me towards freedom,' it read. 'I cannot, alas, leave in such a cowardly fashion. As for you, and in particular for your great country, I never believed for a moment that you would have this sentiment of abandoning a people which has chosen liberty... if I shall die here on this spot and in my country that I love, it's no matter, because we're all born, and we all must die. I have only committed this mistake of believing in you.'†

---

* Up to three million people – almost half of Cambodia's population – were systematically murdered by the Khmer Rouge as part of their attempt to eradicate Western influences and re-educate their people.
† Prince Sirik Matak was shot in the stomach by the Khmer Rouge and died where he lay, three days later.

It is my job to ensure that we act more honourably in Saigon. Evacuate now, as many are saying we should? Pah!

21 April 1975, Saigon

President Thiệu resigned today, after the North Vietnamese took Xuân Lộc, a crucial town guarding the main road to Saigon.

Having led South Vietnam since 1967, Thiệu's resignation speech was almost as vicious as Prince Sirik Matak's letter. Describing the United States as inhumane, irresponsible and untrustworthy, he accused us of breaking our promises and running away.*

'It is so easy to be an enemy of the United States,' he argued, 'but so difficult to be a friend.'

I'm ashamed to say that I think I agree with him.

At least the north might now negotiate.

28 April 1975, Saigon

President Ford gave a speech earlier this week at Tulane University in New Orleans announcing that the Vietnam War was over as far as America was concerned. Cue enormous cheers.

Those of us on the ground are less happy. As well as some 6,000 Americans left in Saigon, there are a further

---

* Not averse to running away himself, President Thiệu took 15 tonnes of luggage out of the country and settled in Surrey, so he could be near his son, a boarder at Eton College.

200,000 people associated with us in some way who might be at risk – translators, drivers, cleaners, wives and 'girlfriends' (some of them more official than others). When you consider that each of those have a family, the potential list amounts to a million people. Now, with all the goodwill – and helicopters – in the world, you can't evacuate a million people. But that doesn't mean we can't help as many of them as we can. We can't simply cut and run. It would be universally interpreted as the most callous betrayal.

Kissinger disagrees. To hell with the Vietnamese, is his view – even though I sent him a cable today stating that Americans could comfortably stay in Saigon 'for a year or more'.

I still firmly believe this, but I have lost this fight, and I have my orders: the President listens to Kissinger, not to me. Tomorrow, at 11 a.m., Armed Forces Radio will play *White Christmas*, the announcer will say, 'It is 105 degrees in Saigon and rising' – and all Americans will head for the embassy.

30 April 1975, US Seventh Fleet, South China Sea

Yesterday was the most extraordinary – and longest – day of my career. It was also a hell of a good job.*

As the North Vietnamese launched their final offensive

---

* This is what Ambassador Martin told the House Foreign Affairs subcommittee which investigated claims that he had mishandled the situation by delaying the evacuation and leaving hundreds of classified documents behind.

SAIGON

at dawn, a mass of 10,000 South Vietnamese gathered at the US Embassy compound, their faces smashed with the butts of US Marines' rifles. American reporters fought and scratched like animals to get over the wall.

Inside the compound, the scenes were no less chaotic. Secretaries tottered under piles of shredded and burning documents, the paper and smoke limiting the visibility of the Chinooks which had come to rescue us. They landed at ten-minute intervals over the next nineteen hours, many of the pilots flying without a break.*

Ignoring the plans to evacuate only Americans, we got over 5,500 Vietnamese out, a fraction of what I would have liked.† A colleague commandeered buses to pick up people on our list, unable to meet the eyes of those who stood quietly by, their suitcases packed, their loyalty betrayed.

At 10 p.m., I was ordered by Washington to leave myself. 'Perhaps you can tell me how to make some of these Americans abandon their half-Vietnamese children or how the President would look if he ordered this,' I cabled back.

At midnight, we withdrew to an inner compound inside the embassy.

By 3 a.m., the siege was so thorough that helicopters could land only on the roof. We were told that there would be only nineteen more flights.

---

* In a further sign of his reluctance to evacuate, Martin refused to cut down the enormous tamarind tree on the lawn of the embassy, which would prevent helicopter pilots from landing, until dawn on 29 April.
† Reports in the immediate aftermath of the evacuation were less convinced that Martin had chosen the right people. According to an article in the *New York Times* in May 1975, dozens of Vietnamese prostitutes were evacuated by American contractors who had listed them as wives or fiancées, whereas the chief spokesman for the Saigon Government and his staff were rejected, despite their vulnerability to communist reprisals.

At 4 a.m., Major Jim Kean, the commander of the Marines, said he had orders to place me on the next helicopter, at the point of a gun if needs be.

We took off at 5 a.m.

Just before 8 a.m., the final group of eleven US Marines boarded a helicopter. Their last act before leaving Vietnam for good was to throw tear-gas grenades over the side to deter the looters.

*

The fall of Saigon was warmly welcomed by anti-war activists who held a 50,000-strong rally in Central Park, New York, on 11 May 1975.

The aftermath in South Vietnam featured fewer cheery songs by Paul Simon. Some 300,000 people were sent to re-education camps, where thousands died. Another 800,000 Vietnamese crammed onto boats and headed for Indonesia, Malaysia or Thailand, 200,000 drowning in the attempt. Around 300,000 of these 'boat people' made it to the USA, where they were met with a mixed reception by an American public who didn't want to be reminded of their humiliation in the war.

Ambassador Martin, who was widely criticised for his handling of the evacuation, worked briefly as a special assistant to Kissinger before retiring in 1977. He was investigated – and cleared – by the FBI over his handling of the embassy files in Saigon, and he died in 1990.

At President Ford's request, Kissinger wrote a paper on the lessons of Vietnam, concluding that the United States was on the right side of history – and that intervention had saved Indonesia and the rest of Asia falling to communism.

SAIGON

Most historians disagree with Kissinger's 'domino theory', not least because Chinese-backed Cambodia and Soviet-backed Vietnam ended up fighting one another for a decade after 1978.

Communists are still running Vietnam today.

Schools

'REQUIRES IMPROVEMENT': INSPECTING THE FIRST 500 YEARS OF BRITISH PUBLIC SCHOOLS

Few topics arouse more excitable and irascible debate in Britain than its so-called public (by which we mean intensely private) schools.* Although attended today by a fraction of British students (about 6 per cent of

---

* Just so we're all clear: 'public schools' in the UK refer to the oldest and grandest private schools. Exactly which schools qualify is up for debate – and it would take at least another book to settle it.

British pupils attend private schools overall), their alumni continue to exert an outsized influence on public life. Boris Johnson was the twentieth prime minister to have attended Eton College, founded in 1440, where fees scraped in at just under £50,000 p.a. in 2023/24. Rishi Sunak, his near-successor in Number 10, was head boy at Winchester College, founded in 1382, making it the oldest purpose-built public school in the country.

As well as educating dozens of generations of politicians, podcasters, judges, generals, explorers, actors, colonial administrators and white-collar criminals, British public schools have also captured the imagination of the rest of the world. J.K. Rowling's Hogwarts, populated with Gothic boarding houses, cliquey teenagers, unfathomable sports and secret lingo, drew upon a rich tradition of school-based literature from Thomas Hughes's Tom Brown's School Days to Enid Blyton's Malory Towers and Jill Murphy's The Worst Witch.

But which real-life schools were those writers drawing upon?

Dust off your lesson plans. Update the Safeguarding register. Tell that struggling Geography trainee to pull a sickie. Here comes Ofsted for an invasive romp through the first half-millennium of British public schools.*

---

* The Office for Standards in Education (the dreaded Ofsted, which can swoop into a school with little warning) wasn't founded until 1992, replacing Her Majesty's Inspectorate for Schools, which was founded in 1839, long after most of these schools themselves, but you get the idea.

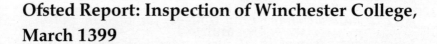

Ofsted Report: Inspection of Winchester College, March 1399

Overall effectiveness: **Good**
Quality of education: **Good**
Behaviour and attitudes: **Good**
Personal development: **Good**
Leadership and management: **Good**

Governance of the school

The inspectors were impressed by the vision of William of Wykeham, the son of wealthy peasants who rose to become Bishop of Winchester and Chancellor of England under Edward III, before founding New College, Oxford, in 1379 and Winchester College in 1382.

A young man when the Black Death arrived in London in 1348, Wykeham was concerned that the disease had killed so many priests, leaving numerous vacancies for new recruits with a good knowledge of Latin and social distancing protocols. An upwardly mobile grammar school product himself, Wykeham's Winchester College accepted seventy poor scholars from 1394. An 'escape clause' in the constitution allows for up to ten sons of noble and influential people to be educated alongside these poor scholars.

A more cynical inspector than me might wonder if this ratio will change over the centuries.

Personal development, behaviour and welfare

Behaviour is excellent. The atmosphere is austere and monastic: students are required to have a 'decent tonsure', may speak only in Latin and study in an east–west-orientated schoolroom based on a church. The school's constitution specifies that the washerwoman, the only woman on the premises, must be old and unattractive in appearance, precluding the temptation for any beastliness.

Outcomes for pupils

Prospects for alumni are excellent, not least because Wykeham set up Winchester College as a feeder school for his other foundation, New College, Oxford. This puts the school at the very top of the Oxbridge league tables, without risking a negative backlash in *Guardian* editorials.

What does the school need to do to improve further?

Admit girls.*

Ofsted Report: Inspection of Eton College, September 1485

Overall effectiveness: **Good**
Quality of education: **Good**

---

* It eventually did so, 640 years after its founding, in September 2022.

Behaviour and attitudes: **Good**

Personal development: **Requires improvement**

Leadership and management: **Good**

Governance of the school

Eton College has had a turbulent few decades after its founding by Henry VI in 1440, with the King poaching Winchester's headmaster, William Waynflete, in order to set up a rival free school for seventy King's Scholars. In 1463, two years after Edward IV had deposed Henry VI, the new King sent a petition to the Pope to close the school down, only to find himself foiled by backstairs lobbying by Old Etonians (hopefully the last time we see any such political shenanigans).

Now on its eleventh headmaster, Eton College seems firmly established.

Quality of teaching and learning

Students start the day with prayers at 5 a.m. and lessons at 6 a.m., which continue until 8 p.m., giving them more than enough time for rest and leisure, with few opportunities for beastliness.

Safeguarding

There is a lack of respect shown to pupils with each form assigned a 'cuss-doss', the weakest boy singled out for testing in front of his peers until he improves and the title is passed on to another unfortunate boy.

If the term 'mental health' existed, we would be concerned about it.

Outcomes for pupils

Outcomes are generally excellent, which is unsurprising given that Henry VI founded the College as a feeder school for his other foundation, King's College, Cambridge.* Outcomes will doubtlessly be even better for the 'Oppidans', students who have to pay for their accommodation. Given its proximity to Windsor and London, the school has started to attract aspirational members of the gentry, including the son of William Catesby, one of Richard III's principal councillors, who died alongside the King at Bosworth last week.

What does the school need to do to improve further?

Admit girls.†

Ofsted Report: Inspection of Barking Abbey, November 1539

Overall effectiveness: **Ineffective**

Quality of education: **Outstanding**

Behaviour and attitudes: **Outstanding**

Personal development: **Outstanding**

Leadership and management: **Outstanding**

---

* Although good luck getting into King's College, Cambridge, in the 21st century if you went to Eton. For several decades the progressive college has taken a far larger percentage of state-school applicants than the rest of the university.
† This still hasn't happened.

Summary of key findings for parents and pupils

Barking Abbey is a brilliant institution with a continuous tradition of female scholarship, including law, history and literacy, stretching right back to 666 AD, when it was founded by a priest named Erkenwald for his sister Ethelburga.

The abbey has since educated the wife of Henry I, the illegitimate daughters of Henry II and John and the sister of Thomas Beckett (as an apology by Henry II for killing the Archbishop).

The education of women is obviously a dangerous and foolhardy business of which no good can come, and we therefore recommend the Abbey be closed down by Henry VIII and its wealth seized as part of the Dissolution of the Monasteries.

Outcomes for pupils

Don't worry: girls can still learn wifely arts elsewhere such as music, needlework and – if they insist – French from a governess or private tutor.[*]

---

[*] This inspector's report was indeed followed, and Barking Abbey – along with other ancient nunneries that provided at least some sort of education for women – ceased to exist in England after the Dissolution of the Monasteries.

SCHOOLS

Ofsted Report: Inspection of Merchant Taylors' School, December 1611

Overall effectiveness: **Good**
Quality of education: **Outstanding**
Behaviour and attitudes: **Good**
Personal development: **Good**
Leadership and management: **Good**

Quality of teaching and learning

Merchant Taylors' School was founded by a livery company in 1561 under the bizarre illusion that a so-called rounded education should extend beyond Latin, Greek and ritual humiliation to include other subjects such as drama, music and sport.

Surprisingly, this unusual approach has already borne fruit, producing Thomas Kyd, the Elizabethan playwright, and six of the translators who worked on the translation of the King James's Bible that was published earlier this year.

What does the school need to do to improve further?

Admit girls.*

---

* This still hasn't happened.

Ofsted Report: Inspection of Westminster School, January 1695

Overall effectiveness: **Outstanding**

Quality of education: **Good**

Behaviour and attitudes: **Good**

Personal development: **Good**

Leadership and management: **Outstanding**

Governance of the school

Richard Busby, the headmaster, has now been in post for a remarkable fifty-seven years, surviving Cromwell's Commonwealth (he boldly led the boys in prayers for Charles I on the day of his execution), Charles II's Restoration, the fire of London and half a century of teenage boys doused in Lynx Africa deodorant.

Outcomes for pupils

Successful Westminster alumnae include the composer Henry Purcell, the philosopher John Locke and the playwrights John Dryden and Ben Jonson, the son of a builder. The school's location in the heart of the capital, as well as its reputation under the Reverend Dr Busby, mean that leading members of the aristocracy are increasingly happy to send their children to be caned at school (the Reverend Dr Busby is an enthusiastic proponent of the birch) instead of being tutored privately at home.

Quality of teaching and learning

The Reverend Dr Busby has introduced modern Oriental languages and mathematics to the curriculum, although it is said that he himself struggles with multiplication (the school's accounts are in an awful state). These struggles are not atypical among London's public schools, according to fellow inspectors. Samuel Pepys, who attended St Paul's, the first public school to admit day pupils, was unable to multiply until he was twenty-nine and working in the Admiralty as a senior civil servant.

What does the school need to do to improve further?

Admit girls.*

Ofsted Report: Inspection of Winchester College, June 1793

Previous inspection (1399): **Good**

This inspection

Overall effectiveness: **Requires improvement**
Quality of education: **Requires improvement**
Behaviour and attitudes: **Requires improvement**
Personal development: **Requires improvement**
Leadership and management: **Requires improvement**

---

* This eventually happened in 1973.

Summary of key findings for parents and pupils

Winchester College is an absolute disgrace and we would be surprised if it lasted another year. If special measures existed, we would place the school in them.

Personal development, behaviour and welfare

Earlier this spring, the Warden (headmaster) of Winchester College, a literary critic called Joseph Warton, forbade the boys from attending a performance by the Buckinghamshire Militia Band in the cathedral close. When one of the boys, a prefect, ignored this ruling, Mr Warton meted out a collective punishment on the student body, preventing them from enjoying the Easter holiday. When he ignored their appeals, written in Latin, against this punishment, the boys rebelled, arming themselves with clubs, marbles and slingshots, smashing the windows, setting the desks on fire and occupying the Second Master's House.

When Mr Warton arrived to negotiate with the students, they seized him and held him hostage.

The following day, the High Sheriff of Hampshire arrived and read the Riot Act, ordering the students to disperse. Armed now with swords and loaded pistols, as well as marbles, they refused. The High Sheriff retreated, returning the next day with three companies of the North Hampshire Militia.

A truce was eventually agreed.*

---

* The Winchester riot of 1793 was not the only armed uprising in a British public school, nor even the first at Winchester, which had had several in the eighteenth century, starting with one in 1710 about the boys not being allowed enough beer. In 1797 the Riot Act was also read at Rugby and the local militia called in. The last great school revolt took place at Marlborough College in 1851, eight years after its founding.

Governance of the school

The Warden has been dismissed by the governors.

Safeguarding

We have some concerns in this area.

Junior boys at Winchester are forced to toughen up their hands, the better to prepare themselves for carrying frying pans for the older boys' breakfasts, by holding white-hot branding sticks. We saw the scars. There is fierce discussion about whether this is worse than the Etonian hazing ritual of prefects pursing younger boys through the countryside with loaded pistols* or the tradition of new boys at Rugby having to swallow a pail of muddy water mixed with salt if their singing is considered below par.

Quality of teaching and learning

Apart from some mindless rote learning of classical texts, we did not see much evidence of teaching or indeed learning.†

Recruiting a mob from the town to help them, students ransacked the school on Bonfire Night, detonating gunpowder in the headmaster's study. The headmaster lost both his handwritten manuscript on the plays of Sophocles and his job.

* William Pitt the Elder, who went to Eton in 1719, home-schooled his own son, who also became Prime Minister, saying that he never knew a boy who had not been broken by Eton.

† This lack of interest in schoolboy learning in the late eighteenth and early nineteenth centuries was by no means unique to Winchester School. John Keate, the headmaster of Eton from 1809 to 1834, used to teach classes of 190 boys at once in order to cut down on staffing costs. Lessons lasted only four hours a day. Percy Bysshe Shelley, who went to the same school from 1804, was pursued by mobs of fellow students, kicking and hurling stuff at him, because they viewed his interest in science as depraved.

Outcomes for pupils

It is difficult to imagine any pupil at this school making much of their lives.*

Ofsted Report: Inspection of Rugby School, February 1838

Previous inspection: **Requires improvement**

This inspection

Overall effectiveness: **Outstanding**
The quality of education: **Outstanding**
Behaviour and attitudes: **Outstanding**
Personal development: **Outstanding**
Leadership and management: **Outstanding**

Governance of the school

Thomas Arnold, who has been headmaster of Rugby School since 1828, is every bit as impressive as we had been led to believe by his legion of admirers. Educated at Winchester College at the beginning of the century, where he was physically attacked by his peers on his first night for kneeling by his bedside in prayer, he has now largely succeeded in his mission to turn out young Christian men,

---

* The leaders of the Winchester rebellion of 1793 included John Colborne, who became Governor General of Canada; Sir Lionel Smith, who became the Governor of Jamaica; and Sir James Charles Dalbiac, who was one of Britain's leading commanders in the Napoleonic Wars.

defined by their strong character, their moral purpose and their ability to govern Britain and its expanding empire in this glorious new Victorian age.

In just ten years Dr Arnold has quintupled the number of boys in the school.

It is no exaggeration to say that he has restored not only the fortunes of Rugby School after decades of turmoil, but also those of the entire British public school system – and maybe even the country itself.

Personal development, behaviour and welfare

Prefects have existed in British public schools since the fourteenth century. Dr Arnold's innovation has been to turn them from unruly adolescents eager to take up clubs and gunpowder against their teachers into a coherent prefect body, an aristocracy of talented, loyal disciples who will guide the younger boys towards better behaviour.

Dr Arnold believes that there are six sins endemic among schoolboys: profligacy, falsehood, cruelty, disobedience, idleness and the bond of evil (although the inspectors couldn't help but wonder if he had missed out a seventh).

We saw little evidence of these six (or seven) sins during our visit. The distinct boarding-house system, another of Dr Arnold's innovations, leads to strong loyalties and coherent discipline, supported by a readiness to use a thin wooden cane, weighted with lead.*

---

* Caning was rife in British schools until after the Second World War – and only made illegal in private schools in 1998, twelve years after a total ban in state schools. One (niche) historian has estimated that half of all erotic works in late nineteenth-century Britain had flagellation as the central theme.

The result is a new generation of young Victorians with stiff upper lips, aching buttocks and a clear understanding that the individual is never bigger than the team. As such, they are ready to fill the upper echelons of the Church, the judiciary, the armed forces, the Civil Service and Soho brothels.

What does the school need to do to improve further?

Admit girls.*

Ofsted Report: Inspection of Cheltenham Ladies' College, October 1868

Overall effectiveness: **Good**
Quality of education: **Requires improvement**
Behaviour and attitudes: **Good**
Personal development: **Good**
Leadership and management: **Good**

Quality of teaching and learning

Earlier this year, the government released the Taunton Commission report, saying that there were two problems with girls' school teaching: one was that the teachers didn't know anything about teaching; the second was that the teachers didn't know anything about their subjects.

Apart from that, they were brilliant.

---

* This happened in 1992.

Our recent visit to Cheltenham Ladies' College, which was founded fifteen years ago, suggests that this might be unfair. Although the young ladies spend a quarter of their time on music and study French rather than Latin, Dorotea Beale, the Principal, has introduced maths and science in the teeth of parental opposition, while encouraging her students to take external examinations.*

What does the school need to do to improve further?

On no account should it admit boys.

Ofsted Report: Inspection of King Edward's Grammar School, Birmingham, May 1895

Overall effectiveness: **Outstanding**
Quality of education: **Outstanding**
Behaviour and attitudes: **Outstanding**
Personal development: **Outstanding**
Leadership and management: **Outstanding**

Governance of the school

This is one of many grammar and public schools in Britain where the headmaster has been directly inspired by the

---

* Miss Beale, who spent almost half a century at Cheltenham Ladies' College, also founded St Hilda's College, Oxford, in 1893, sending many of her students here – an interesting echo of the intentions of William of Wykeham and Henry VI centuries earlier. Cheltenham Ladies' College was soon joined by other girls' public schools, including Roedean in 1885, Wycombe Abbey in 1896 and Downe House in 1907, all catering for a growing number of parents working overseas.

legacy of Dr Thomas Arnold, headmaster of Rugby School between 1828 and 1841. The result is a humane, Christian and efficiently run school.

As the headmaster explained to the inspectors, Dr Arnold's legacy probably owes more to his depiction by Thomas Hughes (himself an Old Rugbeian)* in his bestselling novel *Tom Brown's School Days* than it does to Dr Arnold himself.† We have heard that the headmaster of Rajkumar College, one of the most influential boarding schools in India, founded in 1870, reads out passages from *Tom Brown's School Days* in assemblies to inspire his students. As Japan opens up to the world, their schoolchildren are even attempting to translate the novel into Japanese (omitting some of the technical vocabulary of the cricket matches).

Summary of key findings for parents and pupils

These state-provided grammar schools are now so good that it is difficult to imagine anyone wanting to pay for their children's education in the twentieth century.

---

* A lawyer and a Liberal MP, Thomas Hughes tried to set up a utopian society in America with its own library, croquet lawn and newspaper. He called it Rugby, Tennessee.
† In 1911, the British Board of Education recommended that every school in Britain keep a copy of *Tom Brown's School Days* in its library as an example to pupils.

WHAT DOES A BESTSELLING NOVEL FROM 1885 TELL US ABOUT THE VICTORIANS?

In the autumn of 1885 a small London publishing house released the third book by H. Rider Haggard, a twenty-nine-year-old colonial administrator-turned-barrister-turned-unsuccessful-novelist, gamely touting it as the 'most amazing story ever written'.

Lots of people agreed, including the journal **The Athenaeum** which said its 'fighting scenes were hardly *to be beaten outside Homer and the great Dumas'. Not only did* King Solomon's Mines *become one of the best-selling novels of the Victorian era, it established a new genre of 'Lost World' fiction, inspiring everything from* The Lord of the Rings *to* Tomb Raider, *from* Indiana Jones *to Marvel's* Black Panther.

But what does the novel's success tell us about the Victorians?

1. Haggard was a classic child of Empire

As a boy from a privileged rural background, Haggard was keener on hunting, shooting and fishing than he was on his studies. Like his great admirer Churchill, who sent him fan mail as a schoolboy, Haggard disappointed his father before finding solace in the great playground of the Empire.* While his brothers went to public schools and Oxford, he went to Ipswich Grammar School, failed his army exams, failed even to take his Foreign Office exams – and was bailed out by a family friend who was Lieutenant-Governor of Natal in South Africa.

When he wasn't organising banquets for the Lieutenant-Governor, the nineteen-year-old Haggard spent his spare time hunting in the veld and falling in love with the

---

* Haggard and Churchill are not the only two examples of young men finally finding their feet overseas in the British Empire. Robert Clive, notorious for his role in the Bengal Famine of 1770, was repeatedly expelled from school before his father sent him to India, where he made his fortune with the East India Company. Cecil Rhodes was sent to live with his uncle in South Africa in 1870 in order to recover his health. By the age of 37, he controlled 90 per cent of the world's diamond production, making him feel a lot better.

grandeur of Africa. In 1876, as Britain was on the verge of annexing Zululand, he was struck by his encounters with 'great primeval nature... not nature as we civilised people know her, smiling in cornfields, waving in well-ordered woods, but nature as she was on the morrow of the creation'. But he also had a sneaking admiration for what he perceived as the Zulus' unspoiled, authentic fighting spirit – a warrior potency that many felt was vanishing in Britain.

Haggard got to see this fighting spirit at first hand when he visited the battlefield of Isandlwana, shortly after the Zulus had routed the British there in January 1879. Two years later, after the Boers had disgraced themselves by rebelling in the Transvaal and defeated the British at Majuba Hill, the peace terms were negotiated at Haggard's nearby ostrich farmhouse.

As the junior official who had proudly read out the proclamation of annexation in Transvaal in 1877 and hoisted the Union flag over Pretoria, he took this defeat especially personally, blaming Gladstone and his liberal government. After five years in Africa, a disconsolate Haggard returned home in 1882 and decided to become a barrister.

2. Victorian Britain was ready for a racy, pacey read

Soon after returning to Britain, Haggard found himself on a train to London, discussing *Treasure Island* with one of his more successful brothers. Published in 1883, Robert Louis Stevenson's novel had been an immediate hit, reaching a new generation of readers who had benefited from the Education Act of 1870. Victorian Britain was rapidly becoming more literate, more urbanised, more widely enfranchised and increasingly accustomed to tales of derring-do thanks to a rapidly expanding newspaper market. As Lord Northcliffe, later the founder of the *Daily Mail*, said after a revolt in Egypt in 1882: 'The British people relish a good hero and a good hate.'

Treasure Island, a fantastical tale about pirates, was perfectly designed to tap into this new, burgeoning market.

Rider Haggard wasn't impressed, however. 'I think I could do better,' he told his brother, who bet him five shillings that he couldn't.

The manuscript for *King Solomon's Mines*, which Haggard bashed out in six weeks in 1885, was rejected by a number of publishers, some of whom objected to scenes that included a young Zulu boy being torn apart by an elephant. One editor remarked: 'Never has it been our fate to wade through such a farrago of obscene witlessness. Nothing is more likely in the hands of the young to do so much injury as this recklessly immoral book.'

But one publisher, Cassell, saw the potential in a novel that spoke directly to the dreams – and fears – of so many Victorians.

---

3. The European scramble for (King Solomon's) Africa reached its peak in the Victorian era

The basic plot of *King Solomon's Mines* sees a group of British adventurers and hunters navigate the unknown interior of Africa in search of a lost kingdom, a lost brother and King Solomon's lost treasure mines.

The story could not have been more perfectly pitched to feed the insatiable Victorian demand for exploration and heroism. Men such as Richard Francis Burton, John

Hanning Speke and David Livingstone were already major nineteenth-century celebrities, whether competing to find the source of the Nile, enjoying private audiences with the Queen or selling out the Royal Albert Hall while addressing the Royal Geographical Society (easier in the days when there were fewer rival podcasts). Even before he went missing near Lake Tanganyika in 1871, Livingstone had been described as the most famous man in the world.

Africa was, therefore, both tantalisingly exotic and increasingly familiar, impossibly remote and partially mapped. And into the many remaining lacunae there was plenty of scope to insert some highly dubious history.

Haggard was not the first person to posit the theory that Ophir, the wealthy region visited by King Solomon in the Old Testament, was in Africa. The notion of a lost rich kingdom had fascinated Europeans since the medieval period, and had become conflated with similar myths about the Queen of Sheba, who might not have existed, and the lost Christian king Prester John, who definitely didn't exist.

These myths were turbocharged in 1871 when a German explorer called Karl Mauch discovered the spectacular ruins of Great Zimbabwe in the south-east of modern Zimbabwe. 'I do not think that I am far wrong if I suppose that the ruin on the hill is a copy of Solomon's Temple on Mount Moriah,' he said, 'and the building in the plain a copy of the palace where the Queen of Sheba lived during her visit to Solomon.'

As it turned out, Mauch was very far wrong: Great Zimbabwe was actually constructed by Africans between the eleventh and fourteenth centuries. But many Europeans agreed with his conclusions that only a 'civilised nation must once have lived there'.

Haggard himself wrote a preface to a history of Great Zimbabwe, expressing his hope that 'in centuries to come, a town will once more nestle beneath these grey and ancient ruins, trading in gold, as did that of the Phoenicians [who, Haggard had somehow concluded, must have been the original inhabitants], but peopled by men of the Anglo-Saxon race'.

Haggard's wish was fulfilled well before the end of the century. After the Berlin Conference in 1885, the same year as the publication of *King Solomon's Mines*, European powers accelerated their scramble for African territory, claiming 90 per cent of the continent by 1900 (up from just 10 per cent in 1870). By 1890, Cecil Rhodes's British South Africa Company controlled the site of Great Zimbabwe as part of Mashonaland, which was incorporated into the new country of Rhodesia five years later. Similarly obsessed with the erroneous founding myth of Great Zimbabwe, Rhodes even set up a company called Rhodesia Ancient Ruins Limited to claim the exclusive tourist rights.

4. Victorians had a complicated relationship with imperialism

There is clearly a deep strain of racial superiority underpinning the belief that a complex, beautiful city such as Great Zimbabwe could not have been built by indigenous Africans. This reflected the temper of the times, not least among the men who carved out Britain's new African empire. 'I contend that we are the finest race in the world,' said Cecil Rhodes, 'and that the more of the world we inhabit the better it is for the human race.'

Colonial administrators such as Joseph Chamberlain, Lord Curzon and Lord Milner all expressed similar views – as, indeed, did Haggard himself. He saw life as a constant struggle, a Social Darwinist view shared by many during the heyday of the 'New Imperialism'. As late as 1913, Haggard was still writing letters to *The Times* stating that the 'future of Africa will not be a conflict between the Britons and the Boers, but the inevitable, though let us hope, far-off struggle for practical supremacy between the white blood and the black'.

When Haggard died in 1925, the *Edinburgh Review* praised his novels for 'filling many a young fellow with longing to go into the wide spaces of those lands and see their marvels for himself... they have thus aided far more than we can ever know in bringing British settlers and influence into the new country. They have helped to accomplish the dreams and aims of Cecil Rhodes.'

Haggard, though, was far too complicated – and talented – to be reduced to merely a racist propagandist. Ignosi, the noble Zulu character in *King Solomon's Mines*, ends up regaining his kingdom and banning Western missionaries and exploitative traders. Meanwhile, Allan Quatermain, the British leader of the expedition, returns unhappily home, laden with diamonds, as restless as he is rich.

Such self-awareness reflects a nascent home-grown criticism of the excesses of imperialism, which can be traced back to Gladstone's tirade against Disraeli's expansionist adventurism in the 1870s. After a decade of silence during the 1890s, the voice of British liberal conscience came briefly back to life in 1901, the year in which the Boer War turned sour and Queen Victoria died.

5. Queen Victoria's Britain was a man's world

King Solomon's Mines is probably not a book club staple for fans of Jane Austen, Sophie Kinsella or Marion Keyes. The introduction contains a dedication to 'all the big and little boys who read it'. The first chapter goes on to boast that 'there is not a petticoat in the whole history'.

There is, however, a pervasive nervousness and schoolboy fascination concerning women. The love interests are beautiful, black – and swiftly dispatched. Two mountains are described as 'swelling gently up from the plain, looking at that distance, perfectly round and smooth... covered with snow, exactly corresponding to the nipple on the female breast'. And it doesn't take too much Freudian flimflam to notice the men's unease as they go deeper underground, to be trapped in tunnels by a fabulously ancient witch.

Meanwhile, the male characters are maverick, virile and eccentric. Quatermain was based partly on a Scottish geologist gored by a buffalo while climbing Mount Kilimanjaro, partly on a Prussian game warden who worked for Rhodes and shot seventy-eight elephants in three years. His men are bound together with bonds of masculine brotherhood that would have been familiar to other garlanded Victorians such as General Gordon, Lord Kitchener or Lord Milner. One even admires the 'magnificent physique' of his travelling companion when he dons 'savage dress'.

6. The Victorians' legacy lives on

What have the Victorians ever done for us – apart from pioneering sewers and snooker, railways and rugby, telephones and tennis balls, packaged holidays and political parties, standardised clocks and central heating?

The answer, of course, is that they also gave the world Rider Haggard. His mainstream literary legacy can be seen everywhere from J.R.R. Tolkien to L.P. Hartley (who based Brandon Hall, the setting of *The Go-Between*, on Haggard's childhood home). And he also invented many of the 'lost world' tropes that we now take for granted across numerous forms of media, notably the archetypal evil-but-sexy empress that first appeared as the character of Ayesha in *She*, another hugely successful Rider Haggard novel, published in 1887.*

In other words, Rider Haggard has probably had a greater influence on Hollywood, the games industry and the modern imagination than all those people who *did* pass their exams in the 1870s put together.

---

* Ayesha, a white queen ruling over Africans in *She*, is thousands of years old, eternally youthful and known as 'She Who Must Be Obeyed', a name based on Haggard's childhood rag doll.

The Tichborne Claimant
A REAL VICTORIAN POTBOILER

It was the case of the century, the O.J. Simpson trial of mid-Victorian Britain. Full of melodrama, mystery and madness, the extraordinary case of the Tichborne Claimant gripped the public imagination, containing more plot twists than a hefty Victorian novel.

Unfortunately, Charles Dickens died just before the trial began: he would have loved the combination of interminable legal proceedings and gasp-inducing content as much as the enraptured audiences who gathered every day to watch the courtroom battles.*

But if he had been able to hang around a bit longer and draw on it for his next novel, here is what Dickens's draft synopsis of The Tichborne Claimant *might have looked like.*

Part I: The Curse

Our melodrama opens with a period prologue about an ancestral curse. In twelfth-century Hampshire, a miserly old nobleman called Sir Roger Tichborne lived with Lady Mabella, his kind-hearted wife. Crippled by a wasting disease, Lady Mabella was desperate to help the local poor folk before she died. Sir Roger wasn't keen, so she persuaded him to agree to a bet.

Lighting a candle, Lady Mabella would traverse as much of her husband's land as possible before the flame went out. Anything that grew on the land she covered would be given to the poor. Unable to walk, the dying Mabella crawled instead, managing to earmark an astonishing twenty-three acres for her charitable cause.†

---

* Although we can't call on Dickens to tell the story in all its intricate glory, Zadie Smith's novel, *The Fraud* (2023), tackles the subject with customary aplomb.
† This field is still called The Crawls, and can be visited to this day – if you're interested in an average-looking plot between Tichborne and Alresford.

Not fully trusting her miserly husband to honour the arrangement, Lady Mabella sealed the deal with a curse before she died. If Sir Roger, or any of his descendants, stopped giving out this Tichborne Dole, there would be a generation of seven sons, followed by seven daughters – and then the family would fall into ruin and the Tichborne name would die out.

Part II: The Heir

After 600 years of paying this dole, the Tichbornes felt that too many commoners were taking advantage of the system. They shut it down in 1796 – and the curse kicked in immediately. Sir Henry Tichborne, the eldest of seven sons, fathered seven daughters. A terrified Sir Henry revived the Tichborne Dole – but was it too little, too late?

Roger, Sir Henry's nephew and heir, was a slim, underwhelming young aristocrat with a violent streak: he loved his gun and his tuba, both of which put the servants on edge. However, he was adored by his mother, a half-French noblewoman called Henriette.* Thanks to Henriette, French was Roger's first language (make a note of this: it's going to be important later on). In 1853, aged twenty-four, he set off for a gap year in South America.

---

* Roger's father, James Tichborne, had been a prisoner-of-war during the Napoleonic Wars, along with his future father-in-law, Henry Seymour. While in prison, Seymour had managed to have an affair with the daughter of the Duke of Bourbon, fathering Henriette, who ended up marrying her father's old cellmate. Any Victorian novelist worth their salt could have got 200 pages out of this subplot without breaking a sweat.

Roger had a grand old time abroad, until his ship capsized on the way to Jamaica. Everyone on board drowned. And that – probably – was the end of Roger, the Tichborne Heir, his gap year cut cruelly short before he could tell everyone about it in Freshers' Week. Or was it?

Henriette, however, refused to give up on her darling son. She consulted clairvoyants, who consulted their crystal balls and their wallets (if not their consciences) and told her: *don't lose hope. Roger is still alive.*

Part III: The Claimant

Henriette now did something rather foolhardy. Ignoring the advice of her Tichborne in-laws,* she placed advertisements all over England – and subsequently across Europe and Australia – offering larger and larger sums for the return of her son. In Australia, there were agents whose business was to track down missing people and claim their rewards. The temptation for fraudsters was obvious.

Enter the titular Tichborne Claimant: apparently named Arthur Orton, a heavily overweight butcher from Wapping, east London, who had wound up in Australia, where he was rumoured to be a bushranger. He did not appear to have much going for him as a potential Roger Tichborne returned from the watery deep of the

---

* Henriette hated her in-laws. No doubt, by the end of all this, the feeling was mutual.

Atlantic. But he did have one remarkable ace up his sleeve: Andrew Bogle.

Originally a plantation slave in Jamaica, Bogle had spent twenty years as the valet to Roger's uncle Edward (who had become Baronet after Sir Henry's death) and was now living in comfortable retirement in Australia on a Tichborne pension. He was universally liked and respected, with an innate grace and nobility. So it was an enormous boost to Orton's case when Bogle said he was certain Orton was the long-lost Roger Tichborne.

Was Bogle sincere? Was he duped by the Claimant? Or were they in it together? No one seems to know. In any case, twelve years after the shipwreck, in 1866, Bogle and the Tichborne Claimant set off from Australia to claim the Tichborne inheritance.

There remained one huge obstacle: convincing the Tichbornes themselves. When the Claimant arrived in Paris to see Henriette, he was understandably nervous about being found out. Lying low in a darkened hotel room with a handkerchief over his face, the Claimant said he wasn't feeling well. Henriette came to his room, coaxed him into lowering the handkerchief and said...

'That's my son!'

Part IV: The Trials

The other Tichbornes were more sceptical, pointing out that the Claimant, who had a cockney accent, had inexplicably forgotten how to speak French. When Henriette died in 1868, the surviving Tichbornes ended her payments to Bogle and Orton. In response, the Claimant boldly sued the family to eject a tenant from Roger's house, so he could move into his 'inheritance'. Thus began one of the greatest legal battles of all time.

Courtroom highlights included the revelation that the Claimant had gone to Wapping to inquire after the family of Arthur Orton. The Tichbornes thought this was a bit of a giveaway, but the Claimant insisted that he'd met Orton in Australia and had been asked to pass on a message. Meanwhile, he secretly bribed his Orton siblings to say they didn't recognise him.

Unable to access his 'inheritance' to pay his legal fees, the Claimant was funded by crowdsourced donations from the working people of England. The legal system had always been stacked against them, and they saw this trial as a way of getting their own back. (There's a paradox here. If the Claimant was one of their own, he wasn't the heir to Tichborne. If he was, as they insisted he was, they were helping an aristocrat.) The case became a form of popular entertainment. Hundreds of witnesses were called. Andrew Bogle, the star witness, was adored by early fans of courtroom drama.

Regardless, the Claimant lost. The court found that he was not Roger Tichborne at all, just plain old Arthur Orton. And now the tables were turned: Orton found himself prosecuted as a fraud.

His defence lawyer was Edward Kenealy, an eccentric Irish poet with a tenuous grip on reality. He claimed to be the Twelfth Prophet sent by God – the other eleven included Adam, Jesus and Genghis Khan, all of whom were supposedly his ancestors. Perhaps unsurprisingly, Kenealy's erratic defence failed to save the Claimant. The killer piece of testimony was provided by one of Roger's boarding-school friends, who said that the boys had all given each other distinctive tattoos during their schooldays. Unable to produce any such tattoos, the Claimant's case collapsed. He was convicted of fraud and imprisoned for fourteen years. The Tichborne case remained the longest legal wrangle in English history for the next century.*

Part V: The Outcome

Kenealy was not put off by his client's defeat. He built a political movement around the Tichborne case, called the 'Magna Charta Association'[sic], which was pro-workers' rights, obsessed with conspiracy theories and fiercely opposed to compulsory vaccinations against smallpox. Rallies were held up and down the country, with banners and memorabilia and hundreds of attendees, before interest eventually dried up.

The court decided that Andrew Bogle, the Claimant's key witness, was an honest man who had been deceived. The Tichbornes were pressured into reinstating his pension, but he died a pauper in King's Cross, north London.

Released from prison after ten years, Arthur Orton spent time as a bartender in New York before admitting in a paid interview that he was Arthur Orton after all. He used the proceeds to start a cigarette shop in Islington,

---

* It was finally superseded by the McLibel trial in the 1990s, which featured neither tattoos nor shipwrecks nor ancient curses.

north London. But his business collapsed and he died destitute. Prior to breathing his last, he had retracted the confession made in his newspaper interview. He went to the grave insisting that he was actually Roger Tichborne all along.

In a dramatic twist in the final chapter, allowing for a really good emotional climax to the novel, the Tichbornes had a baffling moment of magnanimity, allowing Orton's coffin to be buried with a cardboard sign labelling it as Roger Tichborne's.

THE END

Uprisings

WAS THE 'PEASANTS' REVOLT' ACTUALLY A PEASANTS' REVOLT?

On 14 June 1381, a fourteen-year-old Richard II met Wat Tyler, a rebel leader, at the gates of London and acceded to a wide range of demands. To those on the intellectual Left, this famous meeting at the peak of the so-called Peasants' Revolt is celebrated as the foundational moment of English radicalism. Medieval kings had often overthrown medieval kings before. Barons

had sometimes joined in too. But this was the first time that the common people of England had made their entrance into the history books.

That, at least, is the traditional textbook narrative of the Peasants' Revolt, a waypoint between the thirteenth-century Magna Carta and the seventeenth-century Civil War in terms of England's shifting balance of power. In 2011, the veteran left-winger Tony Benn, introduced by his fellow-traveller Jeremy Corbyn, unveiled a plaque to the revolt in Islington, north London, praising 'the first of a long series of campaigns to secure freedom and democracy in Britain'.

But is it more complicated than that? Is there an argument that, instead of being a proto-socialist revolution, the 'peasants' revolt' was actually a proto-Protestant, proto-Thatcherite or even proto-American revolution?

Here is the now mainstream left-wing understanding of the Peasants' Revolt, followed by three rather different interpretations of the same narrative.

1. It was a proto-socialist revolution

Capitalist causes

The Peasants' Revolt was caused by a rapacious capitalist class plundering the poor in order to fight a vainglorious war overseas.

When Richard II succeeded to the throne in 1377, at the age of ten, the French promptly restarted the Hundred

Years' War. Facing a much larger country and fed up with shouldering the burden of the cost of the war themselves, an English Parliament dominated by landowners introduced a new poll tax in January 1377. Applied to everyone over the age of fourteen who wasn't a beggar or a vagrant, it led to a second poll tax two years later, much of which was ploughed into building a fleet that was shipwrecked in its entirety off the coast of Cornwall in December 1379.

Unfamiliar with Lenin's seminal work of 1917, *Imperialism, the Highest Stage of Capitalism*, the governing class foolishly introduced a third poll tax in November 1380 to pay for their doomed foreign war. This raised the lowest level of taxation threefold, from four pence to twelve pence per person. And although it was assumed that the well-off would help the poor to pay, there was no mechanism to force hard, avaricious men (whose natural, co-operative natures had been contaminated by capitalism's false consciousness) to do so.

The condition of the proletariat was further damaged by the Black Death, which hit England in the late 1340s and had reduced the population by up to seven million by the 1380s. When a labour shortfall led to higher wages, desperate landowners introduced a raft of rebarbative measures. In 1351, the Statute of Labourers imposed a massive pay freeze, accompanied by a reassertion of landowners' 'rights' over unfree labourers. Villeins were not allowed to sell their land or leave it for more than a day without permission. Most had to work for several days a week on the land of their lord and attend his court every three weeks. When they died, the lord could claim the *heriot* tax, which entitled them to the villein's most valuable possession: usually an ox or cow that the villein's family could ill afford to lose.

Given all these injustices, Marx's notion of historical materialism and dialectical change made it inevitable that a revolt would soon break out.

Workers of Essex unite

In the spring of 1381, the ruling classes sent their lackeys of capitalism to collect their unpopular poll tax.* In Oxfordshire, the vanguard of the proletariat beat up the Dean of Bicester's tax collector, cut off the ears and tail of his horse – and nailed them to the local pillory.†

It was in Essex, however, that the revolt really kicked off. When representatives from sixteen villages were summoned to the town of Brentwood on 30 May by two bourgeois members of parliament, a comrade called Thomas Baker declared that he refused to pay a penny more in tax. The members of parliament tried and failed to arrest Comrade Thomas – and then beat a retreat, like capitalist running dogs.

Realising that by the strength of their common endeavour they would achieve more than they could achieve alone, villagers from all over Essex met on 2 June, near the town of Chelmsford, and swore a formal oath to 'destroy diverse lieges of the king, and to have no law in England except only those which they themselves moved to be ordained'. As with many revolutions, this new 'law' led to an intense period of lawlessness, in which comrades torched MPs' houses, cut off the head of the Essex official

---

* It is no coincidence that this is the period when the legends about Robin Hood, who stole from the rich to give to the poor, started to gain traction.
† The Dean of Bicester's unfortunate tax collector was called William Payable. Fans of nominative determinism can only hope that his friends called him Bill.

responsible for collecting the poll tax and burned as many documents as they could.

This unrest spread to neighbouring Kent, where the aptly named John Legg, a royal sergeant-at-arms, made himself especially unpopular by upskirting young women to check if they were sufficiently mature to pay the poll tax. But by this point, the comrades were developing a class consciousness that went well beyond their initial grievances at an unpopular levy. Led by Wat Tyler,* they set off on the Pilgrim Road from Canterbury to London on 10 June, ready to ask the King not only to abolish serfdom entirely, but also to recognise a worker's right to work for whom he chose, where he chose, on whichever wage he could command.

They had nothing to lose but their chains (and maybe their heads).

March on London

By 13 June 1381, the eastern entrances to London, a city of 50,000 people, were effectively under siege by up to 200,000 comrades from Kent, Essex and Suffolk, gathering at Blackheath and Mile End†. Meanwhile, the elites cowered inside the impregnable Tower of London, including the King, his mother, the Archbishop of Canterbury and John Legg, the Upskirter.

When Richard II sailed down to Rotherhithe to try to meet the comrades, he quickly turned around when he saw how

---

* Frustratingly, we don't know that much about Wat Tyler, who may or may not have been a tiler. We don't even know where he comes from: one chronicler says Maidstone, in Kent; another says Essex. There are also unconfirmed suggestions that he had fought in the Hundred Years' War.

† See the Chaucer chapter on page 58 for another account of this experience, from the perspective of someone trapped inside the city.

many there were. Incensed, the comrades stormed London Bridge, the only crossing point into the city, and set about righting the wrongs of capitalism. The Savoy Palace, which belonged to John of Gaunt, the King's uncle and the richest and most powerful man in England, was so thoroughly razed to the ground that not a single brick was left standing. This was not wanton destruction. Vowing to kill anyone found looting (one thief was thrown into the flames), the comrades made a point of destroying John of Gaunt's property (all of which was, after all, theft), burning furs and tapestries and throwing gold plates into the River Thames.*

Unsure what to do next, Richard II's advisers tried to persuade the comrades to disperse by offering them a general pardon. They rejected it on the grounds that they wanted social justice and equality of opportunity, not forgiveness for trying to achieve them. On 14 June, the teenage King met for the first time with Comrade Wat and several hundred of his companions at Mile End. Listening to their tales of intolerable servitude and oppression, Richard II agreed to abolish serfdom altogether, a radically egalitarian promise which, had it been implemented, would have changed the entire shape of England's social and economic order.

But of course, the ruling classes had no intention of honouring their promises. The following day, the King met the comrades for the second time, on the west side of the city of London, at Smithfield. Why have you not gone home, demanded the King. Because we want more, said Comrade Wat. We want the poaching laws abolished, so

---

* John of Gaunt was in the north in June 1381, negotiating a treaty with the Scots. Some thirty rebels broke into his wine cellar in his absence, got riotously drunk and died of starvation after the palace collapsed on top of them.

we can shoot deer whenever we want. We want the manorial courts abolished.

This was too much for the King and his retinue. When Comrade Wat called for a jug of ale, one of the King's men denounced him as a thief and a robber. Comrade Wat drew his dagger and lunged at Sir William Woolworth, the Mayor of London, who struck back, catching him on the shoulder. Bleeding badly and slumped in his saddle, Comrade Wat made it as far as the hospital of St Bartholomew before he was arrested by Woolworth's men, dragged into Smithfield and summarily beheaded with no trial.

Meanwhile, Richard II tricked the remaining comrades by crying out, 'You shall have no captain but me. Just follow me to the fields without, and then you can have what you want.'

Lured in this way to Clerkenwell Fields, the comrades were kettled by the King's lapdogs in the army and forced to surrender.

The counter-revolution

Although most of the comrades were allowed to return peacefully to Kent, Essex and Suffolk, it did not take long for counter-revolutionary forces to reassert their authority. On 2 July Richard II reversed all the promises he had made, telling a group of Essex comrades: 'Rustics you were and rustics you are still. You will remain in bondage, not as before, but incomparably harsher.'*

In total, almost 300 leading comrades were tried and executed. Traces of serfdom remained until the late Tudor period.

---

* At least, that's what chronicler Thomas Walsingham claims the King said: it is widely disputed whether Richard II actually said this.

So was it all in vain? No. The still, small voice of the silent majority had spoken for the first time – and it was a voice that would never be fully quietened again. The next time the petit bourgeoisie tried to introduce a poll tax – over 600 years later – it brought down the capitalist government of Margaret Thatcher. And speaking of Margaret Thatcher...

2. It was a proto-Thatcherite revolution

There is a strong argument that the revolt of 1381 was led by the kind of go-getting, aspirational people who represented what came to be known as 'Middle England' in the twentieth century – and not proto-socialist comrades.

It is no coincidence that the unrest was heavily concentrated in East Anglia, Essex and Kent, affluent areas that were beginning to share in the wealth generated by the wool trade with Flanders. The people who led the mood of insurrection were the ambitious and the assertive, not the downtrodden labourers at the bottom of the feudal pile. This can be seen in Essex where the revolt was carefully coordinated by men with horses, able to gallop across the county to establish links with fellow rebels, and not in a piecemeal fashion by peasants with pitchforks.

These rebels systematically targeted repositories of documents, aiming to destroy the apparatus of government that recorded the dues and obligations owed. Giant bonfires were lit across Kent and Essex. Cambridge University, founded in 1209, has no records preceding 1381, because they were all destroyed.

The rebels who marched on London went to considerable pains to stress their loyalty to Richard II, the son of the iconic Black Prince and the grandson of Edward III. Indeed, one of the reasons they respected the King so much is that they preferred to owe their lands directly to the monarch, whom they could trust, than to feudal intermediaries, whom they did not.

Once in London, the rebels found themselves among many sympathisers, including a gatekeeper who disobeyed orders and opened London Bridge for them. Some of these sympathisers were undoubtedly well connected. Sir Richard Lyons, a wealthy financier with a monopoly on the sale of sweet wine, was publicly beheaded on Cheapside, not just by horny-handed Essex sons of toil, but with the collusion of commercial rivals within the city. Similarly, no one is entirely sure how the rebels penetrated the previously impregnable Tower of London on 14 June, where they executed the Archbishop of Canterbury, Legg the Upskirter and John of Gaunt's physician. It is highly likely that a distinguished fellow-traveller smooth-talked his way in.

That same day, the rebels' demands agreed on by Richard II at Mile End included the proto-neo-liberal measure of abolishing monopolies and allowing commoners to trade as and where they pleased.

So is it too much of a stretch to point out that upwardly mobile, patriotic and fervently royalist Essex, Kent and East Anglia also became Margaret Thatcher's heartlands in her three election victories between 1979 and 1987? Maybe. But there is no doubt that ascribing the events of 1381 purely to the peasants does not give the whole picture of a more complicated uprising. Tellingly, Juliet Barker's brilliant book *England, Arise* is subtitled *The*

People, the King and the Great Revolt of 1381 – the *people*, not the peasants.

3. It was a proto-Protestant revolution

But just as Essex, Kent and East Anglia became a hotbed of Thatcherism in the 1980s, they were also the centre of Protestantism in the sixteenth century.

There was a strong religious – but anti-clerical – element to the revolt in 1381, embodied most famously by John Ball, an Essex priest excommunicated by the Archbishop of Canterbury for preaching in public places and attacking wealthy landowners and the hierarchy of the Church in his sermons. Drawing upon the Christian strain of radical egalitarianism, notably the Apostles who held their possessions in common, Ball famously asked 'when Adam delved and Eve span, who then was the gentleman?'

The more affluent clergy were a key target for angry rebels who destroyed the London home of Simon Sudbury, who held the position of Lord Chancellor as well as Archbishop of Canterbury. When Tyler met Richard II at Smithfield on 15 June, his unmet demands included the abolition of the entire hierarchy of the Church and the division of the clergy's property among their parishioners – a foretaste of some of the more successful attacks on the established Church in the Reformation of the sixteenth century.

4. It was a proto-American revolution

The Home Counties' hotbeds of Protestantism in the sixteenth century were also the starting point for many of the emigrants to the American colonies in the seventeenth century. So are there perhaps some parallels between two groups of hotheads, reluctant to pay a tax to fund an unpopular war, who unsuccessfully petition a treacherous king to restrain his overzealous ministers? Can the causes of the American War of Independence actually be traced the whole way back to the Peasants' Revolt 400 years earlier?

Maybe that's another stretch too far. But what these different interpretations of a single event really show us is that history is a complicated intersection of the economic, the political and, sometimes, the spiritual.

Just don't tell Benn and Corbyn that.

Vesuvius

#POMPEII: HOW THE FIRST-CENTURY NATURAL DISASTER UNFOLDED IN REAL TIME

When Mount Vesuvius erupted in AD 79, the pyroclastic flows famously buried Pompeii, a bustling town of around 12,000 inhabitants on the Bay of Naples, and Herculaneum, an upmarket resort a few miles further along the coast. In the space of only fifteen minutes, an estimated 2,000 people died in Pompeii. After two terrifying days, the total death toll in the region was as high as 16,000.

The Romans did not know that Vesuvius was a volcano – although they understood that its unusual ash could be mixed with water to build harbours and that its rich volcanic soil made the area spectacularly fertile. They believed the mountain was the resting place of giants, and it towered over a central part of the newly minted Empire: a wealthy bay of fashionable villas, the headquarters of the Roman navy and the great ports where grain was brought from Egypt to feed the Roman people. The thousands who perished must have thought it was the end of the world.

We are fortunate to have insight into the apocalyptic events from two remarkable sources. The first is a series of letters written by Pliny the Younger, an eighteen-year-old eyewitness, at the request of the Roman historian, Tacitus. The teenager was staying with his uncle, Pliny the Elder, the great encyclopaedist and admiral of the fleet, at Misenum, a nearby port on the Bay of Naples, when the volcano erupted.

Our understanding is also furthered by volcanologists and archaeologists. After lying buried for centuries, Pompeii was rediscovered by a group of explorers in 1748, its human – and, famously, canine – remains preserved for almost two millennia by calcified layers of ash. Frozen in their moment of death, holding hands or clutching valuable objects, they provide a terrifying lesson in our own mortal vulnerability, as well as an unusual insight into a remarkable historical event.

But what if there had been a third source for the eruption of Vesuvius? What if social media had existed

VESUVIUS

in the first century AD*? Here's how the disaster might have unfolded on your timeline in October 79* AD.*

---

17 October

@cavecanem – 07.21

Beautiful day here in Pompeii!

#dogsofinstagram

#blessed

#bestlife

@mayorofpompeii – 08.01

Speaking to #TheMorningShow in a few minutes. Will be denying rumours that springs on the slope above the city are drying up. Yes, there have been a few tremors from Vesuvius in recent days, but these are only reverberations caused by the giants striding over the landscape. Many of you will have seen them. Meanwhile, donkeys are milling bread, grapes are being gathered – life carries on.

#keepcalmandcarryon

---

* Although we have a fairly accurate understanding of the hour-by-hour events following the eruption of Vesuvius, no one is entirely sure of the date – or even the month. Pliny the Younger's letters refer to 24 August. However, eighteenth-century archaeological discoveries of thick clothes and the remains of crops pointed to a date in the autumn – a theory given further credence by the uncovering of a charcoal description found on a wall in 2018, dated 17 October 79, which we've decided to take as the first day of the eruption.

THE REST IS HISTORY RETURNS

@gaiuspliniusmaximus – 13.00

Was just doing some reading for revisions to *Naturalis Historia* when my sister ran into my study at Misenum and begged me to come outside. I'm glad I did because it was the most extraordinary sight I have ever seen. Have a look at this massive cloud: it looks like a pine tree in the heavens, doesn't it?* I have ordered a galley to take me south down the Bay of Naples to see what it is and where it's coming from.

#photooftheday

#beauty

#amazing

@herculaneumherald – 13.02

It's only just after midday in Herculaneum and it's suddenly gone pitch black. There appears to be a column of ash, miles high in the sky, blocking out the sun.

#breakingnews

#wtf

#middaymadness

@reuters – 13.23

Reports of black drizzle falling on Herculaneum on Bay of Naples. City in darkness.

#breakingnews

---

* Modern volcanologists continue to refer to this form of volcanic blast, where ash and volcanic matter rises high into the stratosphere before spreading out in a cloud, as a 'Plinian eruption'.

VESUVIUS

@michaelfishbbcweather – 13.33

Meteorological reports in Bay of Naples vastly exaggerated. Nothing to worry about.

#notthe1987hurricane

@mediolanummailonline – 13.34

Herculaneum Hottie, 21, flaunts her beach-ready body in a daring one-piece swimsuit.

#tasty

#tasteful

#middaymadness

@mayorofherculaneum – 13.32

No need to pile up wagons with your possessions. The north-west breeze from Naples is blowing the black drizzle away from Herculaneum and towards Pompeii.

#keepcalmandcarryon

@gaiuspliniusmaximus – 14.40

Aborted natural history expedition and took entire fleet to Pompeii to attempt evacuation of city by sea. Pitch black, impossible to land. Situation much worse than in Herculaneum. Thick black scum on the face of the sea preventing ships from getting in or out. Difficult to breathe. Huge crowds holding torches in the middle of the day trying to escape from the harbour. Fragments of rock falling out of the sky. Roads blocked with wagons. Run or hide: no good options for the inhabitants. No good options for the fleet either. Winds make it impossible to return to Misenum. Going to sail further south to Stabiae to see if I can help my old friend, Senator Pomponianus.

#fortisfortunaadiuvat*

@pomponianussenator – 20.19

Impressed by the cool, calm head displayed by my old friend @gaiuspliniusmaximus. Unable to evacuate Stabiae and stranded by the winds and the pumice, he remains in good spirits, taking a long bath in my chic villa. Nothing we can do now but sit this out, whatever it is.

Delicious dormice and fish sauce for dinner.

#foodporn
#selfie
#friends

@gaiuspliniusmaximus – 21.00

Just seen pitch black sky above Vesuvius torn with jagged bolts of fire.

#Vesuvius

@mayorofherculaneum – 21.01

The giants are coming. They have broken free of their chains.

---

* Although Pliny the Elder didn't coin the phrase 'fortune favours the bold', he used it to rally his men when they couldn't land at Pompeii. Today it is the motto of numerous army regiments, from South Korea to Sri Lanka.

#Vesuvius
#climatecrisis
#nowpanicandfreakout

---

18 October

@herculaneumherald – 18 Oct, 01.00

Everyone staring helplessly at the sky for hours. Stabs and forks of fire. And then, suddenly, an enormous, glowing red cloud emerging from the column of ash. An avalanche of pumice and gas. Terrible heat. The apocalypse descending at speeds of more than hundred miles per hour. So fast that it's impossible to—

@bbcbreaking – 01.02

Entire city of Herculaneum believed entombed by pyroclastic flows. Five hundred feared dead under millions of tons of volcanic ash.

#Vesuvius
#Herculaneum

@gaiuspliniusmaximus – 03.07

Just dragged out of bed by slaves in Stabiae. More pandemonium. Moon and stars still blotted out. Change in air along entire length of Bay of Naples. Pumice falling more heavily now. Fearing getting trapped in the house, we tried to pick our way down to the docks, but wind still contrary and pumice too thick. Now lying on a sheet in the harbour, head protected by a pillow, waiting for the wind – and our fortunes – to turn. I am too old to flee.

#Vesuvius

#endoftheworld

@gaiuspliniusminimus – 06.59

Woke pre-dawn in Misenum to read in the courtyard. The sun's weak light has just revealed a total transformation in the shoreline. Twitching fish stranded on land that used to be sea. Nothing remains of Herculaneum. The giants are reshaping the very contours of the earth. Worried about my uncle @gaiuspliniusmaximus in Stabiae and others in Pompeii which is very close to the giant mushroom cloud on the horizon. We're heading for higher ground.

#Vesuvius

#newdawn

@cavecanem – 06.59

Can someone untie me?

#dogsofinstagram

#ffs

@pompeiipost – 7.01

A weak dawn in Pompeii reveals collapsed roofs buried under pumice. The men who haven't already left hurry their families towards the city gates. Children hold hands as they run. A temple servant carries precious treasures from the shrine. A woman hugs to herself a tiny statue of Fortuna, the goddess of good luck. All in vain. There is a sudden, monstrous pyroclastic flow, destroying every living creature in its path, impossible to outrun, whether shackled slave or fleet-footed freeman, tethered dog or—

@bbcbreaking – 07.03

Entire city of Pompeii believed entombed by pyroclastic flows. Two thousand feared dead.

#Vesuvius

#Pompeii

@gaiuspliniusminimus – 07.22

Just seen a great avalanche of fire rippling out across the Bay of Naples. A dense blackness sweeping onwards, coming closer to my uncle in Stabiae, coming closer to us in Misenum, a deep, dark prison that has never known night, parents screaming for their lost sons and daughters, people weeping for themselves, for the world itself, a smell of sulphur, a cloud of—

20 October

@bbcbreaking – 11.46

Body of Pliny the Elder found in Stabiae.

#breakingnews

#Vesuvius

@gaiuspliniusminimus – 11.49

Distraught to hear the news about my uncle. I was lucky to survive.

#blessed

@bbcbreaking – 15.01

Syrian observers report spectacular atmospheric displays continuing across the Mediterranean in the wake of Vesuvius eruption

#amazing

#photooftheday

@jersualem4judeans – 15.12

The eruption is surely a sign of heavenly fury at Titus's capture of Jerusalem nine years ago! The end is nigh for the Roman Empire!

#karma

VESUVIUS

@titusimperator – 16.23

Eruption of Vesuvius evidently a manifestation of divine anger that we have done too little to appease the gods. Colosseum opening soon to redeem this.

#watchthisspace

#keepcalmandcarryon

#MondayMotivation

Mount Vesuvius has erupted a further thirty times since AD 79, most recently in 1944. The Italian government has a contingency plan to evacuate 600,000 people should it do so again.

Wilde

THE IMPORTANCE OF BEING OSCAR WILDE

In February 1895 Oscar Wilde was the toast of literary London. *The Importance of Being Earnest,* his seventh and greatest play, had just opened to rave reviews at the St James's Theatre. He regularly dined with Henry Herbert Asquith, the Home Secretary. And yet within the space of three months, he had withdrawn a disastrous libel case against the Marquess of Queensberry, faced two criminal trials and seen his reputation destroyed when he was found guilty of *'committing acts of gross indecency with other male persons'.*

Sentencing Wilde to two years with hard labour, Justice Sir Alfred Wills called him 'dead to all sense of shame'. The Western Mail, *a Welsh newspaper, crowed that 'Oscar Wilde will never be anything but a memory, a beacon light set up to warn youth from the dangers that lurk in a life of ease and pleasure. His personality has been wiped out from the haunts of men, and his name has become a byword and a reproach.'*

Wilde died penniless in Paris on 30 November 1900 at the age of forty-six, only three years after his release from prison. It took almost a century for the Western Mail *to be proved wrong and for his reputation to be widely salvaged.**

How did the greatest aesthete and playwright of his age, a married father of two, end up in jail?† And to what extent was Oscar Wilde a nineteenth-century martyr for gay rights? Was he the sacrificial victim for a repressive, puritanical establishment, the target of

---

* British homophobia remained directed at Wilde for a significant proportion of the twentieth century. In the 1950s, a Sunday newspaper ran a series on how to spot homosexuals, singling out Wildean tropes such as a fondness for the theatre, flowers and dandyish clothes.

† Racked with dysentery and initially prohibited from talking with other prisoners, Wilde was given bromide of potassium to suppress his libido and there were even discussions in Cabinet about whether he was masturbating too much in his prison cell (it turned out that he wasn't). Once moved to the prison in Reading his health – and his prospects – briefly improved. Treated with kindness by the Governor, he was allowed a notebook and a pen, resulting in *De Profundis*, a heart-wrenching letter to his lover Bosie. Admitting that he had grown 'careless of the lives of others' while 'feasting with panthers' and 'taking pleasure where it pleased', it forms a key part of his literary canon.

an 'orgy of philistine rancour', as his friend W.B. Yeats put it? Or was he simply the author of his own demise?

Join us in the Old Bailey on 25 May 1895 for the dramatic denouement of his third trial that year.[*]

JUSTICE SIR ALFRED WILLS: The jury will now hear the closing statement for the prosecution by the Solicitor General.

SIR FRANK LOCKWOOD: Thank you, your Honour.

Gentlemen of the jury, you have heard many lurid and licentious stories over the last four days, and you will have been asking yourself: what sort of a man is Oscar Wilde? Perhaps you are too scandalised by the details to give full voice to your thoughts. So let me help you answer the question I have posed, for I have no doubt that we have reached the same conclusions.

I regret to say that Mr Wilde is a man who has spent a decade deliberately and shamefully squandering his talents, his relationships and his reputation.

Despite being born with every advantage, despite winning glittering academic prizes at Trinity College, Dublin, and Magdalen College, Oxford, he has posed as a professional aesthete, producing thinly disguised novels and plays that mirror his own perverted duality.

Mr Wilde is an unfaithful husband who has committed gross misdemeanours in the eyes not only of God, but also of the Law.

---

[*] While the barristers' words have been invented in this chapter, the thrust of their arguments accurately reflects their respective cases.

Despite marrying Constance Lloyd in 1884 and siring two sons, from 1886 onwards he indulged in numerous acts of indecency with other male persons.* You have heard from many of them: William Parker, whose brother repeatedly accepted preserved cherries from Mr Wilde's own mouth during dinner at Kettner's; Alfred Wood, into whose trousers Mr Wilde inserted a hand during dinner in a private room at the Florence; Edward Shelley, confessing that Mr Wilde kissed him after supper at the Albemarle Hotel.

Since the passing of the Criminal Law Amendment Act and its Labouchere Amendment ten years ago, the Law has recognised the crime of gross indecency. And Mr Wilde is undoubtedly an indecent man.

What is more, Mr Wilde is also a reckless man.

In his middle of his fourth decade, he had assignations with men fifteen years his junior. By the time his novel *The Portrait of Dorian Gray* was published in 1890, this behaviour was widely known in literary and theatrical circles. It is no surprise, therefore, that the *Daily Chronicle* described the novel as a 'poisonous tale... heavy with the odours of moral and spiritual putrefaction'. Or that the *Scots Observer* thought it would appeal to 'none but outlawed noblemen and perverted telegraph boys'.†

I am sure you have not stooped to read the novel yourselves, so let me briefly state that it describes a beautiful,

---

* Oscar Wilde's first known homosexual encounter took place in 1886 with Robbie Ross, a seventeen-year-old who was already comfortable with his sexuality. It appears that Ross seduced Wilde, who was then thirty-two.

† In 1889, a homosexual brothel had been exposed in the Cleveland Street Scandal. Telegraph messenger boys were selling themselves to aristocrats, most notably Lord Arthur Somerset, equerry to the Prince of Wales.

eternally youthful man engaged in sinister, unspecified deeds, his mounting depravity reflected only by his disfigured portrait hidden in the attic – and leave it at that.

In 1891, when Mr Wilde met Lord Alfred 'Bosie' Douglas, the third son of the Marquess of Queensberry, he became even more reckless. Despite professing a 'fraternal love' for a man sixteen years his junior – and despite being a husband and a father – the defendant descended deeper into a dark world where you seduce rent boys while roller-skating in Knightsbridge and waiters while dining in St James's.

This is not a world that you and I know, but these 'encounters' didn't stay confined to that world. The defendant and 'Bosie' offended public decency by taking a cottage in Goring-on-Thames, where a shocked vicar chanced upon Mr Wilde in the garden, clothed only in a towel and spraying his naked friend with a hosepipe. The local tavern reverberated with the cries of good, honest folk saying that they would like to punch Mr Wilde in the face.

By the spring of 1894, these rumours had reached the ears of the Marquess of Queensberry himself. He confronted them both, threatening to thrash the defendant if he was seen in public again with his son. And yet still they cavorted together, spending that summer in Worthing, where they 'picked up' a trio of three boys on the beach, including Alphonse Conway, who was only sixteen years old.

All this, gentlemen of the jury, under the noses of the defendant's own wife and children who were on holiday with them! And all this, gentlemen of the jury, while putting the finishing touches to a perverted play about 'Bunburying', a duplicitous excuse in *The Importance of Being Earnest* allowing the defendant's characters to behave however they see fit.

No wonder the Marquess of Queensberry couldn't stand the provocation any more. And no wonder he left a note for the defendant at the Albemarle Club on 28 February this year, two weeks after the opening of *The Importance of Being Earnest*, accusing him of being a 'ponce and a somdomite'.*

Rarely has been there been a truer accusation – and yet in reckless response, Mr Wilde performed his rashest act of all: issuing a writ for a criminal libel.

At the committal hearing for that ruinous libel trial, Mr Wilde wore a dark-blue velvet overcoat and a white flower in his buttonhole, a misguided choice for someone attempting to disprove Queensberry's allegations. At first, Mr Wilde dazzled the courtroom with his words as well as with his outfits. But in the end, witticisms were no match for witnesses. The Marquess's solicitors had produced three years' worth of illicit assignations. Mr Wilde's case, which had no more substance than one of his artfully constructed aphorisms, rapidly collapsed. Asked if he had kissed one of Lord Alfred's lovers, he replied that the seventeen-year-old was too plain for him. He even tried to mislead the court about his age.

On the third day of that libel trial, Mr Wilde withdrew his case and his barrister attempted to strike a deal. But it was too late. Queensberry's solicitor sent the Crown prosecutor a transcript of the trial and a warrant was issued for Mr Wilde's arrest.

Now, you might have read about some of the proceedings of that first criminal trial in the newspapers – although by this point in the second criminal trial, you will understand

---

* The Marquess of Queenberry's spelling was almost as bad as his handwriting. It is possible that he was trying to write 'posing [as a] sodomite'.

that many of the details were too salacious for gentlemen to read. But do not let yourselves be swayed by the defendant's rousing speech about 'the love that dare not speak its name'. We are not interested in fine, beautiful, noble forms of affection – the defendant's words, not mine – between an elder and younger man.

We are not examining whether such relationships are indeed described in the works of Shakespeare, Michelangelo and Plato – or embodied by David and Jonathan in the Bible.

For Mr Wilde is not on trial for his 'friendship' with Lord Alfred Douglas.

He is not on trial for his manner of dressing.

Nor his writing.

Nor his recklessness.

Or even his deceit.

No. Mr Wilde is on trial for his unnatural, illegal and well-documented activities with a series of male servants and clerks.

Mr Wilde is not above the law, whatever he might seem to think.

And so I ask that you do your duty and find him guilty under Section 11 of the 1885 Criminal Law Amendment Act.

JUSTICE WILLS: Thank you, Sir Frank. The jury will now hear the closing statement for the defence.

SIR EDWARD CLARKE: Thank you, your Honour.

Gentlemen of the jury, the prosecution has posed the question: what sort of a man is Oscar Wilde?

But the prosecution has not answered the question truthfully.

So let me answer it instead. Mr Wilde is not an ordinary man. He is, rather, a person of extraordinary ability, kindness and generosity – and he does not deserve the malicious slurs and insidious allegations to which he has been subjected by a venal and unwarranted prosecution.

The son of Ireland's leading ophthalmologist and a nationalist poet, Mr Wilde established his initial reputation as an aesthete without a hint of a scandal. Indeed, if anything, he was viewed as a rather prim young man. So why, I ask you, are there no allegations that precede 1886, the year when a married man of thirty-two was just starting to be heralded as a literary genius? And what, you might wonder, provoked these impecunious low-lives to produce such lurid allegations about an increasingly public figure?

The prosecution sees innuendo where there is innocence, dishonour where there is dignity, vice where there is virtue. Would Mr Wilde have asked Lord Alfred Douglas to reside with his family in Norfolk in August 1892 if there was anything indecent about their relationship? Would a man of his intellect have brazenly entertained young men in bedrooms at the Savoy, as the prosecution ludicrously claims? And would he have been so foolish as to issue a writ against the Marquess of Queensberry if there had been any truth in his scandalous allegations?

I regret to say that Queensberry is not a rational man. If this were a boxing match, he would have contravened his own rules.* In June 1894 he confronted the defendant in his own home. When asked if he was accusing him of sodomy,

---

* Although he didn't write the Queensberry rules himself, the Marquess of Queensberry lent his name to the attempt to codify boxing which forms the basis of the modern sport. Published in 1867, the rules included the requirement to wear gloves and to refrain from wrestling or using boots with wire nails.

Queensberry replied, 'I don't say you are, but you look it, and you pose as it, which is just as bad.' He threatened to thrash the defendant. He haunted *The Importance of Being Earnest* on its opening night in February of this year, armed with a grotesque bouquet of vegetables to make a point which defies reason or explanation. Two weeks later, he sent the defendant an accusatory note that misspelt the word 'sodomite'.

You will also remember that Queensberry has called the defendant a 'damned cur and coward of the Rosebery type'.* Now this is not the place to go into the rumours surrounding the Prime Minister—

JUSTICE WILLS: Indeed it is not. Tread carefully, Sir Edward.

SIR EDWARD CLARKE: I apologise, your Honour. But it is no secret that the defendant is familiar with some members of the Liberal government. Gentlemen of the jury might ask themselves: would a criminal trial have been brought if the government hadn't been concerned about appearing lenient towards the defendant, thereby jeopardising the next general election? Would they have proceeded with a second trial if the Prime Minister's name hadn't been whispered around the clubs of St James's? Why has Lord Rosebery appeared to have suffered some form of unexplained breakdown? What exactly has the Marquess of Queensberry threatened to expose?†

---

* There were rumours that Lord Rosebery, leader of the Liberal Party and Prime Minister 1894–95, was also homosexual.

† Queensberry's simultaneous slur against Wilde and Lord Rosebery was given added spice by the fact that Queensberry's eldest son, Viscount Drumlanrig, had been Rosebery's private secretary. Following allegations about the nature of their relationship, Drumlanrig died in a possibly suspicious shooting accident.

JUSTICE WILLS: That's enough, Sir Edward. Stick to the facts.

SIR EDWARD CLARKE: The facts, gentlemen of the jury, are that, despite – or perhaps because of – their associations with the defendant, the government has also made every effort to offer Mr Wilde a way to avoid these embarrassing trials. When the magistrate issued the writ for his arrest on 6 April, he first checked the train timetable for the ferry to France – and timed the writ for fifteen minutes after that train. And yet Mr Wilde remained at the Cadogan Hotel for the police to arrive. When that first trial collapsed without a verdict he was granted bail and again neglected the opportunity to flee.

Why did he not do so? Because, gentlemen of the jury, Mr Wilde is an honourable man. There is nothing indecent about his relationships. A classicist by training, an aesthete by nature, an artist by calling, he has an elevated sensibility. He is generous and kind to everyone he meets, often handing out silver cigarette boxes.

Now you will remember that the prosecution made fun of Mr Wilde's moving speech at his first criminal trial – a speech that has already been described as the finest piece of oratory by an accused man since St Paul before Herod Agrippa. And you will have noticed that the defendant has made no fine speeches at this trial. Instead, you see before you a ruined man, haggard, quiet and withdrawn. Abandoned by Lord Alfred Douglas, who promised to pay the libel writ against his father and instead fled to France, Mr Wilde is staying in the children's nursery of a friend's house. Meanwhile, the newspapers are baying for the blood of the man they hysterically call 'the high priest of decadence'.

But I ask you, gentlemen of the jury: is this a decadent man you see in front of you? Or is he a wronged genius, the victim of mob justice?

I know what I see, and I know you see it too. Mr Wilde is a kind and decent man. For the love of God, do your duty and return him to the loving embrace of his family.

JUSTICE WILLS: Send the jury out.

[The jury deliberates for two hours, giving the defendant hope.]

JUSTICE WILLS: Have you reached a decision on which you are all agreed?

FOREMAN: Yes.

JUSTICE WILLS: How do you find the defendant?

FOREMAN: Guilty.

Witches

WHY WERE THERE WITCH-HUNTS IN NEW ENGLAND IN THE SEVENTEENTH CENTURY?

Although condemnation of 'witches' can be traced back to the book of Exodus in the Old Testament, mass European hysteria didn't start until the fifteenth century, reaching its peak between 1550 and 1660, a period in which tens of thousands of women were hanged or burned at the stake. The Renaissance might have been an age of culture, science and exploration, *but it never questioned the existence of the Devil.* **Malleus Maleficarum,** *a witch-hunting guide written by a German clergyman in 1486, was the second most popular book in Europe, after the Bible.*

However, by the time the first permanent colonies were established in North America in the seventeenth century, Europe was on the cusp of the Enlightenment. Women were still being tried for witchcraft in England, but more than three-quarters were acquitted, because the prosecutors had understandable difficulties producing the hard proof that the increasingly sophisticated legal system required.

So, surely this medieval practice wouldn't be exported to North America, a society attempting to liberate itself from what they saw as the backwards tangle of Old World superstitions?

Here are six reasons why that supposition is wrong.

---

1. There was still a heady background of global religious conflict

It's not a coincidence that European witch panics peaked in the sixteenth and seventeenth centuries: they were largely driven by the tensions and uncertainty that the Reformation had introduced into Christian belief systems. It was suddenly no longer obvious what the right way to be a Christian was – and if your neighbour was doing it wrong, that probably made them a heretic in league with the Devil.

One way to get away from England's religious confusion, where Charles I was suspected of having Catholic sympathies almost a century after Henry VIII's break from Rome, was to start again somewhere else. The early colonists in North America, whether English, Dutch, German or Scandinavian, tended to have uncompromising Protestant religious principles. Many were Puritans, who thought the Catholic Church an enormous heresy and the Church of England populated by vicars primarily motivated by a quick mumble through 'Dear Lord and Father of Mankind', followed by tea and cake in the church hall afterwards.

The Puritans believed that everyone was already damned or saved by God, unlike other Christian denominations who thought sinners could earn redemption later. So every Puritan had to prove that they were one of God's elect, chosen to lead a saintly life on their way to heaven. This created an enormous psychological burden.

2. New England was a more hostile environment than Old England

New England was a challenging place to start afresh. The settlers found themselves in the back of beyond, performing exhausting physical work every day to survive (and build a new civilisation), constantly aware that they were only one war or epidemic away from being wiped out completely. Their contacts with the Native Americans were tense and unnerving, they had no idea what lay further west and their children kept dying.

Other than their own new buildings, nothing felt very Christian at all.

Meanwhile, they had plenty of reasons to hate each other. Many of the settlers were there for economic as well as religious reasons, which put them in fierce competition for land and status.

For the first thirty years after the Mayflower landed at Cape Cod in 1620, the settlers managed to hold off from accusing anyone of witchcraft. But as their imaginations grew more feverish, they started to wonder: if there were monsters lurking close by, what if their horrible neighbour was the monster all along?

3. Their leaders were often no better than today's

When witch panics became serious, it was often in places where authority figures were weak or threatened. A charitable explanation would be that they were less able to resist the pressure of the accusers. A cynic might argue that it suited these leaders to redirect popular grievances against the so-called witches.

One such leader was William Pynchon, who seems to have been a nice chap, so let's stick with the charitable interpretation.* He was a keen businessman who had arrived in New England in 1630 and founded Springfield, Massachusetts, in 1636 (named after his Essex village back home, not the anywhere-town setting for *The Simpsons*).

---

* To find out more about William Pynchon and the Springfield witch panic, you should read Malcolm Gaskill's brilliant book *The Ruin of All Witches: Life and Death in the New World*.

Life was hard in the new Springfield, a remote village in the Connecticut Valley close to a community of Native American beaver-fur traders – although it was slightly less hard for Pynchon than for everybody else, as he was the one who controlled the land and the debts.

All was going well for him until he published a controversial theological book in 1650 that criticised Puritanism. With its catchy title, *The Meritorious Price of Our Redemption*, it was never going to be a bestseller – but the content was viewed as heretical and it became New England's first banned book.

The following year, just as a serious witch panic broke out in the town he had founded, Pynchon found himself in serious danger of losing his position as the top dog of Springfield.

4. There were plenty of scapegoats

William Pynchon had brought a man called Hugh Parsons into Springfield to make bricks, a vital commodity for house-building given the freezing winters. Roaring fires and wooden houses are, famously, a poor combination. Parsons married Mary, the Pynchons' maidservant, and soon started giving everyone the heebie-jeebies.

Although most historians would agree that Parsons was not a witch with diabolical powers, he certainly didn't help himself.*

---

* It wasn't that unusual for a man to be accused of witchcraft. Although the male–female ratio for executions in Europe was around 15:85, more men than women were accused of witchcraft in Scandinavia.

At the risk of sounding victim-blamey, Parsons was an emotionless man with few friends and very few words, except when he got angry. He was also resented by his neighbours for their reliance on his bricks. His brickmaking deals always seemed to involve a row, in the course of which Hugh Parsons would make vague and sinister threats. On one occasion, after he was denied a glass of milk and went away muttering, his neighbour's cow started produced undrinkable, saffron-coloured milk.

Whenever something strange or awful happened – ranging from the relatively mundane to the tragic death of a child – the increasingly jumpy settlers, spooked by the news from England of civil war and royal execution, looked for someone to blame in a world that was being turned upside down.

And so did Hugh Parsons' wife.

5. There was a very limited understanding of mental illness

Even after the hexed cow incident, the Springfield community was reluctant to take the radical step of accusing Parsons of witchcraft, wondering if there might be a natural cause instead.

Unfortunately, Mrs Parsons seems to have cracked under the strain. Plagued by concerns over whether she was a good Puritan, Mary became increasingly paranoid, obsessed with witchcraft and frightened by her husband. Suffering from what was probably undiagnosed post-partum psychosis, she told all her neighbours that he was a witch. Then she started telling people that she was a witch too.

She described visions in which she had seen devils. When one of their children died, she said that she had killed him herself. Had she really done it, or was she so overwhelmed by supernatural dread that she convinced herself she was guilty? We'll never know.

Still facing troubles over his heretical book, Pynchon was unable to assert himself and quieten the growing fever. Having been reluctant to rush to conclusions at the first sign of witchy behaviour, the Springfield settlers now had multiple 'confessions' from Mary. Pynchon felt that he had no choice but to act. Aware that he couldn't hold a fair trial in their tiny community, he escorted the couple a hundred miles east to face justice in Boston.

6. Not everyone was as rational as the Bostonians

The evidence that had seemed so chilling in Springfield was somehow less convincing in vibrant Boston. Mary Parsons was cleared of witchcraft but pleaded guilty to infanticide; she died in prison awaiting execution. Hugh Parsons was initially convicted of witchcraft, but the verdict was overturned and he walked free after the judges concluded that there wasn't proof beyond a reasonable doubt.

It wasn't the gory end you might expect, but neither was it the end to the New England witch panics. The infamous Salem witch trials in 1692 saw 200 people accused and twenty executed. Although some were pardoned and compensated in 1711, a twenty-two-year-old called

Elizabeth Johnson Jr., one of twenty-eight members of her family to stand trial, wasn't officially exonerated until a campaign in 2022 led by a local teacher and her eighth-grade civics class.

X-Rated Novelist
ON THE PSYCHIATRIST'S COUCH WITH THE MARQUIS DE SADE

Pilgrim's Progress, Le Morte d'Arthur, Don Quixote, De Profundis, Long Walk to Freedom – *incarceration has produced some of the world's greatest books (as well as Hitler's* Mein Kampf *and Jeffrey Archer's three volumes of prison diaries).*

Perhaps the most notorious novel to emerge from prison, however, is the Marquis de Sade's The 120 Days of Sodom, or the School of Libertinage, *written in a thirty-seven-day burst at the end of 1785 during the author's incarceration in the Bastille. Denied access to writing materials, Sade composed the novel on a single, continuous scroll of paper, patched together from scraps, which he hid in a crack in the wall during inspections of his cell. Sade thought the manuscript lost when he was moved to an asylum for the insane and the Bastille was stormed by revolutionaries in 1789, but it had been discovered and removed by a guard, passing through the hands of private collectors for over a century.*

First published in 1904, in an exclusive, special edition for researchers into sexual perversion, **The 120 Days** *only gradually became available to the general public as critical interest in Sade grew in the 1940s and 1950s. It continued to undergo periodic legal challenges in the 1960s (when, following the discovery that Moors murderer Ian Brady owned a copy of another of Sade's novels, it was banned in the UK). In 1990 it was issued by Pléiade in France, effectively enshrining it in the literary canon, and Penguin Classics published a new English translation in 2016, giving it the same status in the English-speaking world.*

'Pure filth,' reads one five-star review on Amazon. 'Disgusting to some, but I love it.'

Sade would have been delighted, having described his own novel as the 'most impure tale ever written since the world began'.

But beyond simple prurience and/or revulsion (and if you're under eighteen or of a delicate disposition, we would suggest you skip to the chapter on 'Top ten monkeys in history' at this point), Sade is a figure of significant historical interest. Not only did his extraordinary life reflect the turmoil of French society at the end of the eighteenth century, his legacy also provides a fascinating insight into philosophies as diverse as Nietzscheism, Nazism, Darwinism, atheism, feminism and Freudianism.

Sigmund Freud's contemporary, Richard von Krafft-Ebing, was the first psychiatrist to investigate Sade's works and popularise the term 'sadism', in 1886 (and arguably the first psychiatrist, full stop). But if the discipline had arisen earlier, what might one of his colleagues have made of Sade himself if they had put him on the couch? Here is a report from a pioneering psychiatrist we'll call Professor Dubois.

Name:	Donatien Alphonse François, Marquis de Sade	Birth date:	2 June 1740
Location:	Charenton Lunatic Asylum, Val-de-Marne, France	Age:	74
Date of examination:	9 August 1814	Examining psychiatrist:	Prof. Dubois

I visited the Marquis de Sade in a professional capacity in his eleventh year of incarceration in a lunatic asylum near Paris. Despite his advanced years, the Marquis was in good spirits, and is enjoying an ongoing relationship of a sexual nature with a seventeen-year-old seamstress. One of his guards told me that they had recently conducted a search of the septuagenarian's room and found 'an enormous instrument fashioned out of wax and retaining some traces of its shameful intromission'.

When I asked an unabashed Marquis about this discovery, he said that neither he – nor society – were master of his tastes. Unrestrained by any notion of inherent moral laws, he felt free to follow his own impulses, wherever they took him.

I found the Marquis willing to discuss a childhood which I believe had a significant effect on his later writings and proclivities. He was born in June 1740 to a father who was a diplomat and a friend of Voltaire and a mother who was a relative of the Prince de Condé, one of the most powerful noblemen in France. But his secure world was exploded at the age of four when he punched the eight-year-old Prince in the face and was sent to live in exile with his uncle in Provence.

Before his tenth birthday, his ruined father had been arrested for financial improprieties and his mother had given up on both of them, moving to a convent in Paris on Rue d'Enfer. It is, therefore, unsurprising that the Marquis' novels feature violent parent–child relationships, including patricide, matricide and filicide.

From the age of ten, when he was sent to a Jesuit school in Paris and regularly whipped, he began to show an interest in masochism and sadism that has dominated the rest of the Marquis' life. After military school and service in the Seven Years' War, his sexual tastes extended well beyond *le vice anglais** to include sodomy

---

* i.e., flogging. The French have made a habit of lobbing hypocritical linguistic insults at their neighbours across the Channel. In addition to

and the exchanging of social and gender roles with his valet.

Marriage, in 1763, to Renée-Pélagie de Montreuil, did not temper these desires, and the Marquis continued to seek the delights – if not the tenderness – of sexual union elsewhere. Within six months of his wedding, he had hired a prostitute, forced her to perform various sex acts on crucifixes and boasted to her about masturbating into a chalice. On Easter Sunday 1768 he cut a beggar woman with a knife, pouring wax into her wounds. He also delighted in giving prostitutes Spanish Fly, a cantharidin-based aphrodisiac (albeit an extremely poisonous one) which made them break wind, and soon he was involving his wife Renée in his orgies, having already conducted an affair with her sister. On one occasion they had a run-in with the father of a fifteen-year-old 'housemaid' they had recruited to 'work' in their castle.

Does the Marquis, we must ask ourselves, hate women, having been abandoned at a young age by his mother? Interestingly, he professes himself a believer in female equality and liberation (he also supports abortion, unsurprisingly), arguing that women are just as capable of being monstrous as men.* When I suggested that his books read as if they're written by a misogynist, he retorted that if

---

le vice anglais, there is also *la maladie anglaise*, which refers to syphilis; on the other hand, it was also known at times in England as 'the French disease'.

* Sade fascinated twentieth-century feminists. 'Must we burn Sade?' asked Simone de Beauvoir in an essay in 1951. The answer, in short, was no. 'The supreme value of his testimony,' she wrote, 'lies in its ability to disturb us.' In her 1978 book, *The Sadeian Woman and the Ideology of Pornography*, Angela Carter also defended Sade for placing pornography 'at the service of women' – a view vehemently opposed by Andrea Dworkin three years later, who wrote that his fiction embodied the male sexual desire to 'possess' women.

he hates anything, it is religion. This might explain why every churchman in his writings is a pervert (including a pope who conducts an orgy on the altar of St Peter's). Christians, he told me, are weak for voluntarily entangling themselves in the myth of brotherly relationships, much to the detriment of their true selves.

By 1777, Sade's behaviour was beginning to catch up with him. Lured to Paris by a letter saying that his mother was dying, he discovered that she had already been dead for three months and that his mother-in-law had petitioned the King to have him arrested, which he duly was. Imprisoned and deprived of his liberty to pursue his sexual desires, he turned to writing for the first time. Tiring of penning routine letters to his wife, sending her on shopping missions for eel pâté, apricot marmalade and butt plugs, he wrote *120 Days of Sodom* at the end of 1785. Did he regret, I wondered, any of the lurid tales of coprophilia, necrophilia and child abuse? Yes, he answered, he wished he'd started more slowly in order to create a bigger build-up to the murderous nihilism of the second part.

Released from the Bastille in the spring of 1790, he recast himself as humble Citizen Sade and moved to the Place Vendôme, the radical stamping ground of Robespierre. Now a divorced, penniless aristocrat in revolutionary Paris, he was voted onto a three-man committee charged with inspecting girls' orphanages – an odd appointment given his proclivities. And yet he appears to have discharged his duties responsibly, even passing up an opportunity to seek revenge on his mother-in-law, which led Robespierre to suspect him of counter-revolutionary tendencies.

Jailed for the second time in December 1793 (on political charges, this time) at the height of the Terror, Sade found himself in a prison cell within sight of the guillotine, but escaped the blade only because Robespierre was overthrown on the day of his intended execution.

Released in October 1794, the Marquis was imprisoned for the third time in 1801 when Napoleon's chief of police took exception to his second novel *Justine*, an anonymously published parody of Samuel Richardson's novel *Pamela* in which virtuous girls end up being rewarded: in Sade's version, every time Justine does something good, unspeakably awful things happen to her, while every time her sister does something terrible, she reaps enormous fortunes.

When I asked the Marquis to explain this philosophy, he explained that virtue is no end in itself. The strong kill the weak. Wolves eat lambs. Such is nature. The Roman Empire only fell, he argued, because the Christians started forbidding spectacles of torture and death. And the same will happen, he insisted, when the so-called Enlightenment comes to an end over the next two centuries.* Darker, truer forces will arise, he prophesied. Death camps. Torture chambers. No one will be spared—

But at this point, I must admit that, however interesting the Marquis de Sade is as a potential psychiatric patient, I couldn't take any more of his nihilist nonsense, and so I emerged, blinking, into a summer sunshine undiluted by mysophiliacs, horny middle-aged women with haemorrhoids and murderous bishops with a passion for sodomy.

---

* A direct line can be drawn from Sade's materialist thinking in the eighteenth century to the bastardisation of Nietzsche and Darwin in the nineteenth century that inspired the Nazis and other fascists in the twentieth: on the other hand, Sade's defenders would argue that his focus on individual liberty and hatred of all forms of authority stands in opposition to totalitarian ideology.

I am also beginning to question the received wisdom in our profession that it is such a bad idea to suppress one's innermost desires.

Prof. Dubois

Yuletide

WAS CHRISTMAS REGIFTED BY THE ROMANS?

We've all done it: time is short, and we don't really need (or like) that vase Aunt Felicia gave us last year. If we give it a quick clean and wrap it nicely, it can just about pass as a brand-new Christmas present for Aunt Belinda this year. And it's a common claim that this is exactly what the Romans did with Christmas itself.

In the fourth century, Christianity went from a capital offence to the state-mandated religion of the Roman Empire, a massive shift which required, among other things, changes to the Roman festive calendar. Rather than inventing a religious festival from scratch, so people say, they just tidied up an existing one – borrowing both the date and elements of the celebrations – and tried to pass it all off as new.

But is this true? Let's have a look at the three most common myths about the origins of Christmas.

Myth 1: Christians stole from the cult of Mithras

Mithras, the hero-god at the centre of the shadowy Roman cult of Mithraism, gets a lot of good press these days. Partly because he's mysterious and intriguing: some of his slightly creepy temples have been uncovered by archaeologists, full of bull, snake and scorpion iconography that we don't really understand. And partly it's because to modern eyes, the cult of Mithras seems a bit like an early rival to Christianity, with its charismatic god-human protagonist and its secretive worship practices. Above all, it's fashionable to say that Mithras's birthday was 25 December.

So did Christianity rip off Mithraism? Well, no. The former was secretive because it was illegal; the latter was secretive because it was for Roman soldiers who loved all the mystery, the grades of initiation and the general hocus pocus.* According to the temple carvings, Mithras sprang

---

* According to the early Christian writer St Jerome, the worshippers of Mithras worked their way up through seven ranks, each one more mystic and shadowy than the last. Advancing to the next level required a special ceremony, in which the initiate was instructed in a new set of occult secrets, which he had to swear not to tell anyone of a lower rank. The seven degrees were named Raven, Occult, Soldier, Lion, Persian, Runner of the Sun and Father. It all sounds like tremendous fun, if that's your sort of thing, and excruciatingly self-absorbed if it's not.

from a rock, which some twentieth-century historians argued was a prefiguring of Jesus rolling back the rock covering his tomb on the third day after his burial; but you have to squint very hard before seeing a hazy connection here. For one thing, 'being born from a rock because you're a primordial god at the beginning of time' is a very different situation to 'escaping from a Roman tomb because you've returned to life'. For another, Mithraism wasn't older than Christianity and might even have been younger – the cult seems to have emerged in the first century AD.

In fact, the only cult doing the ripping-off was Mithraism itself: the name of Mithras seems to have been copied from a much more ancient Near Eastern god called Mithra. Like modern European enthusiasts for yoga and healing crystals, the Mithraists liked to borrow elements of Eastern religions to add a touch of oriental glamour to their belief system.

And what about Mithras's birthday? The truth is that we simply don't know when it was – or if he even had a birthday. But it certainly wasn't on 25 December. There's only one reason why anyone has ever claimed that it was: a confusion about Mithras's titles. Mithras was sometimes called 'Mithras, the Unconquered Sun' (Sol Invictus), which has caused some modern scholars to conflate Mithras with a god called Sol Invictus, whose birthday was indeed on 25 December. But in fact Mithras and Sol Invictus were entirely separate gods with entirely separate cults. The Mithraists had simply pinched a cool-sounding name – again.

Myth 2: Christians stole 25 December from Sol Invictus

Sol Invictus, not Mithras, was the pagan god in the Roman Empire whose birthday was on 25 December. So the Christians must have plagiarised the festival from Sol Invictus. Case closed!

Or not.

Sol Invictus, the Unconquered Sun, is a fairly straightforward concept as a god: a big fiery ball in the sky who had been worshipped in Rome as far back as we can trace any Roman religion. In the first century AD, Nero commissioned a thirty-metre golden statue of himself in Rome, known as Nero's Colossus – and his successors, inheriting this embarrassing waste of taxpayer money, hastily rebranded the Colossus as a statue of Sol.

The earliest reference to Sol Invictus's birthday came in a calendar compiled in AD 354, apparently in Rome, by a calligrapher and stone-engraver called Filocalus. This 'Calendar of Filocalus', which dates Sol Invictus's birthday to 25 December, is accompanied by a note saying that the Church Fathers noticed that Christians were big fans of Sol Invictus's birthday, so they decided to move the date of Christmas to the same day.

This statement seems pretty clear-cut, and in the nineteenth century it inspired the modern theories about Christianity having stolen Sol Invictus's birthday. But there's a twist. Modern scholarship has established that this crucial note was added to the Calendar of Filocalus in the twelfth century, 800 years after the calendar was compiled. The meddling Syrian scribe belonged to the

Orthodox Church, which celebrates Christmas on 7 January, and he wanted to explain why the Catholics had 'wrongly' marked the date on 25 December.

So although Sol Invictus probably did have a birthday on 25 December, there's no reason to take the twelfth-century scribe's word for it that the Christians copied the date. In fact, the fourth-century Calendar of Filocalus records a bigger feast day in honour of Sol Invictus on 22 October. If the Christians were simply repackaging the worship of Sol, why wouldn't they go for this one?

Ultimately, in a society with dozens of gods, it would be very hard to pick a date that wasn't already associated with a pre-existing pagan celebration. And for all we know, Sol Invictus's birthday was invented later than Christmas was – after all, the first we hear of it is in this calendar of AD 354. It looks like the overlap on 25 December was just a coincidence.*

Myth 3: Christians repurposed the Roman Saturnalia

The most popular Roman festival was the Saturnalia, a feast day on 17 December of honour of Saturn, a fusion of a mythic ancient king of Italy and the Greek titan (and father-castrator) Cronos. Eventually the Saturnalia crept longer and longer until it was seven days long, ending on

---

* These things happen. Shakespeare, that great symbol of Englishness, was born on 23 April, but he didn't steal the date from St George, that somewhat questionable symbol of Englishness/fictional Turkish knight, whose feast day is also 23 April.

23 December. The Emperor Augustus, who was the sort of person who would have hated Christmas lights being put up in November, thought that this was all a bit much, and limited the Saturnalia to just three days.

For the Romans, the Saturnalia was a fun opportunity to overturn conventions: men put on women's clothing, gambling was temporarily legalised, and slaves got to play at being the masters for a day.* The Romans loved it in the same way that we love Christmas. But was it actually the holiday that Christmas was based on?

With all its subversion of norms and exploration of social tensions, we can be pretty sure that the Saturnalia invented the Christmas family argument. But when we look a little closer, this is more or less the only tradition that the two festivals really have in common.

For one thing, it wasn't quite the same date. In the later Roman Empire, many Christians celebrated both the Saturnalia and Christmas (to the furious disapproval of more serious-minded Christians), showing that the two festivals hadn't been merged. For another, it's hard to identify any elements of the Saturnalia that were stolen by Christmas. It's true that the Saturnalia involved giving each other presents – but that wasn't a Christmas tradition until early modern times, at which point it definitely wasn't inspired by the Saturnalia.

In fact, the only thing that the Saturnalia really had in common with Christmas was that it was a nice morale boost in the depths of winter. The real reason 25 December

---

*Another popular tradition at Saturnalia was for groups of young friends to get together and pick a leader through a game of knucklebones. Nominated *Rex* or *Princeps*, this leader could order his friends to perform pranks and japes for the general amusement of the company.

was chosen as the date of Christmas was that it was nine months after 25 March, the date when the third-century Roman historian Sextus Julianus Africanus believed the Holy Spirit entered the Virgin Mary.

Year Zero

WAS 1974 THE WORST YEAR IN POST-WAR BRITISH HISTORY?

Among considerable competition, 1974 is widely considered to be the worst year (so far) in post-war British history. Quite apart from England's failure to qualify for the World Cup and the loss of the Ashes to Australia, here are the other main reasons why.

1. The year started with the disastrous three-day week

The year 1973 could stake a claim to being the *second-worst* year in post-war British history. When the Yom Kippur War broke out in October, embargos imposed by Arab oil producers led to a colossal increase in the price of oil, causing a huge increase in inflation in Europe and America. Spotting an opportunity to hold Ted Heath's Conservative government to ransom in the middle of an energy crisis, the National Union of Miners called for industrial action and launched an overtime ban. On 13 November, Heath declared a state of emergency for the fifth time in three years. A month later, he announced the introduction of drastic measures to be imposed from 1 January, including a three-day working week, a speed limit cut to 20mph, ration cards for petrol and television stopping at 10.30 p.m. The public would be encouraged to share baths and brush their teeth in the dark.

'We shall have a harder Christmas than we have known since the war,' said Heath, who had felt obliged to rewrite the Queen's annual message because it was too downbeat. Geoffrey Rippon, the Environment Secretary, privately compared Britain to the Weimar Republic.

The only source of festive cheer was Slade's Christmas number one, 'Merry Xmas Everybody', and a cheeky offer from Idi Amin, the Ugandan dictator, to help the former mother country. Launching the 'Save Britain Fund', the one-time officer in the King's African Rifles solemnly told the TV cameras that he had decided to contribute 10,000

Ugandan shillings from his own savings, urging his countrymen to donate generously to rescue their friends. When the Foreign Office ignored Amin's offer of a lorry-load of vegetables, he started sending telegrams to the Queen.

'The Swinging London of the sixties has given way to a London as gloomy as the city described by Charles Dickens,' gloated the German newspaper *Der Spiegel*, 'with the once-imperial streets of the capital now sparsely lighted like the slummy streets of a former British imperial township.'

2. The country's leading civil servant had a nervous breakdown

Heath's gamble was that the three-day week would prove so unpopular that the unions would have to back down in their pay demands. However, the miners attracted a great deal of public sympathy. In *Till Death Us Do Part*, a popular sitcom, the characters defiantly turned on the lights to wind up Heath. A further complication was that many people quite enjoyed not having to go to work during an unusually mild winter. The *Daily Mail* tracked down a psychologist who encouraged people to use the extra leisure time to experiment more in their sex lives.*

Meanwhile, as Heath stuck to his guns and refused to cut a deal with the miners, Sir William Armstrong, the Cabinet Secretary, appeared to be losing the plot. When he

---

* Entirely coincidentally, Dominic was born approximately nine months later, one of the few good things to happen in 1974.

wasn't haranguing a meeting of stunned ministers about the need to resist a communist conspiracy, he was locking a group of permanent secretaries in a room and lecturing them about the Bible and sex. He addressed a delegation from the Institute of Chartered Accountants while lying on the floor – and the Governor of the Bank of England while wearing no clothes.

Eventually, on 7 February, Heath cracked too and decided to call an election for 28 February, framing it as an attempt to answer the question: 'who governs Britain?' The easy riposte was: no one.

3. Irish terrorism moved to England – and the police kept locking up the wrong people

There had been escalating violence in Northern Ireland since British troops were sent to keep the peace in August 1969. From March 1973, this violence spilled over into England as the Provisional IRA attempted to rouse British public opinion against the province remaining in the United Kingdom. Several car bombs had been detonated in London in December 1973, injuring dozens.

'The Troubles' became much worse in 1974. Three days before Heath called the general election, the Provisional IRA set off a bomb in a coach packed with servicemen and their families, killing twelve people (including all four members of the same family) on the M62. The police hurriedly coerced an erroneous confession out of a mentally ill woman called Judith Ward.

This tragic cycle continued throughout a year that saw 300 terror-related deaths (compared to 255 in 1973). Other notable incidents included two bombs in pubs in Guildford on 5 October which killed five people, injured another sixty-eight and led to four innocent men spending fifteen years in prison; and three bombs in Birmingham on 21 November which killed twenty-one, injured 200, and resulted in six Irishmen being beaten, charged, convicted and falsely imprisoned for seventeen years.

4. The February election was a grim unpopularity contest between two ill, tired leaders

Ted Heath, the spoiled, famously rude* son of a Kent carpenter who had adopted a patrician accent at Oxford, looked like a busted flush after four years in office. A frustrated technocrat, he had presided over a string of disasters, from levels of industrial action unseen since 1926 to 'stagflation'. Conservative Young Turks, including future Cabinet ministers Nigel Lawson and Douglas Hurd, wanted him to take a tougher line on the unions, a strategy that went against Heath's corporatist, paternalist instincts.† He was also suffering from an undiagnosed thyroid problem.

---

* Ted Heath once said that there were three sorts of people in his party: 'shits, bloody shits and f***ing shits'. He was also famously uncomfortable with women. When a female journalist was thrown to the airplane floor during heavy turbulence, Heath called for a brandy – and drank it himself.

† It is a myth that union leaders were offered 'beer and sandwiches' in Downing Street (even if that's what they told their members). A typical meeting was accompanied by white wine and smoked salmon – and even Heath treating his guests to a cosy performance of 'The Red Flag' on the piano.

Similarly, the Labour leader Harold Wilson had lost the gloss that had made him an attractive Prime Minister back in 1964. Once a Pooterish economics don with a fondness for golf, tinned salmon and scouting (he was often pictured on holiday in the Scilly Isles wearing very short shorts, with his shirt tucked in), Wilson looked exhausted by 1974. There is some speculation that he was beginning to suffer from the Alzheimer's that later killed him; he was certainly forgetting things, picking up regular eye infections and drinking too much. Bernard Donoughue, his chief policy advisor, described him in his diary as 'slumped, tired, sour, scowling, his eyes dead as a fish'.

Labour's manifesto wasn't especially inspiring either – unless you had a fondness for their proposal to allow the National Enterprise Board to take over the top twenty-five companies in Britain in an emergency. At a time when taxes were already very high, Denis Healey, the Shadow Chancellor, promised to squeeze property developers 'until the pips squeaked' – a remark that right-wing newspapers wrote up as a broader attack on the middle classes.

5. Everyone started banging on about Europe

If you didn't enjoy the Euro-scepticism that dominated British politics from 1988 until at least 2020, you can also blame 1974 for igniting the issue. After Heath finally led Britain into the European Economic Community (the forerunner to the EU) on her third attempt in 1973, Wilson spotted a political opportunity to keep his fractious party together by promising a referendum on membership if he won the next election (sound familiar, David Cameron?).

Although most Conservatives at this stage were in favour of European economic integration, Enoch Powell, a renegade Tory minister best known for his controversial views on immigration (as well as the fact that he became a professor of Greek aged twenty-five and taught himself Urdu), had other ideas. Having been sacked from the front bench by Heath in 1968 following his incendiary 'Rivers of Blood' speech, Powell was still in the Conservative party in February 1974 when he gave an extraordinary speech in the Mecca Dance Hall in Birmingham. Announcing that he would not stand for re-election in this 'false campaign', he instead urged people to 'vote for the only party that will give you a referendum on Europe, which is the Labour Party'.

The newspapers spoke about nothing else for the next few days, or indeed decades (and Powell ended up joining the Ulster Unionist Party before the end of the year).

6. The February election was won by the party who lost it

If you're looking for reasons to change the UK's first-past-the-post voting system, the general election of February 1974 provides a textbook example. Despite the Conservatives remaining 5 per cent ahead in the polls throughout the campaign – and newspaper headlines such as 'A handsome win for Heath' greeting voters on election morning, before they had cast a single ballot – they won only 297 seats to Labour's 301.

Labour's four-seat victory, which fell well short of an overall majority, belied the fact that they had won only 37.2 per cent of the vote, compared to the Conservatives' 37.9 per cent share.

Meanwhile, thanks to coming second in so many constituencies, the Liberals won 19.3 per cent of the vote – and only fourteen seats (a mere 2 per cent of the total).

For a brief moment, it looked as if Heath might go into coalition with Jeremy Thorpe, the Liberal leader, leading to the delicious prospect of Thorpe being the first Home Secretary to preside over his own murder trial.* However, there were too many disagreements between the two parties and it was left to Wilson to form a minority Labour government. Grey, tired and dishevelled, Wilson stood outside Downing Street again with colossal bags under his eyes and announced, 'We've got a job to do.'

7. Wilson's doctor discussed murdering the Prime Minister's secretary

Wilson's ability to do that job – interest rates had just been raised to 13 per cent and the stock market had lost a quarter of its value in a month – was increasingly hampered by his private secretary. Marcia Williams, the

---

* For a full account of Jeremy Thorpe's antics, which led to his acquittal at a murder trial in 1979, see our first book. In brief, the Liberal leader had ended a relationship with a stablehand called Norman Scott who thought that Thorpe had stolen his National Insurance card. Thorpe denied conspiring to have him murdered by a fruit-machine salesman and a carpet salesman, who were either going to drop him down a mine shaft or feed him to alligators in Florida or poison him in the pub. They ended up getting an airline pilot to murder his dog instead.

daughter of a Northamptonshire builder, had worked for Wilson since 1956, acting as his gatekeeper, secretary and political wife.*

After almost two decades, this relationship had started to take some decidedly odd turns. While arguing with other political aides, Marcia would tap her handbag meaningfully and say, 'One call to the *Daily Mail* and he'll be finished; I'll destroy him.' Wilson spent a significant portion of every day trying to appease her, losing trivial battles about whether or not he should eat lunch with his aides. Marcia cancelled his victory party and regularly gave him lengthy, expletive-laden rollickings in front of other people.

Their relationship was further strained by Marcia's brother becoming involved in a complicated scheme during the summer of 1974 that involved a bouffant-haired insurance broker forging Wilson's signature in order to buy a slagheap near Wigan, an activity banned by the Labour manifesto. After Marcia had screamed at Wilson down the phone for failing to protect him, he was so scared to ring her back that he asked Donoughue to do it instead. In July, he gave her a peerage.

Meanwhile, Wilson's personal doctor Joseph Stone, whom he also ennobled, went to see Joe Haines, Wilson's press secretary, to 'discuss ways of taking the weight of Marcia off the Prime Minister's mind'. According to Haines, Dr Stone explained that he could dispose of her in such a way that it looked like natural causes and sign the death certificate himself.

---

* Wilson's actual wife, Mary, was disappointed when her husband left academia for politics, leaving a vacancy for the role of political wife. According to Mary Wilson, Marcia once went to see Mary following a blazing row and said, 'I went to bed with your husband six times in 1956 and it wasn't satisfactory.'

Thankfully for Marcia, Haines appears to have persuaded him otherwise.

8. Britain led Europe – in the cost of living crisis

When he wasn't having his victory party cancelled by an angry Marcia, the first thing Wilson did was settle with the miners' union, giving them a pay rise of 32 per cent (which was double Heath's offer). This was part of the 'Social Contract', an unenforceable quid pro quo whereby all the unions got better benefits in return for a solemn promise not to ask for more. After doctors had received a 35 per cent pay rise, civil servants 32 per cent, power workers 31 per cent and dockers 30 per cent, Tom Jackson, the postmen's leader, compared the government to a giant Las Vegas slot machine that had got stuck in favour of the customer.

Within a year of Wilson's return to Downing Street in February 1974, these wage increases had stoked a rate of inflation that was five times higher than that of any other European country. The price of sugar increased by 184 per cent; vegetables by 137 per cent; and even tinned soup by 54 per cent. It was a cost-of-living crisis on steroids (which had presumably gone up, too).

Had the Labour party taken leave of their senses? No. Denis Healey, now Chancellor, knew that they would soon face a massive economic crisis. But he also knew that, even sooner, this minority government would have to hold another election, so why not throw money at the problem?

9. Lots of people thought that the British Prime Minister was a communist spy

MI5, the British domestic security services, had opened a file on Harold Wilson as far back as 1945, giving him the unglamorous codename of Norman John Worthington. As President of the Board of Trade in the 1940s, 'Norman' had inevitably met communist officials during his visits to Moscow – and he continued to entertain some slightly dubious friendships over the decades. As a result, there was widespread gossip by the early 1970s in Westminster and Fleet Street (especially in the satirical magazine *Private Eye*) that Wilson was a secret KGB agent. James Jesus Angleton, the CIA's counter-intelligence chief, was also convinced that Wilson was Moscow's mole.*

10. There was a high possibility of a right-wing coup

If you read diary entries and newspaper reports from the summer of 1974, there is a lot of discussion of an ungovernable country requiring a right-wing strongman to take over.

This seemed less mad in the context not only of General Pinochet's Chilean coup in September 1973, but also closer

---

* This put Wilson in good company, as Angleton also suspected Gerald Ford, Henry Kissinger, Willy Brandt and the Canadian Prime Minister Lester Pearson. Subsequent inquiries have cleared Wilson of this rather lurid charge.

to home in Northern Ireland. Within two years, the population had been subjected to internment without trial, the closing of its parliament and troops on the street.

So was there a senior British military figure ready to step out of the shadows and run a right-wing dictatorship? There were two!

General Sir Walter Walker, who had crushed communists in Malaya and Borneo in the 1950s and ended his career as Commander-in-Chief, Allied Forces Northern Europe, was more than a little perturbed by the social and political changes back at home in the 1960s. As well as holding strong views on homosexuals ('people who use the main sewer of the human body as a playground') and Northern Ireland ('We should cut off their petrol, gas, electricity and stop food going in, soften them up and then go in'), he also wrote many letters to the *Daily Telegraph* warning that the 'communist Trojan horse is in our midst with its fellow travellers wriggling their maggoty way inside its belly'.

Backed by a handful of fringe right-wing groups (although he rejected an approach from the National Front), he hoped that 'people will choose rule by the gun in preference to anarchy'.

Meanwhile, Lieutenant Colonel David Stirling, the founder of the SAS, set up his own little organisation called GB75, staffed with 'apprehensive patriots' who would keep the power stations running if a full workers' strike ever took place (although he retreated into embarrassed silence when this was leaked to the *Guardian*).

Wilson remained genuinely petrified of a right-wing coup by ex-servicemen for his remaining two years in Downing Street.

11. The second general election was even more depressing than the first

On 18 September 1974, Wilson announced that he would go to the country again, on 10 October. Few were enamoured by the prospect of a second general election within the space of eight months. 'No election since the war had been held in such a mood of public uncertainty and depression,' wrote *The Times*.

The leaders of the main parties stooped majestically to the occasion. Wilson, who got tanked up on brandy before his first television broadcast, tried to promise the exhausted electorate a quiet life. Heath, a distinctly uncongenial man, gamely attempted to portray himself as an avuncular, jovial fellow in a cuddly jumper. And Thorpe took to the campaign trail on a hovercraft that ended up abandoned and destroyed in front of a delighted press corps.

Indeed, the only breakout star of the campaign was Margaret Thatcher, previously Education Secretary, who fronted the Conservatives' market-defying policy of capping homeowners' mortgage rates at 9.5 per cent. Within five months she had ousted Heath as Conservative leader, sending him into a thirty-year sulk (although at least he never considered murdering a secretary, a lover or a dog).

Despite Labour's share of the vote falling to its lowest share since 1945, it didn't fall quite as far as the Conservatives'. Wilson now had a narrow majority of three seats – and Heath's tally of general election defeats climbed to three out of four.

After an attempt to host a victory party was scuppered by yet another row with Marcia Williams, Labour decamped to their London headquarters – which was promptly evacuated by a bomb scare.

---

12. Everyone wanted to emigrate – including the new Foreign Secretary

'This could well be an election which will damage or even destroy the party which wins it,' wrote *The Times*, presciently, in October 1974 (Labour didn't win another election for twenty-three years).

At the end of the month, Healey gathered together his colleagues to tell them that they would have to borrow three times more money than expected and that inflation was already well over 20 per cent. In November, the Cabinet met at Chequers, the Prime Minister's official country residence, where Jim Callaghan, the Foreign Secretary, reflected that 'when I am shaving in the morning, I say to myself that if I were a young man I would emigrate.'

He was only half-joking. It wasn't just that Davie Bowie had fled to New York or the Rolling Stones to the south of France. In 1974, for the first time, New Zealand had to bring in immigration controls to stem the flow of British incomers. Australia followed suit in 1975, the first year since records began that Britain's population had fallen because so many people were emigrating.

Just before Christmas, one of Wilson's aides briefed the Prime Minister that the country was facing an 'economic Armageddon'. As it turned out, the real reckoning was delayed until after Wilson handed over to Callaghan in the spring of 1976. In December that year, Britain went cap in hand to the International Monetary Fund for a humiliating bail-out of £2.3 billion.

The Great Puzzle Section

Indiana Jones and Oscar Wilde

One is fiction, and one wrote fiction. Apart from that, nothing links Indiana Jones and Oscar Wilde – except this puzzle. A number of words linked to both are hidden within the grid. These words are in a straight line, and can run up, down, across, backwards or on any diagonal. One word in the list does not appear in the grid. Which is it?

ARCHAEOLOGY	IMPORTANCE
ARK	BEING
COVENANT	EARNEST
BALLAD	INDIANA
READING	LADY
GAOL	WINDERMERE'S
CAVE	FAN
CONSTANCE	LIBRARY
LLOYD	LORD
FEDORA	ALFRED
GRAIL	DOUGLAS
IDOL	MEDALLION

THE GREAT PUZZLE SECTION

NEPAL
OSCAR
WILDE
PERU
PICTURE
DORIAN
GRAY

PROFESSOR
SALOMÉ
STAFF
SWORD
UNIVERSITY
WHIP

```
B C E C N A T S N O C U R D C
A X D Y O L L T A S Q A R O L
L N G R A Y O A R X C O V E A
L A G S O E R F K S W E L E P
A I N A W S D F O S N C A U S
D R I L H E S E E A N N D N E
Q O D O I M R E N D B A Y I R
U D A M P U E T F C O T F V E
I Y E E T S R D R O S R G E M
N A R C S D A E A E R O A R R
D E I A E B D L N L N P O S E
I P P R R L E R G I L M L I D
A D F A I B A I J U D I S T N
N L B W L E I B N Z O O O Y I
A R C H A E O L O G Y D L N W
```

Solution on page 417.

Festive Fitback

It's the most wonderful time of the year! Celebrate by putting the words back into the grid.

Words can go either across or down. There is only one way to fit all the words back into the grid.

3 Letters
ELF
EVE
FUN
HAT
ICE
IVY
RED

4 Letters
CAKE
GIFT
HOLY
NOEL
POLE
SING
STAR
TREE
YULE

5 Letters
GREEN
HOLLY
LIGHT
MERRY
SONGS

6 Letters
BAUBLE
PARCEL
SLEIGH
TINSEL
TURKEY
WREATH

7 Letters
CRACKER
PRESENT
PUDDING

8 Letters
DECORATE
MINCE PIE
NATIVITY
REINDEER
STOCKING

9 Letters
MISTLETOE

10 Letters
SANTA CLAUS

11 Letters
GINGERBREAD

15 Letters
FATHER CHRISTMAS

THE GREAT PUZZLE SECTION

Solution on page 418.

Oppenheimer

Reveal a controversial quote by the 'communist' Oppenheimer by correctly answering all the below questions and decoding the text. Answer the questions horizontally in the top grid. All answers have eight letters.* Take the keycoded letters and place them in the bottom grid (e.g. the first letter you need is an N in H1) to reveal his famous words.

1 Chemical element

2 Oxide containing only one atom of oxygen

3 Summary

4 Bravely, rise to the challenge

5 Situation

6 To find something out

7 Used for jotting down ideas

8 Event of major significance

9 Many books of synonyms

10 Feeling low, despondent

11 System of beliefs

---

* Column H reading down will reveal a location associated with the scientist.

THE GREAT PUZZLE SECTION

	A	B	C	D	E	F	G	H
1								
2								
3								
4								
5								
6								
7								
8								
9								
10								
11								

H1	B7	C10	■	G8	■	E9	A2	■	■	■	■
E7	C3	H8	H5	A4	G6	■	A6	C11	E5	D8	B9
					■						,
H10	A1	C9	■	A10	G3	C6	C7	D1	F7	H11	C5	D3
			■								
F11	D4	■	H3	B2	H6	F4	B11	G10			
		■						.			

Solution on page 418.

Romans and Sci-Fi

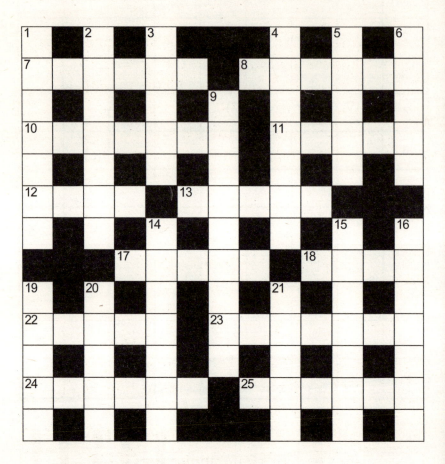

Clues across

7 Only god to share the same name in the Greek and Roman traditions (6)
8 Political institution of the Roman Empire (6)
10 Leader of the Roman Empire (7)
11 Gathering or occasion (5)
12 Performs, such as in a television series or film (4)

THE GREAT PUZZLE SECTION

13 Nickname for a film award; *Gladiator* won five (5)
17 Discovers (5)
18 Diana is the Roman goddess of this celestial object (4)
22 According to the myth, Romulus and Remus were found under this type of tree (5)
23 Actress Portman, who plays Queen Amidala in the 'Star Wars' franchise (7)
24 To take vengeance for another (6)
25 Fictional starship, the Millenium _____ (6)

Clues down

1 1977 novel by Frederik Pohl (7)
2 To calculate or make sense (7)
3 Importance or honour (5)
4 Military leader (7)
5 Fictional setting of *The Hunger Games* (5)
6 Roman goddess of the hearth (5)
9 Clue 5's Coriolanus Snow holds this title (9)
14 Ancestry or pedigree (7)
15 Creature from H.G. Wells' *The Time Machine* (7)
16 Aerial for receiving communications (7)
19 Citizen of Rome (5)
20 Rome is built on the banks of this river (5)
21 2024 film about AI starring Jennifer Lopez and Mark Strong (5)

Solution on page 419.

Downton Abbey

	W			A			B	
O					D	A		
N	B	E						
				T			O	
	W		N		E		D	
	E			D				
					W	T	B	
		Y	T				N	
E				A		N		

The name DOWNTON ABBEY is made up of NINE different letters of the alphabet. In alphabetical order the letters are A, B, D, E, N, O, T, W and Y.

In this puzzle each block of 9 x 9 squares must contain each of these letters. In addition, every row of squares (across) and every column of squares (down) must contain these nine different letters. There is only one possible solution.

Solution on page 419.

Solutions

Love Island Personality Test

Check your ratings.

Mostly A: Charles II – never one to turn down a good time, you'd be the life and soul of Casa.

Mostly B: Mary Fisher – not the most obvious contestant, but your loyalty and strength of feeling would win over fellow residents.

Mostly C: Tony Benn – you'd introduce lively debate and bring leadership to the dreaded challenges.

Mostly D: Catherine Howard – The most decorative, if not the sharpest resident, you'd bring brightness to proceedings. Might need to work on fidelity.

Quick-fire Quiz

Seen on Screen

Answers: 1 Vanessa Kirby, 2 *Dune*, 3 *The Man in the Iron Mask*, 4 Sean Connery, 5 *The Crucible*.

Sounds Interesting

Answers: 1 Bastille, 2 *Hamilton*, 3 'We Didn't Start the Fire', 4 Tchaikovsky, 5 Framlingham Castle.

Grim and Grisly

Answers: 1 Peter the Great, 2 Eleven, 3 Henry I, 4 Canterbury Cathedral, 5 Henry II.

Good Sports

Answers: 1 1968, 2 Biannually, 3 Baseball, 4 Paris 1900, 5 Italy.

The Rest is…

Answers: 1 Harold Wilson, 2 American War of Independence, 3 Anne of Cleves and Catherine Parr, 4 Lighthouse, 5 Pope.

Indiana Jones and Oscar Wilde

The word which doesn't appear in the grid is GRAIL.

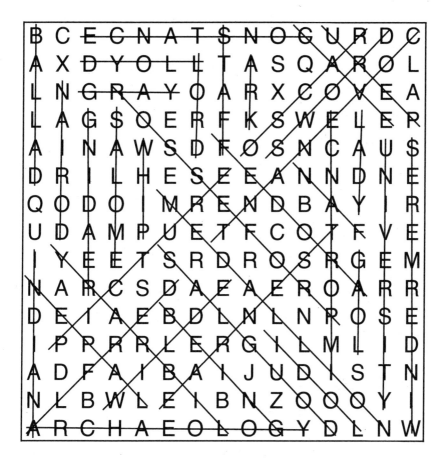

Festive Fitback

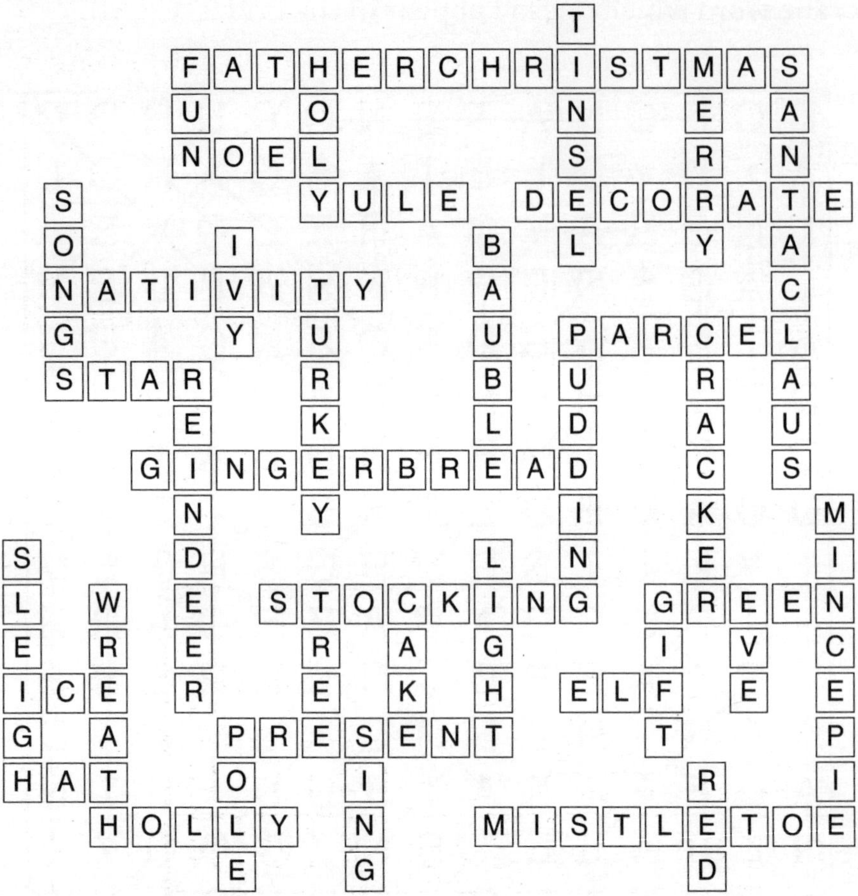

[Completed crossword grid with the following entries: FATHERCHRISTMAS, FUN, NOEL, SOON, NATIVITY, STAR, GINGERBREAD, SLEIGH, ICE, HAT, HOLLY, YULE, DECORATE, PARCEL, STOCKING, GREEN, ELF, PRESENT, MISTLETOE, TREE, CHRISTMAS, MERRY, TRACEY, NUTCRACKER, BAUBLE, CAROL, REINDEER, WREATH, SANTA, DICKENS, PINECONE, SINGING, among others.]

Oppenheimer

1 Hydrogen, 2 Monoxide, 3 Overview, 4 Manfully, 5 Scenario, 6 Discover, 7 Notebook, 8 Historic, 9 Thesauri, 10 Downcast, 11 Ideology. The place associated with Oppenheimer is his birthplace of NEW YORK CITY and the quote is 'Now I am become Death, the destroyer of worlds'.

Romans and Sci-Fi

Clues across

7 Apollo, 8 Senate, 10 Emperor, 11 Event, 12 Acts, 13 Oscar, 17 Finds, 18 Moon, 22 Olive, 23 Natalie, 24 Avenge, 25 Falcon.

Clues down

1 Gateway, 2 Compute, 3 Glory, 4 General, 5 Panem, 6 Vesta, 9 President, 14 Lineage, 15 Morlock, 16 Antenna, 19 Roman, 20 Tiber, 21 Atlas.

Downton Abbey

T	D	W	Y	O	A	N	E	B
Y	O	E	B	N	D	A	T	W
A	N	B	E	W	T	O	Y	D
D	Y	A	W	T	B	E	O	N
O	W	T	N	A	E	B	D	Y
B	E	N	O	D	Y	W	A	T
N	A	O	D	Y	W	T	B	E
W	B	Y	T	E	O	D	N	A
E	T	D	A	B	N	Y	W	O

Acknowledgements

Like its predecessor, *The Rest is History Returns* has been a great team effort. We are, after all, merely the photogenic, charming and humble front men for a vast collective enterprise.

A heartfelt thank you to everybody at Bloomsbury, especially our wonderfully encouraging editors, Jasmine Horsey, Ariel Pakier and Juliet Brooke, superbly assisted by Shanika Hyslop. Thank you to the heroic Florence Dodd at WME. And thank you to everybody at Goalhanger Podcasts. We're especially grateful to our chief puppet-masters, Tony Pastor and Jack Davenport; to the Herbert Henry Asquith of our chat community, James Regan; and above all, to our brilliant, brilliant producers, Theo Young-Smith and Tabby Syrett.

Our podcast would be nothing without its listeners, so thank you to everybody who has ever downloaded it, especially our beloved Rest is History Club members. And this book would be nothing without the ingenuity and effort of our peerless collaborator, Iain Hollingshead. How he comes up with so many superb ideas is quite beyond us, but we're very lucky to work with him.

Thank you all. Onwards!

About the Authors

Tom Holland is the author of a range of books on ancient and early medieval history. He has translated Herodotus and Suetonius, presented TV documentaries on subjects ranging from dinosaurs to the Islamic State, and been described by *The Times* as 'a leading English cricketer'.

Dominic Sandbrook was educated at Oxford, St Andrews and Cambridge, and was an academic at Sheffield before becoming a writer. He is best known for his histories of Britain since the 1950s, most recently *Who Dares Wins*, as well as a series of history books for younger readers, *Adventures in Time*. He has presented many documentaries on BBC Two and Radio 4, and is a columnist for *The Times* and book critic for the *Sunday Times*.

Index

Abbasids, 29–31, 33–4
Abd al-Malik, Caliph, 27
Abitur, 94
Abu Muslim, 29
Abu Qais (monkey), 219
Adams, John, 80
Adams, John Quincy, 114, 122n
African Americans, 115, 178, 243
Agent Orange, 293
Agincourt, Battle of, 141
Aistrop, Charles, 221–2
Aksum, 157n
Aladdin, 32
Aldrin, Buzz, 111
Alexander the Great, 185
Alexander VII, Pope, 123n
Ali, cousin of the Prophet, 29
Ali Baba, 33
Allison, Graham, 287n
Alypius, 75
Amin, Idi, 393–4
Anderberg, Rolf, 227
Angleton, James Jesus, 402
Anglo-Saxon Heptarchy, 92
Anne of Austria, 146
Apollo 11, 283
Arabian Nights, 33–4
Archer, Jeffrey, 377

Archimedes, 158
Aristotle, 185
Ark of the Covenant, 151–8
Armstrong, Sir William, 394–5
Armstrong-Jones, Antony, 106
Arnold, Dr Thomas, 314–15, 318
Artaud, Antonin, 259
Arthur, King, 132
Asimov, Isaac, 284, 287–8
Asquith, Henry Herbert, 358
Assyrians, 32, 155
astrologers, Zoroastrian, 32
Athelstan, King, 130
Attlee, Clement, 213
Augustus, Emperor, 72, 286, 390
Auld Alliance, 132
Aurelian, Emperor, 187–8
Austen, Jane, 326
Austrian *Anschluss*, 212
Aztec (the word), 10n

'Babylonian Captivity of the
    Papacy', 37
Babylonians, 155–6
Baghdad, 24–35
    House of Wisdom, 32
    Karkh market, 31
    Palace of the Golden Gate, 32

INDEX

Bailey, David, 106
Baker, Thomas, 339
Baldwin, Stanley, 192, 202
Ball, John, 345
Barker, Juliet, 344
Barking Abbey, 307–8
Barmakids, 34
Barras, Paul, 238–9
Barruel, Augustin, 116
Basra, sack of, 34
Bastille, 143–4, 148–9, 230, 232–3, 378, 382
Batista, Fulgencio, 164
Battle of Cable Street, 209, 211
Bay of Pigs, 164–6
Beale, Dorothea, 317
Beame, Abraham, 242, 245
Beatles, the, 7, 90, 107, 109, 258
Beauvoir, Simone de, 381n
Becket, Thomas, 65, 283, 308
Bede, 69
Bedford, Duke of, 90
Ben Hur, 288n
Benedict XVI, Pope, 41
Bengal Famine, 81, 320n
Benn, Caroline, 196
Benn, Tony, 192, 195–7, 199, 337, 346
Benzoni, Girolamo, 122
Berkeley, George Charles Grantley FitzHardinge, 221n
Berkowitz, David, 245n
Berlin Conference (1885), 324
Berlin Olympics (1936), 209
Berlin Wall, construction of, 162
Berlusconi, Silvio, 71
Bernard of Clairvaux, 281n
Birmingham, Alabama, 179–80

Black Death, 37, 60, 63, 65n, 138, 304, 338
Blair, Tony, 138n, 196n, 220
Blyton, Enid, 303
Boccaccio, Giovanni, 61, 63
Bodleian Library, 90
Boer Wars, 321, 325
Bogle, Andrew, 332–3
Bond, James, 7, 107
Book of Amos, 182
Book of Chronicles (1 and 2), 155–6
Book of Exodus, 18, 369
Book of Genesis, 157
Book of Isaiah, 182
Book of Kings (1 and 2), 155–6
Book of Samuel (1 and 2), 154
Boothby, Robert, 203n
Borås Zoo, 226–7
Boston Tea Party, 81
Bosworth, Battle of, 307
Bowie, David, 405
Brady, Ian, 378
Brando, Marlon, 103, 180
Brandt, Willy, 402n
Brassau, Pierre, 226–7
Braun, Eva, 209
Breakspear, Nicholas, 283
British Empire, 47n
British Library, 190
British South Africa Company, 324
British Union of Fascists, 200, 204, 208, 211, 213
Brooklyn Bridge, 243
Brotherhood of Sleeping Car Porters, 180
Bubbles (chimpanzee), 227–8

Bugliosi, Vincent, 161–2
Bunker Hill, Battle of, 283
Burns, Robert, 111
Burton, Richard Francis, 33, 322
Busby, Rev. Richard, 310–11
Bush, George H. W., 162
Bush, George W., 122n
Bynum, Caroline Walker, 42n
Byron, Lord, 69
Byzantium, 92

Cadbury, John, 126–7
Calais, 135, 137–8, 140–1, 149–50
Calendar of Filocalus, 388–9
Caligula, Emperor, 286
Callaghan, James, 405
Calvi, Roberto, 118–19
Cambodia, 296, 301
Cambridge University, 97–8
Cameron, David, 398
Capote, Truman, 162
Carnegie, Andrew, 6
Carter, Angela, 381n
Carter, Jimmy, 243
Carthage, 44–57
Castro, Fidel, 164–5
Catesby, William, 307
Ceaușescu, Nicolae, 263
Cecil, Hugh, 146n
Chamberlain, Joseph, 325
Chamberlain, Neville, 213
Charles V, Emperor, 17–18, 21–2
Charles I, King, 80, 371
Charles II, King, 147, 192–3, 195, 199, 310
Charles IV, King of France, 131
Charles V, King of France, 140

Charles de Blois, Duke of Brittany, 137
Charny, Geoffroi de, 137, 139
Charonne metro station, 261
Chaucer, Alice, 66n
Chaucer, Geoffrey, 1, 58–67, 340n
Chaumpaigne, Cecily, 64–5n
Cheltenham Ladies' College, 316–17
cherubim, 153n
Chevalier, Haakon, 249–50, 254–5
chevauchées, 135, 139
China, exam system, 92–3, 95
chocolate, 120–8
Cholula, 15
Christmas, 385–91
Christodoulou, Daisy, 91
Churchill, Randolph, 202n
Churchill, Winston, 3, 87n, 111, 146n, 215, 320
CIA, 164, 166–7, 295, 402
Cicero, 286
civil rights, 115, 167, 171, 177–81, 258
Clarke, Sir Edward, 364–8
Claudius, Emperor, 72
Clement V, Pope, 37
Cleopatra, Queen of Egypt, 185–6
Cleveland Street Scandal, 361n
Clive, Robert, 320n
Cockburn, Rear Admiral George, 4
Colborne, John, 314n
Cole, Nat King, 111
Columbia University, 244
Commodus, Emperor, 68
Common Sense for Housemaids, 86
Conan Doyle, Arthur, 111

Condé, Prince de, 380
Confucianism, 92–3
Connally, Governor, 160–2
Connor, Eugene 'Bull', 179
Constantinople, 29, 92, 157n
Conway, Alphonse, 362
Coppola, Francis Ford, 286
Corbyn, Jeremy, 337, 346
Cortés, Hernán, 1, 9–23, 121
Cortés, Martin, 22
corvus, 53–4n
Courrèges, André, 108
Cranmer, Archbishop Thomas, 194
Crécy, Battle of, 136–9
Cribb, Tom, 222
Criminal Law Amendment Act (1885), 361, 364
Cromwell, Oliver, 80, 124, 147, 149, 310
Cronkite, Walter, 161
CRS, 260–1
Cuauhtémoc, 21
Cuban Missile Crisis, 162, 164–5
Culpeper, Thomas, 194n
Curzon, Lady Cynthia, 203, 205
Curzon, Lord, 87n, 325
Czechoslovakia, Soviet invasion, 257

Daily Mail, 208–9, 322, 394, 400
Dalbiac, Sir James Charles, 314n
Dante, 61, 63
Darwin, Charles, 223, 383n
Dauger, Eustache, 149–50
David, King, 39, 154–5, 364
David II, King of Scotland, 132, 137

de Gaulle, General Charles, 258, 261–6
de Niro, Robert, 244
de Villeneuve, Justin, 106n
Dean, James, 103
Dean, John Gunther, 296
Decimus Meridius, Maximus, 68
Defoe, Daniel, 124n
deism, 114
'd'Éon, le Chevalier', 118n
Der Spiegel, 394
Derrida, Jacques, 259
Desert Island Discs, 216
Diana, Princess of Wales, 161
Diaz, Bernal, 19n
Dickens, Charles, 5–6, 329, 394
Dickier, John, 116
Diderot, Denis, 145
Dior, Christian, 103
Disney, Walt, 111
disputatio, 94
Disraeli, Benjamin, 325
Dissolution of the Monasteries, 308
domestic service, 84–90
'domino theory', 301
Domitian, Emperor, 187
Donoughue, Bernard, 397, 400
Douglas, Kirk, 288n
Douglas, Lord Alfred ('Bosie'), 359n, 362–5, 367
Douglas-Home, Sir Alec, 108
Downe, Viscountess, 207
Downe House, 317n
Drake, Sir Francis, 122
Drumlanrig, Viscount, 366n
Drummond, Stuart, 220
Dryden, John, 310

Dumas, Alexandre, 143
Dunmore Proclamation, 81
Dworkin, Andrea, 381n

earth, circumference of, 185n
East India Company, 81
Edinburgh, Duke of, 111–12
Education Act (1870), 321
Edward II, King, 131
Edward III, King, 37, 60–2, 130–41, 304
Edward IV, King, 306
Edward VII, King, 112
Edward VIII, King, 212
Edward, the Black Prince, 62n, 136–40, 344
Eisenhower, Dwight D., 169
Elizabeth II, Queen, 102, 142n, 145n
Emergency Powers Act (1939), 215
English Civil War, 337
Enlightenment, 113, 115, 370, 383
Epistle to the Hebrews, 16
Eratosthenes, 185n
Erkenwald, 308
Ethelburga, 308
Eton College, 106, 108, 146n, 297n, 303, 305–7, 313
European Economic Community, 397
Evans, Meirion, 274
exams, 91–100

Fall of the Roman Empire, 285n
fashion, 101–10
FBI, 168, 171–3, 246–56, 300
Fellowes, Julian, 84

Fillmore, Millard, 114
fiqh, 32
Fisher, Mary, 192, 196–7, 199
flagellation, 315n, 380n
football, 70–1
Football Pools, 128n
Ford, Gerald, 293, 295, 297, 300, 402n
Ford, Harrison, 151, 282
Ford, Henry, 111
Fort McHenry, 5
Foucault, Michel, 259
Franco, General Francisco, 117
Franklin, Benjamin, 81, 125, 285
Freemasons, 111–19
French Revolution, 116, 230, 233n, 235–7, 239
Freud, Sigmund, 379
Fritz, Captain J. W., 175
Fry, Joseph, 125–7

Galland, Antoine, 33
Gaskill, Malcolm, 372n
Gaston, Duke of Orléans, 146
Gaul, 186n
Gauls, conquest of Rome, 49n
GB75, 403
Gelli, Licio, 118–19
Genghis Khan, 333
George III, King, 2, 77–83, 115
George IV, King, 222n
George V, King, 88
George VI, King, 112, 145n
Gibbon, Edward, 82, 188–9, 287
Gibson, Mel, 76
GIs, black, 7n
Giscard d'Estaing, Valéry, 266
Gladiator, 285n

INDEX

Gladstone, William Ewart, 321, 325
Glorious Revolution, 80
Goebbels, Joseph, 200, 210, 214
Gonne, Maud, 157
Gordon, General Charles, 326
Grand Central Station, 245
Grant, Hugh, 3
Great Fire of London, 310
Great Library of Alexandria, 184–90, 283
Great Papal Schism, 41
Great Zimbabwe, 323–4
Greer, Germaine, 90
Gregory VII, Pope, 280
Gregory XI, Pope, 40–1
Grenada, US invasion, 8
Grenelle Accords, 263
Grenville, Lord, 80
Griffith, Arthur, 157
Groves, Colonel, 249, 251, 253
Guinness, Alec, 285
Guinness, Bryan, 202n, 208n

hadiths, 27
Haggard, H. Rider, *King Solomon's Mines*, 319–27
Haile Selassie, Emperor, 157n
Haines, Joe, 400–1
Hall, Prince, 115
Hallidon Hill, Battle of, 132, 134
Hamilton, Emma, 194n
Hamilton, Sir William, 192, 194
Hancock, Graham, 157n
Hannibal, 57
Hardy, Oliver, 111
Hartlepool monkey, 219–20
Hartlepool United FC, 220

Hartley, L. P., 327
Harun al-Rashid, Caliph, 33–5
Haydn, Joseph, 111
Healey, Denis, 397, 401, 405
Heath, Edward, 8, 393–9, 401, 404
Henry I, King, 308
Henry II, King, 308
Henry IV, King, 62n, 64n
Henry V, King, 129–30, 141
Henry VI, King, 306–7, 317n
Henry VIII, King, 99, 194, 283, 308, 371
Herbert, Frank, 282, 288
Herculaneum, 74, 347–57
heriot tax, 338
Herod Agrippa, 367
Hess, Rudolf, 210n
Heston, Charlton, 288n
Hezekiah, King, 155–6
Hill of Tara, 157
hippies, 108–9
Hiroshima, 251, 256
Hispaniola, 11
Hitler, Adolf, 1, 85, 200, 205–6, 208n, 209–12, 214–16, 247, 377
Holland, Sir Thomas, 138
homophobia, 359n
Hong Xiuquan, 95
Hood, Robin, 339n
Hoover, Herbert, 178
Hoover, J. Edgar, 162, 167–8, 251
Howard, Catherine, 192, 194, 199
Howard, Lady, 207
Howe, George B., 224
Hudson, River, 244
Hughes, Thomas, 303, 318
Huitzilopochtli, 18, 21

427

Hundred Years' War, 37, 61n, 129–41, 337–8, 340n
Hunger Games, 284, 289
Hurd, Douglas, 396
Husayn, grandson of the Prophet, 219
Hussein, Saddam, 122n

Iliad, 185n
Imperial Fascist League, 203
Indian Mutiny, 98
Indiana Jones, 151–8, 282, 320
International Monetary Fund, 405
'Intolerable Acts', 81
IRA bombings, 395–6
Irving, Washington, 5n
Isandlwana, Battle of, 321
ITV, launch of, 105
Iztapalapa, 20

Jacco Macocco (monkey), 221–2
Jack (baboon), 224
Jack the Ripper, 245n
Jackie (baboon), 225
Jackson, Andrew, 114
Jackson, Jesse, 115
Jackson, Michael, 227
Jackson, Tom, 401
Ja'far, vizier, 34
al-Jahiz, 32n
James II, King, 99, 147
Jefferson, Thomas, 78
Jellicoe, Earl, 207
Jenny (orang utan), 223
Jericho, walls of, 153
Jerusalem, Roman conquest, 156, 356

Jesus Christ, 72, 95, 155, 157, 179, 280–1, 333
and Catherine of Siena, 39–40, 42
and Mithraism, 387
jizya tax, 27
Joan, Pope, 275–81
Joan of Arc, 129
Joel, Billy, 282
John, King, 308
John, King of Bohemia, 136
John II, King of France, 137, 139–40
John XI, Pope, 278
John XII, Pope, 278
John of Gaunt, 62, 341, 344
Johnson, Boris, 303
Johnson, Elizabeth, Jr., 376
Johnson, Lyndon B., 167–8, 170–1, 285
Johnson, Samuel, 80, 82
Jones, Carwyn, 274
Jones, Lewis, 269–70, 272–3
Jones, Rev. Michael, 268–9, 271
Jones-Parry, Captain Love, 269–70, 272
Jonson, Ben, 310
Jordan, River, 153
Joseph, son of Jacob, 182
Josephine, Empress, 239–40, 282
Josiah, King, 155–6
Julius Caesar, 71, 185–6

Kabul, US evacuation, 292
Karbala, Battle of, 219
Kasdan, Lawrence, 151n
Kaufman, Philip, 151n
Kean, Major Jim, 300

INDEX

Keate, John, 313n
Kebra Nagast, 157
Kenealy, Edward, 333–4
Kennedy, Joe, 172
Kennedy, John F., 1, 7, 159–76, 179–80, 182, 256
Kennedy, Robert, 167, 172–3, 257
Kennerley, David, 295n
Kéroualle, Louise de, 195
Ketch, Jack, 147n
KGB, 167, 402
Kharijites, 29, 31, 34
al-Khayzuran, 34
Khmer Rouge, 296
Khorasan, 29
Khrushchev, Nikita, 162, 164
King, Martin Luther, Jr., 177–83, 257
King Edward's Grammar School, Birmingham, 317–18
King James Bible, 309
King Solomon's Temple, 112, 323
King's College, Cambridge, 307
Kinks, the, 107
Kipling, Rudyard, 111
Kissinger, Henry, 8, 162, 293, 298, 300–1, 402n
Kitchener, Lord, 326
Knapp Commission, 243
knucklebones, 390n
Koch, Ed, 245
Krafft-Ebing, Richard von, 379
Ku Klux Klan, 118, 171
Kyd, Thomas, 309

La Malinche, 14, 17, 22
La Noche Triste, 19, 21
Labouchere Amendment, 361

Lacan, Jacques, 259
Lafayette, Marquis de, 122n
Lancaster, Duke of, 139–40
Lawson, Nigel, 396
League of Nations, 152
Lee, Richard Henry, 80
Legg, John, 340, 344
Lenin, V. I., 338
Lennon, John, 109–10
Lennox William Pitt, 221
León Pinelo, Antonio de, 123n
Lethbridge, Lucy, 90
Lincoln, Abraham, 1, 81n, 180
Lincoln Memorial, 181
Lionel, Duke of Clarence, 61, 62n
Livingstone, David, 323
Llívia, 218
Lloyd, Constance, 361
Lloyd George, David, 87
Lloyd Webber, Andrew, 138n
Locke, John, 310
Lockwood, Sir Frank, 360–4
London Bridge, 344
London Zoo, 223
Londonderry, Lord, 207
longbows, 134
Loos, Battle of, 204
Lords Appellant, 63
Los Alamos, 246, 251, 255
Louis XIII, King of France, 146
Louis XIV, King of France, 142–6, 148–9
Louis XV, King of France, 145
Louis XVI, King of France, 232, 236, 264
Louis-Philippe, King of France, 264
Louvois, Marquis de, 144

Love Island, 191–9
Lucas, George, 285–6, 289
Lyons, Sir Richard, 62, 344

MacDonald, Ramsay, 3
McKinley, William, 1
Maclean, Gertie, 88
McLibel trial, 334n
Macmillan, Harold, 7
Madison, James, 4
Mafia, 172–3
Magellan, Ferdinand, 268n
Magna Carta, 337
Magna Charta Association, 334
Mailly, Jean de, 276
Major, John, 138n
Majuba Hill, Battle of, 321
'Make Do and Mend', 102
Malcolm X, 180, 182n
Malleus Maleficarum, 370
Man in the Iron Mask, 142–50
Manhattan Project, 246, 249–50
manorial courts, 342
Mansfield, Katherine, 88n
al-Mansur, Caliph, 30–2
Marchiel, M. de, 148
Marcus Aurelius, Emperor, 68
Margaret, Princess, 106
Mark Antony, 186
Marlborough College, 312n
Marozia, 278
Marr, Albert, 225
Marshall, Thurgood, 115
Martial, 73–4
Martin, Bishop of Poland, 276–7
Martin, Graham, 292–300
Martin, Richard, 222
Marwan, 30

Marx, Karl, 1, 339
Massu, General, 265n
Mattioli, Ercole, 148
Mauch, Karl, 323
Maya, 13n
Mayflower, 372
Mendès-France, Pierre, 264
Menelik, King, 157
Mercenary War, 57
Merchant Taylors' School, 309
Mercury, Freddie, 227
Mesopotamia, 26–7, 31
Metropolitan Opera, 244
Mexica, 10, 12, 14–21
Mexico City Olympics (1968), 257
MI5, 402
Michael, Archangel, 157
Michelangelo, 364
Mill, John Stuart, 96
Miller, Arthur, 282
Milner, Lord, 325–6
Miranda, Lin-Manuel, 76–7
Mississippi, River, 5
Mrs White's Chocolate House, 124
Mitford, Diana, 200–3, 205, 208–10, 213, 215–16
Mitford, Jessica, 205, 211, 215
Mitford, Nancy, 201, 211, 215
Mitford, Pamela, 211
Mitford, Tom, 215
Mitford, Unity, 200–2, 205–7, 209–12, 214–15
Mitford family, 200–16
Mithras, 386–8
Mitterrand, François, 264
Mods, 103–4
Mongols, 34
monkeys, 217–28

INDEX

Monmouth, Duke of, 147
Montezuma, 10, 16–19, 21, 121
Montreuil, Renée-Pélagie de, 381
Mortimer, Roger, 131–2
Mosley, Sir Oswald, 200, 202–3, 205, 207, 209–11, 215–16
Mount Gerizim, 156
Mount Moriah, 323
Mount Sinai, 153
Mount Vesuvius, 74, 347–57
Mozart, Wolfgang Amadeus, 111
Muhammad, Prophet, 26–9, 219
Murdoch, Rupert, 243
Murphy, Jill, 303
Musk, Elon, 110
Mussolini, Benito, 203, 210, 212

Napoleon Bonaparte, 2, 99, 229–41, 383
Narváez, Pánfilo de, 18–19
National Association for the Advancement of Colored People (NAACP), 115
National Enterprise Board, 397
National Front, 403
Native Americans, 371, 373
NATO, 167
'Naval Warfare' tactics, 48, 52–3, 55
Nazis, 151–2, 154, 162, 204, 209n, 213, 383n
Nelson, Admiral Horatio, 194–5
Nero, Emperor, 34, 69, 72–3, 193–4, 388
New College, Oxford, 305
New England witch-hunts, 369–76
New Look, 103
New Party, 203

New Reformed Palladians, 117
New Testament Apocrypha, 177
New York City, 242–5
New York Police Department, 243
New York Post, 243
New York Times, 243, 299n
Nietzsche, Friedrich, 383
Nile, River, 323
Nixon, Richard M., 162, 167, 257, 285–6, 292
Nobel Prizes, 183, 261
Norman Conquest, 64n
Northampton, Earl of, 135
Northcliffe, Lord, 322
Northern Ireland, 395, 403
Northern Transoxiana, 29
Nuclear Test Ban Treaty, 163

Octavia, Empress, 193
Ofsted, 303n
O'Hara, General Charles, 237n
Olivier, Laurence, 288n
ollamaliztli, 121
Olmecs, 121
O'Neal, Shaquille, 112
Ono, Yoko, 110
op-art, 108
Oppenheimer, Ella, 248
Oppenheimer, J. Robert, 2, 246–56
Oppenheimer, Julius, 247
orange trees, exported to Spain, 31n
Order of the Garter, 138
Order of the Star, 137–8
Oriflamme, 136, 139
Orton, Arthur, 331–5
Orwell, George, 7n, 128n

Oswald, Lee Harvey, 161, 163, 165–76

Paine, Thomas, 79n
Palace of Holyrood, 112
Palmer, Arnold, 112
panem et circenses, 289
Paoli, Pasquale, 234–6
Papon, Maurice, 260
Paris 1968, 257–66
Paris Commune, 261
Paris Peace Accords, 292
Parker, William, 361
Parks, Rosa, 115, 178
Parsons, Hugh, 373–5
Parsons, Mary, 373–5
Pasiphae, 75
Patagonia, 267–74
Patagotitan, 268n
Paul VI, Pope, 41
Payable, William, 339n
Pearson, Lester, 402n
Peasants' Revolt, 60, 62, 336–46
'People's Budget', 87
Pepi II, Pharaoh, 142n
Pepys, Samuel, 124, 311
Peter (chimpanzee), 226–7
Peter the Great, Tsar, 192–4
Petrarch, 61, 63
Petronius, 72
Phoenicians, 324
Philip II, King of Spain, 122, 128
Philip VI, King of France, 132–3, 134n, 135–7
Philippa of Hainault, 138
Philippe of Orléans, 145n
Philistines, 154
Phoenicians, 47, 155, 324

Pinochet, General Augusto, 402
Pitt, William, the Elder, 313n
Pius II, Pope, 41
Pius V, Pope, 123
Plato, 364
'Plinian eruption', 350n
Pliny the Elder, 348, 352n, 356
Pliny the Younger, 348, 349n
Plutarch, 186
poaching laws, 341–2
Poitiers, Battle of, 139
Pole, Margaret, Countess of Salisbury, 282
poll tax, 338–40, 343
Polybius, 45–57
Pompeii, 2, 74, 218, 347–57
Pompey, 156, 185n
Pompidou, Georges, 264n, 265
Pont Saint-Michel, 261
Poppaea Sabina, 192–5
pornocracy, 278
Port Elizabeth Railway, 224
Portsmouth, burning of, 133
Powell, Enoch, 398
Presley, Elvis, 226
Prester John, 323
Prince Hall Freemasonry, 115
Private Eye, 402
Procol Harum, 216
Prometheus, 75
Propaganda Due (P2), 118
prostitutes, Vietnamese, 299n
Protocols of the Elders of Zion, 212
Ptolemy XIII, King of Egypt, 186
Ptolemy, 185
public schools, 302–18
Punic Wars, 44–57
Purcell, Henry, 310

INDEX

Putin, Vladimir, 192
Pynchon, William, 372–3, 375
Pyrrhus, King of Epirus, 45–57

Quakers, 125–6, 127n, 180, 192, 196–7
Quant, Mary, 104–5
Quebec Act, 81
Queensberry, Marquess of, 358, 362–3, 365–6
Queensberry Rules, 365
Quélus, M. de, 125
Quetzal Owl, 21
Qu'ran, 27–8, 188

Raffles, Sir Stamford, 223
Raiders of the Lost Ark, 151–8
Rajkumar College, 318
Ramsey, Sir Alf, 112
Randolph, A. Philip, 180
raptus, 64–5n
Raymond of Capua, 37n, 38
Ready Steady Go, 105
Reagan, Ronald, 4–8
Red Cross, 225
Redesdale, Lord and Lady, 201, 202n, 212n, 215
Reformation, 345, 370
refugees, 89n
'Requirement, The', 15
Restall, Matthew, 17n, 18n
Revere, Paul, 80–1
Rhodes, Cecil, 111, 320n, 324–6
Ribbentrop, Joachim von, 214
Ricci, Matteo, 93
Richard II, King, 62n, 63, 336–7, 340–2, 344–5
Richard III, King, 66n, 307

Richardson, Samuel, 383
Richelieu, Cardinal, 146
Riley, Bridget, 108
Riot Act, 312
Rippon, Geoffrey, 393
Rivera, Diego, 10
Robespierre, Augustin, 237–8
Robespierre, Maximilien, 116, 237, 382–3
Rockefeller, David, 162
Rockers, 103–4
Roedean School, 317n
Rogers, Clifford, 134n
Rolling Stones, 405
Rome, ancient
  fall of empire, 75, 356, 383
  Gaulish conquest, 49n
  origin story, 49–50
  Punic Wars, 44–57
  and science fiction, 284–90
Rome (city)
  Colosseum, 68–75, 357
  Great Fire, 73
  Nero's Colossus, 388
  Temple of Jupiter, 74
Romulus and Remus, 49
Romulus Augustus, Emperor, 218
Roosevelt, Franklin D., 169, 180
Rosebery, Lord, 366
Ross, Robbie, 361n
Rothermere, Lord, 208
Rowling, J. K., 303
Rowntree Foundation, 87n
Royal Geographical Society, 323
Royal Navy, 82
RSPCS, 222
Ruby, Jack, 172–3, 175
Rugby School, 312n, 314–16, 318

433

Rumsfeld, Donald, 122n
Rundell, Maria, 124–5n
Rustin, Bayard, 180

Sade, Marquis de, 1, 377–84
sadism (the term), 379
al-Saffah, Caliph, 29–30
St Augustine, 75
St Catherine of Siena, 36–43
St George, 389n
St Guglielma, 281
St Hilda's College, Oxford, 317n
St Jerome, 386n
Saint-Mars, M. de, 144, 148–9
St Paul, 39, 155, 367
St Paul's Cathedral, 112
St Paul's School, 311
St Peter's Basilica, 382
Sainte-Marguerite island, 144
Salem witch trials, 375
Salisbury, Lord, 146n
Samaritans, 156
Samarra, 34
Samnites, 50
Sasanians, 29, 32–3
Saturnalia, 389–90
Scatter (chimpanzee), 226, 228
Schama, Simon, 84
Schaw, William, 112
science fiction, 284–90
Scott, Norman, 399n
Scottish Leaving Certificate, 99
Scruton, Sir Roger, 266n
Second Crusade, 1
seditio, 70
Séguy, Georges, 263
Sellers, Peter, 111
serfdom, 341–2

Seven Years' War, 79, 380
Sextus Julianus Africanus, 391
Seymour, Henry, 330n
Shakespeare, William, 364, 389n
  Richard II, 62n
Sheba, Queen of, 157, 323
Sheeran, Ed, 282
Shelley, Edward, 361
Shelley, Percy Bysshe, 313n
Sheshonq, Pharaoh, 156
Shrimpton, Jean, 102, 105–6
Simon, Paul, 300
Simpson, O. J., 328
Sinatra, Frank, 162
Sindbad, 33
Sinn Féin, 157
Sirik Matak, Prince, 296–7
Slade, 393
slaves, 5, 13–14, 20, 27–8, 34, 70,
  73, 80–2, 115, 124, 182, 332,
  353, 355, 390
Sluys, Battle of, 134
smallpox, 18, 30, 125, 334
Smith, Sir Lionel, 314n
Smith, Zadie, 329n
'Social Contract', 401
Social Darwinism, 325
sodomy, 365, 380, 383
Sol Invictus, 387–9
Solomon, King, 32, 155, 157,
  322–3
Somerset, Lord Arthur, 361n
Somme, Battle of the, 225
Sophia-Sapho, Sister, 117
Sophocles, 313n
South African Infantry Regiment,
  225
Soviet Union, 8, 253, 293, 301

INDEX

Spanish Fly, 381
Spartacus, 288n
Speke, John Hanning, 322–3
Spielberg, Steven, 152
Springfield, Massachusetts, 372–5
Stamp Act (1765), 80
Star Trek, 284, 290
Star Wars, 284–6, 288–9
'Star-Spangled Banner, The', 4
Statute of Labourers (1351), 65n, 338
Stevenson, Adlai, 160
Stevenson, Robert Louis, *Treasure Island*, 321–2
Stirling, Lieutenant Colonel David, 403
Stirling Castle, 112
Stone, Dr Joseph, 400
Stone, Oliver, 166
Stone of Scone, 156
Strauss, Lewis, 253, 255–6
Streicher, Julius, 209n
Suárez, Catalina, 12, 22–3
Sudbury, Simon, 345
Suetonius, 72n, 193n
Suez Crisis, 7, 265n
Suffragettes, 88n
Sugar Act (1764), 79
Sunak, Rishi, 303
Sunday Times, 105–6
Swinging London, 394
syphilis, 381n

al-Tabari, 219
Tacitus, 193n, 348
Taínos, 11, 13
Talmud, 27
TASS, 171
Taunton Commission, 316
Tavistock, Marquis of, 207
Taxil, Léo, 117
Tea Act (1773), 81
Teddy Boys, 103, 109
'teenager' (the word), 104
Tehuelche, 271–2
Teller, Edward, 255
Temple of Serapis, 188–9
Ten Commandments, 153
Tenochtitlán, 10n, 15–16, 18–22, 121
Tepeaca, 20
Texcoco, 20
Thatcher, Margaret, 4–8, 343–4, 404
Theodora, Empress, 192, 195
Theroux, Paul, 8
Thiệu, Nguyễn Văn, 294, 297
Thorpe, Jeremy, 399, 404
three-day week, 393–4
Thucydides, 286
Tiberius, Emperor, 290
Tichborne, Henriette, 330–2
Tichborne, Sir Henry, 330
Tichborne, Sir Roger and Lady Mabella, 329–30
Tichborne, Roger, 330–1
Tichborne Claimant, 328–35
Tigris, River, 26, 31
Till Death Us Do Part, 394
Time magazine, 107, 183, 295n
Tippit, J. D., 175
Titus, Emperor, 73–4, 356
Tlaxcalans, 16, 19–20
Tolkien, J. R. R., 327
Torah, 27
Totonacs, 12

Toulon, 236–7
Tower of London, 344
Townshend Acts, 80–1
Toxcatl, feast of, 17
'Treachery of the Blue Books', 269n, 274
Treaty of Brétigny, 140
Treaty of Edinburgh-Northampton, 131
Treaty of Paris, 77
Trubshaw, Pansy, 88n
Truman, Harry S., 112, 252
Trump, Donald J., 167, 245
Twiggy, 106
Tyler, John, 5
Tyler, Wat, 336, 340–2, 345

Ulster Unionist Party, 398
Umayyads, 26–32, 219
United States of America
  Civil War, 115
  Constitutional Convention, 285
  Continental Congress, 82
  Declaration and War of Independence, 2, 76–83, 346
  Emancipation Proclamation, 180
  Founding Fathers, 114–15
Upstairs, Downstairs, 90
Urban VI, Pope, 41
US Capitol, 114
Ustinov, Peter, 288n

Velázquez, Diego, 12–13, 17–18, 22
Vespasian, Emperor, 73–4
Victoria, Queen, 146n, 222n, 223, 325
Vietnam War, 7, 109, 166–7, 170, 183, 257–8, 261, 285
  fall of Saigon, 291–301
Vietnamese boat people, 300
Virgin Mary, 13, 39, 391
Virginia Almanac, 124n
Vogue, 104
Voltaire, 143–4, 149, 380

Wagner, Richard, 216
Walker, Major General Edwin, 174
Walker, General Sir Walter, 403
Walker, Wyatt Tee, 181
Wallace, George, 179
Walsingham, Thomas, 342n
War Powers Resolution, 293n
Ward, Judith, 395
Warren Commission, 170–1, 175
Warton, Joseph, 312
Washington, George, 76–7, 79–80, 114, 237n
Watergate scandal, 7, 285
Watt, James, 126
Waugh, Evelyn, 202n
Waynflete, William, 306
Weimar Republic, 393
Wellington, Duke of, 111, 229
Welsh Assembly, 273
Western Mail, 359
Westminster Abbey, 59
Westminster School, 310–11
Weyand, General Frederick C., 295
Wide, James, 224
Wife of Bath, 66–7
Wilde, Oscar, 1–2, 111, 358–68
William of Wykeham, 304–5, 317n
Williams, Marcia, 399–401, 404
Wills, Justice Sir Alfred, 359–60, 364, 366–8

INDEX

Wilson, Harold, 108, 196, 397, 399–405
Wilson, Mary, 401n
Winchester College, 303–5, 311–14
witchcraft, 197, 282, 369–76
Witsius, Hermann, 153
Wood, Alfred, 361
wool industry, 37, 61–3, 66, 133
Woolf, Virginia, 88
Woolworth, Sir William, 342
Wren, Sir Christopher, 112
Wycombe Abbey, 317n

Yazid, Caliph, 219
Yeats, W. B., 157, 360
yeshivas, 27
Yom Kippur War, 393
Yorktown, Battle of, 77, 237n
Younge, Gary, 182n

Zab, Battle of the, 30
Zhou Enlai, 293n
Zoe, Empress, 192, 195
Zoroastrianism, 27–9
Zubaidah, 34
Zulus, 321–2, 325